THE
EMERGENCE OF
LOS ANGELES

THE EMERGENCE OF LOS ANGELES

POPULATION AND HOUSING IN THE CITY OF DREAMS

1940-1970

B MARCHAND

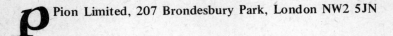
Pion Limited, 207 Brondesbury Park, London NW2 5JN

© 1986 Pion Limited

ISBN 0 85086 088 1

Printed in Great Britain by Page Bros (Norwich) Limited

The main aim of this book is to describe the changes experienced by the population of Los Angeles, California, between 1940 and 1970, the transformations that occurred in the housing stock during the same period and the evolution of the relationships between these dwellings and the dwellers.

A further purpose is to adopt new approaches to this description, both mathematical and philosophical, and to employ various methods and techniques in order to focus on the main question, the description and explanation of the change in an urban structure.

Given the importance, the size, and the originality of Los Angeles, such a study is likely to produce important material for the building of urban theory. Because Los Angeles has been one of the fastest growing metropolises in the industrial world, detailed knowledge of its development should permit an evaluation of the main models of urban growth and of the classical models of urban structure. The theories of the city that have already been proposed remain few and are based on weak ground. This is an opportunity, then, to put them to work, to evaluate them, and eventually, should this evaluation be negative, to try and propose a new model of urban growth.

These ambitions explain some of the particularities of the study. First, it deals only with residential topics (population and housing); this is not to say that urban functions, location, nature, and growth of services or industries, are not important, but only that they have not been taken into account because that would have been an encyclopedic and mammoth task; second, it focuses on *change*, which explains the complexity of some of the mathematical methods used and the reliance, in some chapters, on dialectics; third, the detailed analysis of the change in Los Angeles is preceded by a critical evaluation of leading urban theories, and is followed by a re-evaluation of those theories in the light of this study's conclusions, accompanied by the proposition of a new model of urban growth.

This book should be of particular interest to graduate students in geography and in urban or city planning by its emphasis on population, housing, and urban change. An obvious basis for teaching a seminar, the text could also be used as material in courses on urban structure as well as courses on research methods. The development and the application in the book of new mathematical methods (like three-way factor analysis, the theory of regionalized variables, or the mapping of urban social space) never before used in urban analysis will present teacher and student alike with modern and powerful tools of analysis. The philosophical approach, based mainly on semiological and dialectical analyses, is also quite new in urban research, in spite of its exceptional capacity for exhibiting hidden connections between phenomena, basic factors at work, and intricate relationships. Up to now, such philosophical approach has been little used or dangerously distorted and monopolized by traditional marxist analysis, although it is much wider than and largely independent from such ideology.

Graduate students, professors and researchers in other fields of Social Science should also find the book interesting, particularly if they work in urban history, urban sociology, or systems analysis.

Finally, the large amount of empirical data treated in this research, the information extracted from this material, and the general findings which conclude the book make it a basic document for urban practitioners and elected officials, as well as for urban planners.

I am particularly grateful to Madame Beaujeu, Professeur à la Sorbonne, for supervising this research; to Marc Barbut, Peter Gould, Allen Scott, Alan Wilson, Gunnar Olsson, and Jean Serra for advising me; and to Geoff Matthews and Jennifer Wilcox who drew the maps so diligently. The University of Toronto, by means of two grants, and Northwestern University, through the use of their computer facilities and their libraries, made this book possible. Marie-France Ciceri and Debbie Pile helped me to gather the data and to treat them. John Offord proofread my manuscript. To them I am most grateful. To the staff at Pion and particularly to Dr John Ashby, I owe more than I could say for their help, their understanding, and their patience.

From there, after six days and seven nights, you arrive at Zobeide, the white city, well exposed to the moon, with streets wound about themselves as in a skein. They tell this tale of its foundation: men of various nations had an identical dream. They saw a woman running at night through an unknown city; she was seen from behind, with long hair, and she was naked. They dreamed of pursuing her. As they twisted and turned, each of them lost her. After the dream they set out in search of that city; they never found it, but they found one another; they decided to build a city like the one in the dream. In laying out the streets, each followed the course of his pursuit; at the spot where they had lost the fugitive's trail, they arranged spaces and walls differently from the dream, so she would be unable to escape again.

This was the city of Zobeide, where they settled, waiting for that scene to be repeated one night. None of them, asleep or awake, ever saw the woman again. The city's streets were streets where they went to work every day, with no link any more to the dreamed chase. Which, for that matter, had long been forgotten.

New men arrived from other lands, having had a dream like theirs, and in the city of Zobeide, they recognized something of the streets of the dream, and they changed the positions of arcades and stairways to resemble more closely the path of the pursued woman and so, at the spot where she had vanished, there would remain no avenue of escape.

The first to arrive could not understand what drew these people to Zobeide, this ugly city, this trap.

Invisible Cities I Calvino¶

¶ Calvino I, 1974 *Invisible Cities* (Harcourt, Brace, Jovanovitch, New York) pp 45-46

To my father and mother

Pickford, Fairbanks Studio,
Santa Monica Blvd,
staging 'Ali Baba and the
Forty Thieves (c.1926):
where is the limit between
stage and city?

The Bonaventure Hotel, Downtown Los Angeles: stage for the Annual Meeting of the Association of American Geographers, 1981.

Contents

1

Introduction

1.1 The choice of Los Angeles

For one whole year I lived and taught in Los Angeles, and my visits to the city have been numerous. I have learned to love it and to enjoy its variety, its beauties, and its madness. On the other hand, it is certainly hell when one is really poor, but then this is true of all American cities, and the big metropolises in the East and the Midwest are probably worse places to endure from this standpoint. It is probably the most disparaged city in the United States: excessive size, excessive disorganization, excessive pollution, excessive reliance on the automobile, most people find it excessive on all accounts. However, *vox populi*, like *vox dei*, is often wrong and I feel this is the case here, but one cannot discard such common feeling without looking for its causes, and this also formed a reason for writing this book.

As a subject for the study of urban growth, Los Angeles is an obvious choice: third metropolis in the USA, one of the largest cities in the world, and probably the most widely spread, it has grown faster than any other US city (Harris, 1943; Forstall, 1970; Nelson, 1955). Its behavior has been so peculiar that it has been pointed out as one of the more blatant exceptions to the rank–size rule (Berry, 1971). Actually, its ability to attract migrants has been much stronger than for all other comparable cities in the USA. As a result, any study of Los Angeles is necessarily a diachronic study of urban change.

The regional role of Los Angeles reflects its size: its influence extends over all the southwestern part of the USA, as far as the Mississippi valley (Taaffe, 1956). Although a very important industrial center, mainly with high-technology industry (electronics, aerospace), it is also one of the major regions of the Union for agricultural production; Los Angeles County is one of the main producers of dairy products, fruits, and vegetables, employing very modern techniques based on irrigation.

In urban studies, Los Angeles often plays another role, namely that of a model towards which most large cities of the industrial world are supposed to tend. Very low population densities, extraordinary dispersion of urban life, multiplicity of centers without any clear hierarchy among them, a paramount role played by the freeway network, an enormous accumulation, apparently formless, of individual houses simply juxtaposed across the townscape, forming, to paraphrase Pirandello, "six suburbs in search of a city" appears to many authors (most of whom deplore it) as the natural, unavoidable form of urban evolution in the western world.

Such a belief may well be mistaken, but one would expect it to foster innumerable studies of such a model city; surprisingly enough, nothing of the kind has happened. Most urban researchers have kept away (or rather shied away) from such a fascinating case. New York City has been analyzed in great detail, particularly by Hoover and his co-workers (Hoover and Vernon, 1959), and Jean Gottman has described in detail the north-eastern megalopolis (Gottman, 1961). The classical studies by Park et al (1925) and by Hoyt (1939), or Wirth (1938) on Chicago, have led to the building of urban models which are the basis of any urban study course today. For twenty years, Brian Berry and his students have analyzed Chicago in such detail that it is certainly the best understood city in the world.

Los Angeles, on the contrary, remains largely an uncharted land. Although the third city in the Union, with an extraordinary growth record, and in competition with New York as a center of culture and modern art (painting, dance, music, television, and more generally, show business), there are no more than half-a-dozen good studies available: an excellent history of the city's development from its origins until 1920 (Fogelson, 1967); a seminal but quite limited sociological analysis at the end of World War II (Bell and Shevky, 1948); a beautifully written, and subtle presentation of the city's architecture (Banham, 1971); an interesting and useful geographical analysis, but limited in its scope (Nelson and Clark, 1976); and finally, a discussion of the city's urban role, a sort of plea by urban planners (Hirsch, 1971). Hopefully this book will be another contribution to the discovery of this badly neglected metropolis (see also Nunis, 1973).

1.2 The methodological purpose

There is a second purpose in this research: the combination of methods, very different in nature, to focus on the problem at hand. Two basic approaches have been used:

1.2.1 The mathematical approach

A battery of statistical and mathematical methods, based of course on factorial analysis, but also on information theory and spatial autocorrelation have been used. The purpose, actually, was twofold:

First the adaptation of classical and newer methods, which have not yet been used in urban analysis, to study change over time. This is a fundamental problem urban analysts must face, although they have not often directed their attention to it. Classical methods, such as time-series analysis, are useless in such cases, because they call for a large number of measures (more than one hundred) extended over time, whereas censuses are very few: there were only four during the thirty years covered by this study.

Second, the convergence of different methods to crack the nut. Too often, urban researchers (and this author among them) have written papers about one particular method, treating urban questions mainly as examples to exhibit the usefulness of the approach, and concluding with the usual words: "Further research is needed ...". This study takes an opposite stand: it focuses on a problem, the evolution over time of population and housing, and uses any method which may be useful and reliable in its elucidation.

1.2.2 The philosophical approach

This is quite a lofty name for a rather obvious endeavor: the demonstration through structuralism and dialectics, of hidden logical structures. Such an approach puts the emphasis on *qualitative change*, that is on processes which cannot be efficiently measured, and where inner alteration through self-contradiction is the main object of study.

Trying to use mathematics and philosophy simultaneously is not a common practice in urban analysis, although it is clearly the best approach to the joint study of quantitative and qualitative change. The main difficulty is to integrate such different logics harmoniously. From this viewpoint, the shortcomings of the book are obvious, even to the author, who realized only too often how wide apart some chapters and paragraphs stood, the one from the other, and this is where the indulgence of the reader will probably be needed most.

1.2.3 Theories of the city

After several years of teaching in US universities I could not help feeling dissatisfied with the current state of urban theory. Classical models and theories, mainly from the Chicago school, are fed to students without much discussion of their pertinence in the modern urban situation. Von Thünen's rings are often identified with those of Burgess; spatial forms discovered through factorial ecology are given names coined by authors for similar forms long before factor analysis was applied to cities. The result is a startling cacophony which is barely hidden behind the peremptory statements of most urban geographers. To study change in such a huge, wide, and fast-growing city as Los Angeles was an obvious opportunity to test, corroborate, or replace some of those leading urban theories and models.

1.3 Limits of the study

The evolution of population and housing in Los Angeles has been analyzed from 1940 to 1970, the censuses for those years being included.

How to delimit the geographical space under study was less obvious. Los Angeles SMSA, with its eight million inhabitants, and an overall diameter of almost eighty miles, was obviously too large for the study to be significant. Hence it was necessary to limit the urban space, and two possible approaches were available. It was possible, on the one hand, to choose a certain human group and to follow it in its drift across the city. On the other hand, it would be very interesting to select some portion of space from the city and adhere to it while studying the various groups of people as they move in and out. This second approach was chosen because it puts emphasis on space, land rent, land use, and spatial structure, and corresponds better to a geographer's task; sociologists know well enough how to follow groups of people as they change.

   Suburbs are where fast and surprising evolution takes place, but the city
heart is where spatial forms are anchored, where they are particularly
clear, and where their inner logic is more apparent: this is the part of the
city that was chosen.
   There remained the problem of choosing the limits for this urban area.
Los Angeles City forms only one-third of the population of the SMSA
(table 1.1).   Administrative limits do not make sense: they are the result
of a short but complicated history where the shock of conflicting
interests, the desire to control a wide fiscal basis, the amount of municipal
taxes available, and the protection of land property through building
codes and zoning laws have led to the carving of city space in the most
absurd and intricate ways.   Los Angeles, *stricto sensu*, is made up of two
pieces of land: the larger one includes the city center, but also includes
independent municipalities like Beverly Hills, Santa Monica, and Culver
City;   the smaller one, in the south, is squeezed between the independent
cities of Torrance and Long Beach, and actually includes a part of Long
Beach harbor.   Both parts of Los Angeles are united by a long and narrow
stretch of land (eight miles long, less than a mile wide).   The whole point
behind such a strange pattern was to ensure that Los Angeles would have
access to the sea without paying taxes to another municipality, a kind of
small Dantzig panhandle.
   Three constraints have been taken into account.
(1) It was desirable to choose urban districts of different age, as far as
possible in such a new city, to allow the observation of different types of
evolution which might correspond to different stages in the city's evolution.
Downtown had thus to be included, as well as districts which were
practically rural in 1940, such as the slopes of the Santa Monica mountains,
the south between Los Angeles CBD and Long Beach, and the ocean
shore (land where the International Airport is located today, was rural
thirty years ago).
(2) Districts should be different from a socioeconomic viewpoint, so as to
allow the taking of 'vertical' slices through the population to study their
behavior through time.   Beverly Hills (and Bel Air, one of the wealthiest
neighborhoods in all the United States), are included in the study, as well
as Watts, a very poor black ghetto famed for its riots of 1965, which
became a model of urban disorders at the time;   Little Tokyo, with its
population of Japanese origin;   Westwood Village, and its upper-class

Table 1.1.   Population of some municipalities in Los Angeles SMSA, 1970.

Los Angeles	2816061	Beverly Hills	33416
Long Beach	358633	Culver City	31035
Santa Monica	88289	Inglewood	89985
West Hollywood	29448	Los Angeles County	7032075

Source: US Bureau of the Census, 1970.

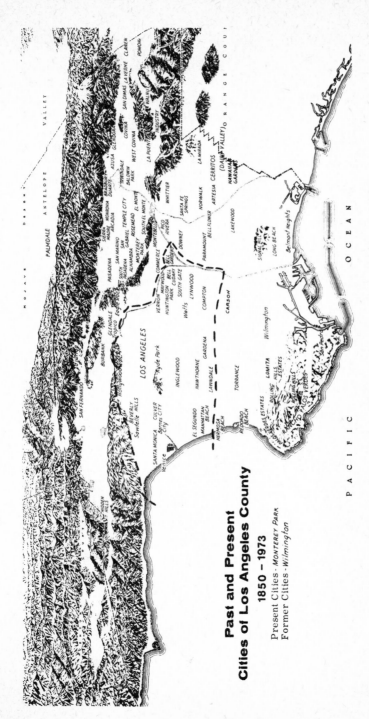

Figure 1.1. Los Angeles—the general surroundings and the study area.

families; Culver City with the black middle class; and Manhattan Beach with its white upper-middle-class population.

(3) It was necessary to choose districts with very different sites, relief, and accessibility in order to evaluate the role of such fundamental geographical variables as mountain slopes, seashore, central plain, etc.

All in all, the portion of space which is studied here forms a vast diamond of 20 miles by 20 miles, with 2·5 million inhabitants in 1970, that is, four to five times the area of Paris (*stricto sensu*), with a population slightly smaller (figure 1.1). Throughout the book the term Los Angeles will represent this portion of space, which includes most of Los Angeles City, plus Beverly Hills, Santa Monica, Culver City, Huntington Park, South Gate, etc.

This book begins with a presentation of the methods used in the analysis which is followed by an evaluation of the main urban theories and models, with their particular bearing on the case of Los Angeles. The evolution of the population, of the housing, and of the relationships between these dwellings and dwellers forms the substance of what follows, with a particular emphasis on the four kinds of value as defined by Baudrillard (1972). Lessons taken from the evolution of Los Angeles lead on to a re-evaluation of urban theories, and to the proposal of a new one.

Studying urban change: concepts and methods

The static study of a metropolis involves difficult questions about the nature, the reliability, and the volume of the data. However, to study *change* in an urban context opens a whole new field of questions dealing mainly with methods and logic. It is one of the most fascinating and most difficult aspects of this study.

A technical question, albeit a difficult one, is posed by the comparability of data over time. Although the answer is far from straightforward, it can be settled by technical procedures.

To choose a logical approach suited to the analysis of data variations with time is a wholly different task. Mathematical methods are powerful and useful in the description of change, but the introduction of time into the usual linear models creates certain delicate questions. Whatever the model used, however, mathematics can only decompose, describe, simulate, or test: they are not really equipped to explain change in its whole complexity. The object which is changing must simultaneously keep its identity and somehow remain the same, so we can identify what is changing, whilst altering its nature because it is becoming something else: dialectics are the necessary form taken by change.

Finally, it will be necessary to substitute Los Angeles in the general framework offered by the classical urban theories. These theories and models should be able to tell us beforehand what we can expect in studying change in Los Angeles, what urban forms are likely to appear, which mechanisms should be at work. Conversely, it will be important later (chapter 7), after a detailed analysis of change in Los Angeles, to make clear what it can teach us about urban theory.

2.1 Variables and census tracts through time employed in the study
Measurements describing population and housing are not stable over time, and this is one of the main difficulties met in the study of change.

2.1.1 Variables over time
Most of the data used in this analysis were extracted from the successive censuses of Population and Housing taken by the US Bureau of Census in 1940, 1950, 1960, 1970. Other sources of information did not offer data sufficiently stable to be compared over a thirty-year span; thus, statistics from Real Estate Agents, Insurance Companies, even from the City Department of Traffic or the Bell Telephone Company, did not prove very useful. In any case, the US Census is so rich in information that it has not been possible, given the limited scope of the study, to use it completely or to exhaust its potentialities. The variables that were used are listed in table 2.1.

Table 2.1. List of variables used in the study.

Variables measured as %

1 Whites	11 Professionals
2 Blacks	12 Proprietors, managers
3 Young (19 years and less)	13 Clerical and sales workers
4 Old (65 years and over)	14 Craftsmen
5 Bachelors (14 years and over) (missing in 1940)	15 Operatives
6 Owner-occupied dwellings	16 Service workers
7 Renter-occupied dwellings	17 Laborers
8 Vacant dwellings	
9 Single-dwelling units	
10 Five- and more-dwelling units	

Variables measured as median value

18 Income (missing in 1940)	21 Number of persons per room
19 Housing value	22 Number of school years completed
20 Contract rent	

Variables measured as absolute value

23 Total population	25 Total number of dwellings
24 Total employment	26 Construction year

Variables describing population

Most of the variables employed have been used elsewhere in many studies and are self-explanatory. Only one or two choices need to be justified.

Ethnic composition of a census tract, a measure so important in American urban geography, is described by two variables, the percentages of Whites and Blacks in a tract. Other ethnic groups (Orientals, persons of Chinese and Japanese origins; and Chicanos, from Mexican stock) appear by subtraction. They are located in a few districts (Downtown, Little Tokyo, Chinatown) and never played the important role that black migration did across the city.

Distribution by age has an important economic meaning: figures for young (up to 19 years) and old (65 and over) have been used, which indicate, by subtraction, the active population (20–64). Since censuses divide this variable by groups of five years, with different limits for each census, a quite lengthy aggregation of the data has been necessary.

The proportion of bachelors among people older than 14 years is particularly useful to study the recent return to the city center of young unmarried professionals. This variable, unfortunately, is not available for 1940.

A tract's social level is measured in two ways: household median income, and median number of school years completed. Both variables are strongly correlated, but the first one, which is the more interesting, does not appear in 1940. In later censuses, distribution of incomes per tract is indicated, but class limits vary so widely from one census to the next that comparisons would be meaningless in practice.

Socioprofessional composition, on the other hand, is indicated in great detail: nine groups in 1940 and 1950, eighteen in 1960, twenty-one in 1970, excluding the classification 'Occupation not reported'. These groups do not remain stable: 'professionals' were separated from 'semi-professionals' in 1940, but joined in the following censuses. Conversely, 'sales workers' and 'clerical workers', counted together in 1940, are separated later; eventually, seven categories were chosen (cf table 2.1, 11–17), and the principle of distinction was professional rather than social—a 'manager', for instance, may be the man in charge of the small shop round the corner, or a director at General Motors; 'proprietors' are no less heterogeneous.

There is a difficult problem here, one rooted in a society's dominant ideology. John Adams, in conversations held at the University of Minnesota, insisted on the fact that these categories had been chosen by the US Congress at the end of the nineteenth century with an ideological purpose in mind, namely to give researchers the ability to prove that European immigrants, once settled down in the USA, did climb the social ladder, from one generation to the next—in other words, that American society was fluid and that capitalism gave everyone his chance. During the 1920s, Congress debated the opportunity to modify these categories to make them conform to modern society, but the Director of the Bureau of the Census defended the existing classification. The existing grid exhibited social status and occupation, whereas a Marxist one would have manifested the way the means of production were controlled. Such arguments, reinforced by the fear of Bolshevism, saved the old classification, except for some minor revisions. It has proved very useful for the purpose of this study, but it would not do for an analysis trying to establish who controls the economy (where the French census, for instance, would be more convenient). No partition imposed by the government is good or bad in an absolute way; each one favors a particular kind of research, but obstructs others.

The housing variables
Two types of dwelling have been singled out for inclusion in the study: single-dwelling units, that is one-family homes, and buildings with five units or more, the true apartment buildings.

Land rent is assessed in two different ways: (1) as the median of the contract rent, which is the rent paid directly to the owner, other charges (heating, utilities, telephone, etc) being excluded, because this represents the owner's income; (2) as the market value of the dwelling, as estimated by the owner. Here, there is an important point to make. This value does not coincide necessarily with the actual price the landlord would get, should he actually sell his property, but represents rather what he hopes it is worth. Actual rent is closer to the real equilibrium value of the market, so an eventual disparity between both values may indicate an evolution of the neighborhood. Too high a value expected in relation to the rent paid is likely to forecast a decline of the neighborhood, not yet recognized by the landlords. Too low an estimation, conversely, would indicate a short-term increase in market prices. The basic assumption underlying such remarks is that the rent market is more exact and more fluid than the real estate market, where there is a time-lag with respect to the movement of the rent over time.

The important link between housing and population housed is well represented by the 'median number of persons by room', actually a measure of crowding very useful for identifying ghettos, large houses from which the children have left, and so on. Evolution of the housing stock is indicated by the 'year built', but unfortunately its modalities change so often from one census to the next that it does not carry as much information as one might hope to get from it.

Problems in using the variables
The most delicate problems are due to the diachronic nature of the study, though some problems of sampling, albeit classical, did occasionally arise. Census mechanical errors may be spectacular (Coale and Stephan, 1962), but the most important ones have been corrected in the data used here.

The problem of comparability over time. Choice was necessarily restricted to the variables measured at each period, and since the 1940 census was the oldest and the poorest, it had to determine the indicators chosen. One of the further difficulties of a diachronic analysis is the need to limit information to that encompassed by the intersection of successive censuses.

The definition of most variables remained fixed for the four censuses, although there were unfortunately some slight alterations, as in the case of the 'year built'. In particular, the value of the dollar has fallen during the thirty years studied, and it was necessary to correct incomes and land rent into constant dollars. All prices have been expressed, prior to any computation, in 1940 dollars, by using the following deflators taken from the corresponding *US Statistical Yearbooks*:

Year	1940	1950	1960	1970
Deflator	1.00000	0.58253	0.47333	0.36119

Table 2.2. Original number of observations available before aggregation.

Year	Number of observations per tract	Number of census tracts	Total number of observations
1940	32	316	10112
1950	39	395	15405
1960	51	553	28203
1970	50	621	31050
		Total	84770

Preparation of the data before any mathematical treatment is a long and delicate task—many variables were extremely subdivided and had to be aggregated. The initial 85 000 observations (table 2.2) were concentrated by summation in each of the 1940 tracts, and by logical aggregation into some thirty variables, to produce finally 9500 pieces of information, which form the empirical foundation of this study. Such a condensation loses information, but also suppresses eventual errors among the data and decreases their relative importance, producing in this way a very solid core for the mathematical treatment.

2.1.2 The geographical units

The US Census of Population and Housing is based on two spatial units: the block group (a union of several city squares) and the census tract. The first unit is too small for such a study as this one; data from old censuses are not always available, and the limits of the groups have often been changed. The analyses in this book are based on the larger units, tracts made up of several contiguous block groups and limited by avenues or large streets. Census tracts have been designed with a view to encompassing a population as homogeneous as possible, although the effort has not always been successful. Unfortunately, administrative divisions are so complex and intricate that they frequently clash with the desirability of drawing out a homogeneous cell. For example, many tracts are divided between two different municipalities and are reported in the census under two distinct entries (these are known as 'split tracts'). In some cases, fortunately quite rare, a tract is not in one piece, but is divided into two parts, one of which is included in the territory of some other administrative unit (as in the case of Culver City) or of another census tract (as in the case of Beverly Hills, for instance).

The population of a tract can vary quite widely from 1000 to 10 000 inhabitants, though the more usual size is 5000 to 7000 persons.

2.1.3 Stability of the census tracts over time

The limits of the census tracts have changed over thirty years, and this constitutes one of the worst problems of any diachronic study and explains in part why there are so few of them in geography (Coulter and Couralmick, 1959; Duncan et al, 1961; Foley, 1953; Mabry, 1958). The same spatial areas have been subdivided into a different and increasing number of smaller administrative areas, and the problem is to render these comparable (see table 2.3).

To try to retain the 621 tracts of the last available census was not satisfactory, since this would have involved the use of a model to 'add'

Table 2.3. The evolution of the spatial units.

Census year	1940	1950	1960	1970
Number of tracts	316	395	553	621

information into the poorer censuses.   To do this it would be necessary to
assume that each 1940 tract was homogeneously inhabited to the extent
that it is reasonable to apply the values of the variables for the larger tract
to each of the later smaller subdivisions.

To avoid distortion of the empirical information gathered in the census,
the safer way to proceed was to use the 1940 grid, aggregate the data
from the more recent censuses, and attach them to each of the 1940
tracts.   Of course, such a procedure loses some information: in the worst
case (assuming that the values of all variables are equiprobable, that is,
carrying the maximum information) the information loss is given by

$$\lg 621 - \lg 316 = 0.29 \text{ dits},$$

which is quite low.

One important task of tract aggregation remained, in order to reduce the
621 units to the 316 existing at the beginning of the study period.   In most
cases, territorial units had only undergone successive splits as their
population increased.   The space was then structured by inclusion;   it
was cumbersome but easy to reaggregate the pieces of an old tract and to
sum up the variables of the different elements.   However, for variables
which are not absolute (such as number of dwellings) but represent a
statistical moment, there is no unique solution when the variables to be
aggregated are medians, we know only that the global median is strictly
included between the largest and the smallest medians (Kendall and Stuart,
1966).   In such cases, the global median of the large 1970 tract has been
estimated as the weighted arithmetic mean of the medians of each
elementary tract included in the 1940 one.   Clearly, this is not an elegant
solution, and it mixes quite awkwardly two different types of central
tendencies;   but it is the only solution available and, in practice, the error
is extremely small, particularly when elementary medians are distributed
symmetrically.

New tracts created after 1940 with pieces taken from neighboring units
are the worst cases to deal with: variables corresponding to these new
cells have been estimated by weighting their values in the small elementary
tracts by their relative area in the earlier larger tract.   Typical of the
problem is tract 264 with its 1940 limits.   In 1970, it corresponds to
tract 618, half of tract 399, and a third of tract 400.   It goes without
saying that such an elaborate process of aggregation makes it necessary to
write special computer programs to check and recheck the coherence of
the process and to ensure no spatial unit has been forgotten or counted
twice, and that the variables are adequately redistributed.

The result of this long and arduous process applied to the 1950, 1960,
and 1970 census figures is to map all the census data onto the 1940
partition of space, and to render all measures spatially comparable over
time.

2.2 The mathematical approach and time
The mathematical approach has been used to analyze changes over time by employing three different techniques.
(1) Differential calculus and connected methods are among the most powerful tools for the study of change when differentiation can be carried out with respect to time; but it assumes the variables changing over time are well defined and continuous functions with derivatives. Variables used in urban analysis are in general discontinuous, with abrupt and often unpredictable jumps; practically none of them can be formalized in mathematical functions other than linear (and this simpler approach will be treated below), and the measures available are so few (once every ten years for the censuses) that it would be meaningless to build a discontinuous curve from them step by step and to look for a continuous function as its envelope. Calculus is quite useless to deal with the data.
(2) Probability calculus is a most useful tool to simulate and try to predict the evolution of a system after a satisfactory model of the system has been built. This study, however, never reaches such an advanced point: before constructing a model, we need to describe and to understand the phenomena at least roughly—in this case, the very evolution of the city. Here again, we have far too few points in time to be able to use models of stochastic processes.
(3) Linear analysis, the most usual approach, remains in fact the only tool we can rely upon, mainly for its simplicity and the small requirements it makes on chronological data. It is not so well equipped, however, for dealing with such a complex and subtle category as time: limits, difficulties, and even paradoxes appear when it is used as a variable in a linear model, and these must be carefully taken into account.

2.2.1 The regression paradox
Trouble begins when we try to relate the changes in two variables [cf Harris (1963), by far the best text on the subject], or in the same variable at two different times. Consider the household median incomes of a group of census tracts in 1950 and 1960 (figure 2.1); incomes are measured in deflated dollars. Let us plot the values for the tracts on a graph defined by a horizontal axis (incomes in 1950) and a vertical one (incomes in 1960). The points are likely to form an elliptic cloud, quite thin and elongated, because incomes in the same tracts over a ten-year time span are related. The B line bisecting the quadrant contains the tracts where income did not change; tracts above this line have become wealthier, tracts under the line, poorer. However, all this is quite trivial.

Now, draw two vertical lines R and P isolating the two extremities of the cloud S_1 and S_2. On the right of R are the wealthiest tracts in 1950; on the left of P, the poorest this same year. The graph then shows clearly that the wealthiest tracts have become poorer, and the poorest ones wealthier: there is a global drift towards the mean, and this turns out to be a general phenomenon. Whatever the variable being plotted is and which is exhibiting change (with the rare exception of abnormally behaving variables), time appears as a universal equalizer. Now this is most surprising, because experience shows, particularly with income, that disparities tend to grow, not to disappear. Clearly, we are not observing an actual phenomenon here, but an artifact, owing to a wrong way of representing change.

The consequences are still worse when we try to relate change in two different variables, looking for an eventual effect of one upon the other. For instance, median income usually shows a strong correlation with the number of school years completed. In the common situation used above as an example, one would be led to infer that people with a low educational level tend to become wealthier and vice versa—education appears as a factor of poverty, an absurd conclusion.

This paradox is so important that it gave its name to the regression model. Galton, at the end of the nineteenth century, observed that tall fathers had, on average, sons of a smaller size; there was a definite 'regression'. This was, in fact, the beginning of the statistical analysis of change: Galton, and later Karl Pearson were trying to substantiate Darwin's thesis, which can certainly be described as a most diachronic theory (Benzécri, 1976).

All these paradoxical observations are real; they are produced by the disparities between the initial positions of the variables. Figure 2.1, however simple it may appear, actually compares different objects: tracts, which were rich in 1950, with other tracts which were poor. So, differences in the final measure (income in 1960) may point, in a very ambiguous way, either to differences in change (which is what we are

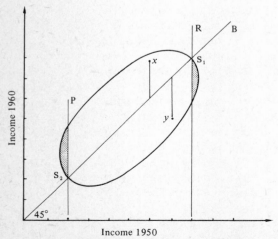

Figure 2.1. The regression paradox.

interested in), or to differences in the starting condition, a completely
independent point. Pure change can be exhibited only if all the changing
objects are similar at the beginning of the period—in this case, if all the
tracts in 1950 have the same median income. Practically, this condition
is never met, but it can be realized through statistical manipulation.

A common method consists in dividing, for each tract, the final value
by the initial one; change is then expressed as a percentage. But each
tract is then treated independently of the others, and so the global
evolution is lost. A much better approach would be to regress the income
in 1960 on the income in 1950, for every tract in the city, and to study
the residuals. In this way, the global evolution of the city is represented
by the regression line, and the residuals express change in each census
tract once the effect of the initial income value has been removed.
Geometrically this is equivalent to measuring a tract's income by its
projection not on the abscissa but on the regression line, thus taking into
account the global evolution of the city. Let us now try to relate income
and education, this time by first regressing income and education in 1960
on the same variables in 1950, and then by correlating the corresponding
residuals for the two variables. This is comparing changes after all starting
points have been equalized. From an algebraic viewpoint, this is equivalent
to using partial correlation, and correlating income and education in 1960,
after partialing out, or freezing, income and education in 1950. Only this
partial correlation compares and rightly relates true change in both
variables. Of course, this approach assumes that the linear model fits the
data well, but this is easy to check by using the F coefficient, usually
computed in any regression model.

To compare only the raw values taken from the census in order to
study change may lead to serious mistakes. Consider for example the
situation exhibited in figure 2.2. This time, regression line R is not the
same as the bisectrix B of the right angle, which is the common case.

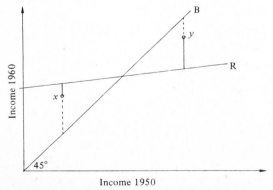

Figure 2.2. The regression paradox: affine function.

Consider census tract x: it is plotted above line B, which means its income in 1960 is larger than in 1950. Conversely, we see that tract y has a lower income in 1960 than in 1950. A careless observer will next look for reasons to explain why x has gained and y has lost, and he will undoubtedly find good ones! The form of the cloud, however, and its regression line R show that x has lost in relation to what tracts of its kind (that is, with the same initial income) have experienced; on the other hand, y has gained relatively more than other comparable tracts. So the interesting question is to explain a relative loss in x and a relative gain in y—relative—changes which should attract the researcher's attention once he has defined the city's global evolution.

Because of this paramount importance of the starting values, the regression effect may alter and even reverse the situation presented by the raw figures taken directly from the census. In the following chapters, I have systematically analyzed relations between residuals after an auto-regression of each variable on itself at two different points in time.

2.2.2 The problem of time

The main goal of data analysis by linear methods is to break down a complex set into a sum of elementary components which are independent from each other; this is the purpose of the various methods of factor analysis as well as those using Fourier analysis. When time, however, is introduced as a basic variable, new problems arise. Time may load mainly onto one particular factor; this is what some economists, quite naively, are aiming at. It thus looks possible to study change as an almost pure, independent category in its own terms, represented by a particular factor in the vector space where the data are embedded; the other groups of variables loading onto the other factors can then be analyzed as if they were independent of time. But such an approach assumes time to be some external characteristic which can be absent in some variables; in other words, that a number of phenomena can be described outside of the category of time, and remain meaningful: this is absurd. The other alternative is to consider time as a necessary, unavoidable component of any variable, but then the basic methods used in the social sciences come into question.

Geographers do not seem to have been bothered very much by such a problem; psychologists, who have made a better and more advanced use of analytical methods, have recognized this stumbling block. Cattell writes: "[the trend concept] ... may represent one, two or more time-associated factors acting together, and we want to know what they are. There is no reason why any real factor or factors should not show a time-trend ... . Time is associated with factors but there is no reason to posit that it is itself a factor or to treat it in this respect as a privileged variable ... . Consequently, (a) to partial out 'time-trend' from the correlations among other variables in the matrix before factoring, or (b) to rotate to set aside a factor running through the time vector after factoring, is to wreck the whole purpose of the analysis. In the first case, ..., selection on one variable will distort all the correlations among the factors and, of course, obliterate their relation to time. In (b), we are most likely to rotate to a quite artificial factor—a monster possessing no natural hyperplane—thus adding to the distortion of the factors left by (a), the final confusion of entertaining a truly nonexistent factor. In either case, we throw away a great deal of valuable information about the covariance of variables. Anything that happens over time is excluded from our science. It is the supreme example of throwing away the baby with the bath water" (Cattell, in Harris, 1963, pages 177–178). Note particularly that the use of partial correlation I have advocated above and employed frequently in this study is not the one alluded to by Cattell in (a) but has, on the contrary, the opposite aim.

2.2.3 Methodological choices for this research

Most geographical studies of change are based on comparing different moments in time, like the examination of instant photographs taken at different periods to suggest evolution. Change is supposed to emerge from a juxtaposition of these synchroneities. Such a traditional approach is convenient, useful, and can hardly be dispensed with.

But it is not completely satisfactory. One cannot help looking for methods which would describe and analyze duration itself, the actual flow of time which forms change. Time-series analysis is closer to a solution, but it needs a large number of observations through time (a hundred at least; Box and Jenkins, 1970) and there are only four censuses available. One way of circumventing the difficulty is to imitate the progress from still photography to cine film; that is, to advance from the separate pieces of information given by individual pictures to a global understanding gained from a sequence of pictures united or synthesized by some careful process. In linear methods, three-way factor analysis corresponds to the running film or the rotating disk of the cinema.

Three-way factor analysis
Consider the usual data matrix where each line represents a tract, and each column, a variable; it contains information taken from the census at a particular year. In the case of Los Angeles, four matrices of this kind are available, one for each of the four censuses (1940, '50, '60, and '70). These four matrices juxtaposed in chronological order form a cube, or rather a parallelepiped, which we wish to analyze. More formally, define three sets: L (tracts), V (variables), and T (periods); the problem is then to analyze the cartesian product (LVT). Since eigenvalues and eigenvectors are defined only for two-way matrices, the solution consists in unfolding the data cube by combining in all possible ways two of the three initial sets. There are three different ways ($3!/2!$) of unfolding the cube. The analysis produces three principal component analyses related to one

another by a small 'cubic' matrix. For each census tract, for instance, it is possible to sum up the evolution of all the variables chosen during all the periods. The method, remarkable for its power of synthesis, has been proposed in psychology by L R Tucker, but has practically never been used in urban analysis, or for that matter in geography. It has produced some very important results in this analysis of change in Los Angeles (see chapter 6 and appendix A).

The use of information theory

The methods presented above are varieties of linear analysis. All assume that variables have a vector structure and are measured on a ratio scale. This assumption is usually met, but it would be reassuring to be able, at some point, to avoid it. Methods using 'weaker' spaces and assuming less of the variables are always welcome.

What is more, although most data are scalars, easy to compare by subtraction or division, some are percentages (socioprofessional groups, for instance) which it is more tricky to treat algebraically. In order to compare socioprofessional structure among city tracts, various approaches have been proposed: indices (Duncan et al, 1961), the chi-squared distance, or the coefficient of linear correlation, if we are ready to assume a linear structure among the variables. A different method has been used here to investigate social relations in Los Angeles—not less precise, but safer than the others, because it makes practically no assumption about their hidden structure—it is 'information theory'.

The basic tool is the concept of *entropy*, a measure of disorder in a system, of the dispersion of a distribution, or of the information contained in a message. Because of these different meanings, and because of its paramount role in thermodynamics, the concept has been given too many interpretations and some authors have warned against its careless use (see in particular Georgescu-Roegen, 1971, page 141 et seq). However, entropy is used here only as a measure of dispersion, without any attempt to infer anything about the eventual order or disorder of a social structure. It is treated only as a convenient tool for studying social change, as it works as a monotonic function of social segregation.

In any tract, consider the probability p_i for the head of a household to belong to one of the seven basic socioprofessional categories.

Information, H, contained in the census when it describes the social distribution in a tract is given by

$$H = - \sum_{i=1}^{7} p_i \lg p_i .$$

This is the classical definition of entropy (Marchand, 1972), and is the *linguistic* information in a message. The *semantic* information, H_S, however, is exactly the measure we are looking for: it compares two pieces of information, the piece we had first before receiving the message, and the piece contained in the message. In other words, it measures how much we are surprised by the message, or rather, in the present case, the way two social distributions in the same tract vary between two censuses (Goldman, 1953). This measure of social change is defined by

$$H_S = + \sum_{i=1}^{7} p_i \lg \left(\frac{q_i}{p_i} \right),$$

where q_i is the frequency of a social category in the first census, and p_i its frequency in the following census. The scalar H_S measures, in each tract and for each decade between two censuses, the stability of the change in its global social structure.

The analysis of spatial structure
Spatial autocorrelation has become an important branch of quantitative geography. In the English speaking world, however, it has led mainly to the development of statistical tests devised to check if, after fitting a regional model to the observed data, there is not some remaining correlation indicating that the model has failed somehow to take into account all the regional relations.

In this study we are more interested, however, in exhibiting, describing, and measuring a variable's spatial structure, that is its spatial organization. Let us take an example: assume we know the median income in a census tract. Clearly, income in the adjacent tract should not be too different. As one moves away from the first tract to increasingly remote tracts, their median income tends to bear less and less relation to the first measure. After a certain distance, income has become completely independent of its value in the initial tract. In other words, a variable is usually correlated with itself over a certain distance, and the way this autocorrelation changes describes its spatial structure.

This is the basis of any urban spatial analysis: a variable with no spatial autocorrelation at all is not a geographical variable, its distribution over space is purely random. It can be analyzed as a global measure like those which interest economists, for instance, but cannot tell anything about the inner mechanisms of a city. The 'theory of regionalized variables' has been developed to describe such spatial autocorrelation, (1) to acquire knowledge over spatial structures, and (2) to interpolate, that is to transform discrete measurements made at a few points into a continuous map. It is a powerful solution to the problem of building a continuous contour map from a few scattered data; that is, to the problem of 'kriging'. The theory has been developed in South Africa by Krige (Krige) for gold mining, and in France (Matheron, 1965). Unfortunately, in the English speaking world, engineers have preferred to use trend analysis for the same purpose, and the method, although easily available in English (Davis, 1973), is not widely used. Certainly, it has never been applied to urban data. It will be employed below to analyze the urban space of Los Angeles (appendix B).

Mapping the results of the study

The four censuses available produced some thirty variables to describe the urban space of Los Angeles. To map all of them was out of the question. Apart from the overwhelming amount of illustration submitted in this way to the reader, the fact that very many of the maps would have been redundant, telling the same story over again in different colors, made the whole process senseless, and in addition the 'regression effect' would have magnified the role of the initial situations and masked the real change.

In the chapters which follow, information, each time it was possible and meaningful, has been concentrated through a principal components analysis followed by a Varimax rotation. The mapping, then, of the factor scores, displays in a concentrated but convenient way, the information of interest. The use of the euclidean metric (principal component analysis) answers perfectly well for the purpose of concentrating the data, avoids any controversy over all the flimsy assumptions one must make while performing a factor analysis with communalities less than one, which are unfortunately so popular in North America, and finally, allows a unique and clear solution to the computation of the scores.

I have tried to avoid mapping absolute values because of the problems this creates in the comparison of one map with another, and also because they are often factor scores or residuals from regression analyses, without any easy intuitive meaning. On most maps, values have been ranked in decreasing order; the first and last thirds of the distribution being represented with a number of colors (or rather shades) corresponding to the precision needed. The value of such ranking is twofold:

(1) it makes the comparison of one map with another much easier; parts of the city are grouped naturally and blocks of the same spatial type are more easily identified;

(2) it maximizes the information carried by the map (Marchand, 1972; 1975). A computer program, written for this purpose, ranks the 316 tracts and then prints the first 120 (those with the highest values) and the last 120 (those with the lowest values). Two different symbols represent the maximal and minimal values; tracts with median values remaining blank. In this way, tracts are divided into three groups on the maps, almost equal in number, and this maximizes the map information.

2.3 The philosophical approach

The whole of this book, each of its chapters, whatever the method used in it, is based on one fundamental postulate: that observations, facts, mere recordings of events, be they qualitative or quantitative, expressed in careful statements or measured in numbers, are only appearances concealing the true reality, which is made up of logical structures hidden behind these appearances and is in general very different from them. The role of science is to penetrate beyond the illusory veil presented by superficial observations in order to get at the truth: if appearances were not illusive, if simple observation and true knowledge were one and the same, there would not be any need for science.

This position will hopefully be clarified rather more later; at this point, it is only necessary to underline some basic epistemological consequences. If appearance and reality are different, then so-called 'common sense' is a very dangerous tool, which can lead one to accept pretences and make-believes as truths. The usual opposition between hard, 'real' concrete facts and abstract, theoretical ideas based on flimsy ground, becomes inverted: "These real relations thought has to ferret out because they are hidden by the appearance of things. For this reason, thought is more 'real' than its objects" (Marcuse, 1960, pages 72–73).

Latent structures underlying facts have their own inner logic, but this does not mean the logic has been planned or wanted by any human being, or by any other kind of being for that matter; a system of coherent relations may develop without the conscious intervention of anybody, take on a power of its own and act as a subject. There is no mysticism or occultism in such a process, only a truer and more subtle definition of the nature and relations of subjects and objects, and this leads us directly into dialectics.

2.3.1 Dialectics
At this point, the reader must be cautioned about language. Reliance on different methods and different concepts makes it necessary to use language that is different. This may take the form either of a particular jargon, or of a common vocabulary to which new meanings are attached to some usual words. There is no way around the difficulty. Most people are quite ready to do it when they deal with mathematics; for instance, geographers using factor analysis learn the meaning of technical terms like eigenvector, and understand 'discrete' and 'continuous' in their particular mathematical meanings.

Unfortunately, such understanding and such modesty are not usually shown when reading texts dealing with certain philosophical approaches, at least they are certainly infrequent in such texts in English. To impose one's usual 'language' grid to interpret a very different text is certainly mis-leading and probably dishonest, though this has usually been the case with dialectics. Too many readers, refusing to learn the specific language and to adopt the concepts, are necessarily unable to understand the ideas, and so they reject them as 'fuzzy', 'obscure', or 'unintelligible'. Would any geographer so describe topology, although very few master the subject?

The word 'logic' is very general. It represents any coherent system of discourse and of thought. Formal logic, as used in mathematics, is the most widely known type of logic, but it is not the only one. It is paramount that the reader, at this point, recognizes there are various levels of logic, each one playing an important role in the operation of the mind. Formal logic, with its basic principle of noncontradiction (A is not at the same time not-A) is but one of them. Negation also has a powerful and a positive role.

Negation as a positive category

There is no need to present formal logic, but dialectical logic, on the contrary, is too often misunderstood by geographers and misrepresented in a partisan way by Marxists: some clarification is in order. Unfortunately, this is a truly formidable task given the complexity and the subtlety of dialectics as created by Plato, developed from Aristotle until Kant (for example, the famous antinomies of the reason), and elevated to the main constituent of logic by Hegel; it would take a gifted philosopher an enormous volume to do justice to this mode of reason. I can only undertake here to dissipate the worst sources of misunderstanding and to emphasize a few key points.

Negation stands at the very basis of dialectics, but the meaning of the term must be clarified. Any finite thing contains in itself something different from itself: in the jargon, it is called self-contradiction, or self-negation, but the true meaning is *otherness*. A city neighborhood, for instance, is not only defined by what it is, that is the architecture of the buildings, the socioeconomic status of its inhabitants, and so on, it is also defined by what it is not, such as by the nature and form of the other neighborhoods, and of the parts of the city which are not constituted as neighborhoods (CBD, industrial districts, etc). All these elements are necessary in the definition. Actually, this is not very far from the concept of a closed set in topology, that is of a set including its limit, that is something which is not the set anymore. There is no place here for fuzzyness or imprecision but only for the realization that things, when they are finite, are limited, are as much characterized by what they are not (their negation) as by what they are. The words negation or contradiction are taken here in a particular sense.

Dialectics deal with *quality* rather than with quantity, which explains the incessant self-contradiction by which a quality changes into another one (its 'contradictory'), and also the difference from mathematics .

Negation is a positive character and plays a most important role: a thing (a neighborhood, a family, a transportation system, ...) could exist in many different ways, but at a certain moment in time only one of them is realized. Reality destroys and conceals most potentialities. To refuse a given state of affairs or, to use the jargon, to negate reality, is to open the way to all hidden potentialities. Hidden behind dialectics is the belief that change, that transformation is life, and cannot and should not be stopped.

In this way, change becomes a basic constituent of everything. Any being exists only inasmuch as it changes, that is transforms itself into something else or, in other words, turns into its contrary (into the other). Science is historical. An object's complete definition must include the history of this object, how it has been formed, and how it has become what it is now. In the same way, truth is not, in Hegelian logic, conceived as something given once and for all, but as a concept perpetually changing, whose scars indicate the progress of inner coherence.

The three levels of logic
This positive role of negation, by which qualities turn into something else, is clearly expounded in Hegel's *Logic* (Hegel, 1975). The process of thought goes through three different stages:
Stage 1 Understanding: "Thought sticks here to fixity of characters and their distinctness from one another" (Hegel, 1975, page 113). A rose is a rose is a rose is a rose. The mind puts objects of thought into boxes, labels them and insists on their differences. 'Common sense' works in this way, but this way of thinking is aptly criticized as "abstraction from reality"; things are in fact much more complex. One feels often that in dividing the world into distinct, separated elements, what one gains in clarity, one loses in reality and actually kills the world. Most thought, unfortunately, stops there, justifying the common impression that thought is abstraction from reality: indeed, at this stage, it is.
Stage 2 Dialectics or negative reason: Dissatisfied by such clear but so rough apprehension of the world, thought negates this stage and focuses on what the things are not, on their negation, on their relation with other things. Negation of a thing is here a positive act, putting emphasis on its links with the rest of the world. A neighborhood is not defined any longer by what it is but what it is not: what is was, what it could be, what the other districts are. Concepts then become dynamic, and change is introduced into the very nature of things. This is a return to the very complexity of things and to concreteness, a negation of the abstraction away from the thing which characterized understanding.
Stage 3 The synthesis: positive reason: The "speculative" stage "apprehends the unity of terms or propositions in their opposition". To keep the same example, although a little oversimplified, a neighborhood is thought of as what it is and what it is not, what it has been or could be, and is perceived dynamically as a living entity whose truth lies in its inner laws of evolution.
   Clearly, each stage is necessary (no one is better than the other). They are presented here separately only according to the category of understanding which makes things clearer, but destroys the all-important relations between stages. If most people, unfortunately, stop at the first step (understanding) and conceive thought only as a way of severing links, gluing labels, and forcing objects into distinct boxes where they do not fit, it is not surprising that thinking is interpreted as a dangerous abstraction from the real world. It remains true, however, that this 'real world' is thought in man's mind, and the danger of limiting oneself to the operation of understanding appears immediately: models and theories are too often seen as purely artificial tools made in order to describe the 'real world out there'. Such a criticism is right because understanding is abstraction away from reality. But if thought were in effect radically divorced from reality, then the 'real world' people talk about would be only an idea in their mind, something completely unreal; and pure Empiricism turns dialectically into its contrary, pure Idealism.

All steps are necessary: "Apart from Understanding, there is no fixity or accuracy in the region of theory or of practice" (Hegel, 1975, page 114). "The dialectical principle constitutes the life and soul of scientific progress ... Wherever there is movement, wherever there is life, wherever anything is carried into effect in the actual world, there Dialectic is at work" (Hegel, 1975, page 116).

It is easier now to come back to the existence of hidden structures behind the veil of appearances: the dialectic subject–object throws light on their nature. A *subject*, in dialectical terms, is whatever maintains its identity through change; it is not necessarily provided with consciousness, not necessarily a human being. A coherent system of rules, built spontaneously, may have inner forces maintaining its equilibrium in such a way that it reacts to external events and acts as a subject upon different objects, which may be men. There is no need to imagine a god or a hidden providence: the system has been created by man, in general unwillingly, but takes on a life of its own, turns against man, and largely determines his behavior. Man creating the system of social rules acts as a subject, but turns into its contrary and becomes an object, submitted to the influence of the object he created turned into a subject.

To understand this phenomenon is essential: it would let so many Marxists avoid the ridicule of finding plots everywhere, as if landlords or businessmen were 'bad' and were meeting together in smoke-filled rooms in order to devise new means to 'exploit' the workers. The situation is far more complex. It has been traditionally oversimplified by Christian and by Marxist researchers, calling upon some Providence or some scape-goats to help. The whole of this book is based on the fact that most forces acting in society, and particularly in the city, are man-produced but not man-controlled, and that most phenomena must be explained by the complex actions and reactions of hidden or latent structures which need to be exposed, either by mathematical analysis (like factor analysis), or by qualitative investigation trying to uncover the dialectical forces which make things move. This is obviously an ambitious enterprise, opening quite new ground. It is hoped the reader will be intrigued by the compound approach through dialectics and mathematics, and have patience with the results achieved.

2.3.2 Order versus disorder

Urban theories and models try to define and to explain order in the city. The concept of order, however, is a very tricky one and needs to be elaborated, in particular in its relation with the geographical scale of the study.

The concept of order

Order in a system is indicated by the complexity of the definition needed to give a true and complete picture of it. A disordered system can be described fully with very few terms, or with very few mathematical laws.

Order is often measured today by negentropy, that is, by the entropy (with its sign reversed) of a distribution. Such an approach tends to follow Brillouin's way of thinking, although strong criticism has been levelled against it, for instance by Georgescu-Roegen (1971). This is, however, secondary in the development here, and we shall not enter into it. Only two pertinent points need retain our attention: (1) disorder, as measured by entropy, tends to increase without any external action, and (2) change, as a consequence, is irreversible. Since energy (and order) are *qualitatively* changing when abandoned to themselves, it is impossible to come back to a past situation without the intervention of some external agent; but even then, the situation A' which is restored in this way is never identical to the past one, A: it bears the marks of its past history, of the starting point A, and of the foreign agent necessary to reconstitute the past. This poses the basic problem of the reversibility of Change.

The role of scale
Order corresponds in fact to the way microstates are grouped into macrostates. As noted by Georgescu-Roegen (1971, page 143): "... the degree of disorder ... depends upon the manner in which microstates are grouped in macrostates". Consider, for instance, the distribution of ethnic groups in the blocks and neighborhoods of a city, and in the city as a whole. Assume the number of White and Black blocks is given and fixed. At the block level, order can be computed from the probability that a block is White or Black, and is fixed, whatever the block location in the city. If blocks are grouped in two huge neighborhoods, one Black and one White, we shall speak of a strong racial order; conversely, if blocks are distributed randomly throughout the city, we shall say we have a completely disordered racial map. Order changes strongly at the neighborhood level but, in both cases, it remains the same at the block level, and also at the city level. In other words, defining macrostates and microstates is quite arbitrary but will serve as the very basis for the definition and computation of spatial order.

2.3.3 Time and change
Change is basically a dialectical process, which means it is irreversible.

On change
The notion of change assumes stability and alteration simultaneously: there must be something stable in the changing object so that we can still recognize it, but of course, some qualities must have turned into others. More specifically, in urban analysis there are a certain number of agents representing the 'motor' of change, and spatial forms which tend to organize and order those elements in transformation. The problem is to identify what fuels change and what keeps it in a stable frame, and to investigate the dialectical relationship between one and the other.

More deeply, the problem is to distinguish 'true change' from 'quasi-change'. Let us say there is change when an object V_i at time i is other than the object V_j at time j, with i and j different. We say there is 'quasi-change' if, for some finite k, we have $V_i = V_k$. Such an identity may obtain in two ways:

(a) In the case of a cyclical change of period p: for j smaller than $i+p$, there is change; for $j = i+(np)$, with n any integer, there is no change; actually, there is stability modulo p.

(b) In the case of random change, as in Brownian movement; the probability that the system will come back to a past state is close to zero, but it is quite certain it will come 'near to it' (cf a famous theorem by Henri Poincaré, quoted in Georgescu-Roegen, 1971, page 152).

Here again, the scale of analysis is fundamental, but in this case it is a time scale and not a spatial one. In quasi-change, change happens only in the short term, but there is stability over the long term.

True change, on the contrary, is irreversible: V_i is different from V_j for any time j different from i. This true change corresponds to a qualitative change, and is nothing other than a dialectical change: A turns into not-A which becomes in turn not-not-A different to A. The difference stems from the fact that there is some memory, or rather some hysteresis in the concept or in the object in the process of change; it is no longer the same, even while passing through a preceding step.

Georgescu-Roegen argues that reversible change exists only in some small parts of physics, where everything is explained by 'locomotion' (that is, pushing and pulling), whereas in most other fields, time has one direction only and quality changes in an irreversible way—that is, processes are dialectical. Even in physics, however, the entropy law stands beside and above the narrow mechanical laws based on locomotion (Georgescu-Roegen, 1971).

What makes change irreversible?
If true change is irreversible and if dialectics are the true way of reaching the logical structures hidden behind the mass of facts and observations, what exactly are the processes which ensure change is irreversible?

A fascinating lesson can be learned from Biology. There, the problem is to explain evolution, a qualitative change in living species which is irreversible and unplanned. What mechanisms can be found which would represent mutation and reproduction, without having to rely on some absurd finality mysteriously inscribed by which hand? The French biologist Jacques Monod, Nobel Prize winner, has proposed one interesting solution (Monod, 1970). For him, change is produced by the interaction of two independent processes, and the irreversibility of change is ensured by their independence. On the one hand, strong preservation mechanisms ensure massive reproduction of an organism—codings contained in the DNA control reproduction as a *necessary* process. On the other hand, *random* mutations change some codes in the DNA double helix, representing the other element of the dialectic. As a result, randomness induces mutations which, if advantageous, necessity ensures are so quickly and so widely multiplied that they extend to the whole species and become the new norm. Such mutations are filtered by the life process of adaptation to external conditions.

Irreversibility is due to the combination of two independent processes, necessity and randomness. If only random mutations happened in an otherwise unchanging population, individuals would change, but not the species. Even a large number of isolated mutations would not lead to anything other than quasi-change, with alterations at some microstates, but immutability at the macrostate. Massive reproduction of the existing species would, of course, produce no change at all. Change happens only because individual mutations, if they have survived the contact with the external world, are extended to the whole of the species.

This is not the place to describe the deep dialectical structure of the process described by Monod: dialectic between individual and species, stability and change, randomness and necessity. It is an example, however, well worth keeping in mind when we try to analyze and to explain change in an urban structure because, as will be shown later, we have here the basis for a new model of urban change.

2.4 Los Angeles and theories of the city

What is a city? How do its inhabitants live? What functions does it fulfil in the nation? How does it grow? How are people, housing, commerce and services, and industry distributed inside the urban space? An urban theory should try to answer such questions and to propose a set of laws explaining present life in the city and the spatial forms it takes, allowing a reasonably good forecast of their evolution in the near future and thus paving the way to planning, an activity supposedly dedicated to the correction of disharmonies and dysfunctions, to ease away the worst tensions, and to maximize the happiness of city dwellers. Of course, such a program is utopian and no so-called urban theory has come even close to such an ambitious goal, but it is useful to recall the overall importance of the task to avoid mistaking a minute description of some urban regularity for a theory or even an urban model.

Surprisingly enough, the few systematic urban analyses which might pretend to the status of a theory have been produced by sociologists and have very little to say about the geographical layout of the city. Max Weber's thesis that the city is characterized by a particular social class, the bourgeoisie, whose appearance has spelled the end of feudality, does not tell us anything about spatial patterns (Weber, 1958). The Marxist theory (or rather theories: Castells, 1972; Lipietz, 1977; Lojkine, 1977; Preteceille, 1975; Topalov, 1974) of the modern city analyzes the role of capital invested in land rent, of the banks as principal agents on the real estate market, and of housing as a basic factor for reproducing the labor force. Whatever the insights and the flaws of Marxist urban theory, it is mainly socioeconomic and throws very little light on urban geography. One wonders sometimes, while reading Lipietz for instance, if the author has ever read a geographical textbook. Marxist mavericks, like Henri Lefebvre, may emphasize the role of the city in the modern world so much that he is able to see in it as the mark of a new civilisation, a "post-industrial society", but he fails to tell us anything about its inner structure (Lefebvre, 1972). It is characteristic that Smith, while reviewing various social theories dealing with the city, finds only one, that of the Chicago School, with spatial insights (M P Smith, 1980)—and among the various models of urban structure classically presented by geographers it is the only one, by virtue of its scope and coherence, to deserve the name of theory.

2.4.1 Classical urban models

So, in order to consider the evolution of Los Angeles in the light of current theories of urban growth, it is necessary to content ourselves with the classical models so often presented in geography textbooks—that is, to demonstrate their spatial patterns and inner mechanisms, and to evaluate their coherence and the way they may predict the growth of Los Angeles over a thirty-year period.

Classical models: spatial forms and inner mechanisms

The concentric model of successive rings surrounding the city center is usually presented as the most important discovery of the Chicago School of Urban Sociology, but this is largely false. Actually, at least three currents of thought are grouped in a very confusing way under this heading.

The publications of the Chicago sociologists, in the late 1920s, insist on an anthropological process of acculturation: migrants from central and mediterranean Europe, poor, unskilled, generally ignorant of the English language, and grouped in large patriarchal families, settle down in the city center, where housing is cheap. Their children and grandchildren, however, working their way up the social ladder, move toward the periphery of the city as their customs change, as they become better and better integrated into American society, and as their income consequently increases. Clearly, this complex process of integration into a new culture, and of social promotion from one generation to another (a cherished theme in American sociology of the time) constitutes the main interest of *The City* by Park et al (1925). This is why they also study the way information flows across the city through the local press, as well as the eventual failure of the social improvement process, exemplified in the fate of the hobo, falling down the social ladder and back to the dilapidated city center. These two basic topics are treated in two important chapters of their book. Cultural progress takes the form of a natural process: because the city grows outward, like a tree fed by the sap of social promotion, urban ecology appears as the basis and the justification of American society. In comparison with such global and important concepts, the ring pattern of the concentric model, so famous among geographers, obviously plays a secondary role, and one cannot help wondering how much of it comes from a careful analysis of urban dynamics, and how much from the image of the natural growth of a tree, so central to the argument.

Louis Wirth, in a seminal paper published over ten years later (1938), develops the idea of the Chicago School in a direction which, characteristically, forgets completely about spatial patterns, but puts the emphasis on conflicts, tensions, and consensus in the city. Urban life is increasingly divided into segments of activity and interests, and the individual dweller lies at the intersection of several of them, losing his equilibrium and his autonomy. For three reasons, its large size, its high densities, and its social heterogeneity, the modern city induces dangerous contradictions— men cannot avoid simultaneous engagement in, and withdrawal from, public life. Social consensus, that is, what individuals take for granted and what forms a common ground for understanding and action, is undermined. Wirth predicts and deplores the decline of the neighborhood as a homogeneous group of households. Actually, he misses the dialectical process by which the loosening of the family and the dispersion of social ties reinforces, instead of weakening, the neighborhood, but the interesting point here is that the only concept which might still have a spatial basis in the whole of Wirth's analysis is in the process of vanishing. Such a pessimistic view was certainly justified in 1938, as the economic crisis and the resulting unemployment were exacerbating social tensions and undermining the very structure of American society.

Geographers, unfortunately, have retained only the less important part from this rich current of thought, namely the ring pattern, throwing away most of the fascinating social and anthropological content of the Chicago urban theory. When, twenty years later, factorial ecology exhibited concentric rings in most American cities, these spatial patterns were identified with the Chicago rings, and a surprising confusion ensued. Murphy (1974), for instance, relates Burgess's model to von Thünen's rings and, seeing in the rings a land-use pattern although it was a dynamic socioanthropological system in the Chicago theory, he writes: "The general concept involved is that rent or land values (sic) is inversely proportional to distance from the central area" (Murphy, 1974, page 294). Not only are rent and land values considered proportional, although we know that the main problem in the city center is, conversely, the discrepancy in this relation, but the ring pattern is supposed to represent decreasing land rent (a distortion of Burgess's ideas), a variable which, as we shall learn a few pages further on, is distributed rather in sectors, whereas rings represent, according to factorial ecology, stages in the family cycle. Actually, Murphy is well representative of the confused way in

which geographers interpret the ring pattern. Distorting the Chicago
theory, they see social status as increasing away from the center; but
factorial ecology shows the rings represent life stages, independent of the
social level, and land values and income are also distributed in sectors, as
is well known. Quite obviously, the spatial form is clear, but its content
quite elusive.

   One reason for this confusion is that the so-called 'Hoyt's sectorial
model' has not been better understood (Hoyt, 1933; 1939). Wealthy
households constitute the motor of the process: rapidly dissatisfied with
their home, they move away from the center into still free land to build
more modern homes, and poorer families move into the empty dwellings
the rich leave behind them. "High-grade residential growth tends to
proceed from the given point of origin along established lines of travel ..."
(Hoyt, 1939, pages 117–118). The model is thus a dynamic one, with
the rich moving outward inside a sector but not laterally. Again,
unfortunately, more than ten years later factorial ecology exhibited a
sectorial pattern containing the various socioeconomic levels of the city,
and mental confusion again mixed up Hoyt's model of sectors, containing
the outward expansion of successive and different social groups, with the
sectorial distribution of quite homogeneous and static social groups (Hoyt,
1964).

   The multinuclei model is certainly more coherent, but it has also
suffered from a drift in its interpretation. Harris and Ullman (1945) showed
that in modern American metropolises, and particularly in Los Angeles,
important commercial activities drifted away from the city center and that
several separated centers appeared in the city, forming distinct nuclei
around which space was organized. Urban functions and activities are
beyond the scope of this study, but again a multinuclei pattern was
frequently exhibited by factorial ecology, which represented the location
of distinct ethnic groups, and in current publications the multinuclei
model is believed to represent ethnicity.

   In the use geographers make of all these theories and models, there is
an impressive tendency to keep the spatial patterns, even where they are
only slightly suggested, and to forget the content of these spatial forms.
As a result, geographical theories of the city today suffer from a surprising
number of weak assumptions, incoherences, inconsistencies, and distortions.

Evaluation of the classical urban models
Fundamental to the purpose of this book are the implicit *assumptions*
hidden behind the classical urban models, and it will be a quite straightforward task to demonstrate the weaknesses of these models as they are
described today in geographical textbooks and put to use in urban analysis.

   The concentric ring model is based on an unwritten postulate: that the
city is circular with radial transportation axes. Three assumptions are then
necessary and sufficient for the model to work:

1. There must be a constant influx of poor, foreign migrants. This is by far the most important assumption, the very motor of the model, which is, unfortunately, absent from practically all geographical literature.
2. Urban growth is based on individual ascension of the social ladder, accompanied by a complex aculturation process.
3. The ideal dwelling for most families is the individual house, away from the center and on a large piece of land.
In this model, families in social progress lead the way.

The sectorial model also postulates a circular city with radiating axes. Its assumptions are not very different from the preceding ones, but the emphasis is placed differently, viz:
(a) New buildings are more desirable; here also, the detached house on a large piece of land is the ideal dwelling, and the area needed increases with wealth (Alonso's land-rent model starts from here and develops this concept).
(b) There must be a constant increase in population, particularly of poor families, to explain why the houses left behind by the rich are occupied. Both assumptions form the motor of the model, explaining the sprawl of the city. Two other assumptions explain the form of this sprawl:
(c) Radial transportation axes play a basic role in ordering spatial growth.
(d) Local amenities, also important, are linear and radiate from the center of the city; in other words, the old center stays at the point of convergence of linear local amenities.
In this model, wealthy households lead the way.

The multinuclei model, if applied to residences (our sole concern here), assumes only that strong tensions oppose people of different kind (with a loose definition of the term 'kind', namely social, racial, cultural, linguistic, or a combination of these characteristics) and that they react by flocking together. There is necessarily an upper limit to the size of the homogeneous group formed in this way, but what is it? Here, urban growth is fueled and led by minorities.

All of these models are actually socioeconomic models with strong anthropological meanings; they contain few, if any, indications of spatial patterns. These are implicit: the city is assumed to be circular, with a center from which important axes radiate, and there are strong gradients of different kinds between center and periphery. For instance, at the time the Chicago sociologists were publishing elements of their theory, a geographer tried to describe the forces at work in the city (Colby, 1933). The points made by Colby were that:
some forces attract toward the center—site attraction, functional convenience, functional magnetism;
others act in a centrifugal direction: spatial force (congested versus empty land), site force, situational force, plus
a force of social evolution and the opposition in status and organization of occupance.

Colby's distinctions may be open to discussion, but they boil down to the same thing, that is an assumption of a center with radiating lines, and strong gradients toward or away from this center.

The *weaknesses* in the subsequent development of these models are of two kinds: insufficiencies due mainly to the fact that practically all theoretical content has been watered down in subsequent expositions, so that in their present forms they are not able to explain anything anymore; and inconsistencies in their inner structure due to later confusion and misunderstanding.

Insufficiencies are many and it is not difficult to select a few examples. Almost all American cities, with the famous exception of Washington, DC, have gridiron plans. Yet such a spatial pattern never appears in these models. If the reason is that only axes bearing important traffic play a structuring role in the city, a reasonable suggestion, the problem remains to determine at what point in time this important network did structure the city—the rails of the electric streetcars in the 1920s, the important avenues open to cars in the 1930s and 1940s, or the urban freeways, from the late 1950s until today? Their patterns are very different. Hoyt himself is not clear: "High-grade residential growth tends to proceed from the given point of origin along established lines of travel" (Hoyt, 1939, pages 117–118)—but which lines? And if they change over time, according to which law? It is quite likely there is a kind of spatial memory, a hysteresis fixing for some period (of what duration?) the effect on urban land of a particular transportation network, but how is it fixed? At which moment? Why?

Other questions remain unanswered, or are not even asked: what about black migration across the city? Characteristically, this factor does not play any role in the Chicago models: Blacks were not, at the time, an important part of the urban population. They play a role in the multi-nuclei model, but an inverted one: the model is based on the congregation of similar households in homogeneous neighborhoods. Black migrations, however, represent the opposite tendency: families leave the security of their community to try and infiltrate a different and often hostile neighborhood.

Factorial ecology as used in American geography has often been discussed and criticized. Let us consider here only one basic point, the identification of the main axes, that is the meaning of the observed spatial patterns. Usually, socioeconomic status, life cycle, and ethnicity form the first three factors, the main spatial patterns, respectively in sectors, in rings, and in several separated nuclei. These factors are orthogonal by construction, but it would be absurd to pretend that age of the head of the family, income, and race are not correlated. The axes are linear combinations of these variables. Income, for instance, loads on most axes, but more so on the so-called socioeconomic status factor—it is only by an abusive extension that factorial ecologists act as if the whole variable was represented by only one factor. Of course, most know that reality is more complicated, but they remain lax in identifying the factor. The result is a false identification of the logical content of the patterns: income is not distributed only in sectors, but also (albeit to a lesser degree) in rings and in patches. Thus, the interpretative content of the models in their modern version is not only small, but also misleading and incomplete.

Furthermore, these fairly weak models are plagued with logical inconsistencies. Geographers are fond (cf Murphy, 1974, page 293) of identifying Burgess's model with von Thünen's rings, but the analogy holds only externally as far as the forms are concerned. The inner mechanisms of both models are exactly opposed: in von Thünen's model, differences in quantity (transportation costs) induce differences in quality (the type of product); that is, a continuous function (cost as a function of distance) determines a step-wise function (discrete)—a suitable model choice for agricultural production. As a result, spatial patterns are very clear and definite: the line separating wheat from vegetables may be mapped precisely. Conversely, for the Chicago School model, qualitative differences between families (in their qualification, their culture, their income, their morality, etc) induce quantitative differences in space (in density, land rent, dwelling size, distance to the center, etc). In this case, a discrete distribution induces a continuous function: it should not surprise us that the rings are largely artificial, as are their limits and their number; the only resulting clear pattern is an ordinal succession of types from center to periphery—a ranking of areas, but no clear delimitation.

Let us point to another inconsistency in the opposition between sectors and rings: for Homer Hoyt, each sector corresponds to a centrifugal direction along which different social groups move in succession, ranked in order of increasing income from the center to the periphery, and following the leading group, the wealthiest. Actually, Hoyt's pattern is made of concentric waves inside each ring. In Burgess's model, architectural and anthropological rings are immobile, each one characterized by a certain type of building and of housing, as well as by a certain kind of family. People move outwards on a stable backcloth. In other words, Hoyt's model is probably as dynamic as the Burgess model, probably more so; and differentiation in land use exists inside each ring as waves move inside each sector. There is a dialectical relationship between the two models, but much more complex than modern texts would have us believe.

Theories of the city and urban geography
Let us now consider what is the present status of urban theories. The fascinating theories elaborated in Chicago some sixty years ago have now been largely emptied of their content by subsequent urban studies, for reasons largely as follows.

From the very beginning, the theories have been poor in their account of spatial patterns. The fundamental form, the all-important center with radial axes, is actually assumed before any discussion starts. This does not mean the models do not imply some spatial organization, but they do so in a subtle and complex way which has been badly distorted by later urban researchers.

The models describe dynamic processes, which explains their partly dialectical structures and makes it very difficult to extract from them a simple spatial order.

The original urban theories have been subsequently misunderstood and mutilated. Above all, these dynamic models have been rendered static: Burgess's system of dynamic and expanding rings of moving individuals has been changed into stable rings of land uses, and Hoyt's waves moving inside a sector along a radial axis have been changed into homogeneous and static sectors.

Social and economic theories have been abandoned for spatial patterns which were only partly explicated in those theories but which corresponded to the forms empirically discovered through factorial ecology. The names of Burgess and Hoyt have been kept, however, thus increasing the confusion.

But most important of all, the inner mechanisms of the theories have been destroyed since 1931, but this seems to have been noticed by very few workers. While the USA was for centuries the main country in the world accepting immigrants, it changed, in 1931, into one of the most closed lands in the world. The importance of such radical change cannot be exaggerated, and in particular its impact on models based on foreign immigration. After 1931, the Burgess and Hoyt models simply could not work anymore: their basic condition (a steady flow of poor foreign families) did not hold any longer.

Nor can they be replaced by black immigrants to the city: these immigrants do not (and do not want to) follow a similar process of aculturation; rampant racism efficiently forbids their harmonious diffusion throughout the city. The 1970 Census data begin to show an important distinction between patterns for new middle-income Blacks and those for poorer Blacks. Both groups, however, are deserting the city center for the fringe areas.

Finally, all the models assume a growing city whose population, and particularly its poor population, increases constantly. But since the late 1960s in California, and since an earlier time in the East, huge metropolises do not grow anymore, at least not in their centers. Instead they tend, like New York, to lose their population.

Thus we are left with quite a curious state of affairs. The few theories of the city that we have do not hold anymore—the images of them given in most textbooks are caricatures, distorted simplifications which keep the form but drop most of the theoretical content. At the same time, however, empirical analyses carried out by factorial ecologists in many cities (cf the work by Brian Berry and his students) continue to exhibit regularly the three spatial patterns which apparently correspond to these theories. And this is the source of the bad confusion in which we find ourselves: there is no doubt that these urban forms do exist, but the old contents which so many still try to find in them are now illusions, and they have been so for many years. We must therefore ask ourselves whether this strange resilience of spatial forms to change means they are independent of any content we might find in them. Such an explanation would account for why past theories have been so well fitted to the conditions of their time and have then broken down as these conditions changed without a concomitant change in the patterns they assumed. There is another clue: in their authentic form, the classical theories had little to say about spatial patterns; to begin with, at least, they were largely autonomous constructs. This provides an interesting indication of what a new urban model might be. I suggest it should develop as two independent entities: (1) as a model of the spatial patterns in the city, thus organizing space; and (2) as a theory of forces at work, thus explaining changes in the city; it should then indicate the way these two autonomous processes combine. Stable forms would thus integrate change, the main topic of this study.

2.4.2 Classical urban models and change
Stability and alteration are built into the classical models as interesting inner contradictions, sometimes giving the impression of a dialectical process. But is it really the case? Are they models of real, authentic change, as defined above, or only of quasi-change?

The positive aspects of models: the stable components
In the three models, the position of social groups in relation to one another remains constant. They are ranked in an immutable order for the Burgess model, along an anthropological and radial line; for the Hoyt model, along a socioeconomic line, which also forms a radius; Harris sees different homogeneous groups juxtaposed in fixed locations. In all three cases, groups are definitely ordered in one-dimensional or two-dimensional space.

There is also a general stability of spatial forms: circles around the center are fixed in their relative order of land uses and building types, and even, in the recent distorted versions of the models, in their distances to the city center. Sectors are also fixed, along the main axes and by linear local amenities, and by the directions taken by the leading groups.

So, how can change take place? It happens precisely in the relationship between spatial forms and human groups. The suitability of the assignment of each social group of households to a particular piece of land, be it a part of a ring, a segment of a sector, or some nucleus, is what changes over time. In other words, change arises from the contradictory contact of two stable sets of elements, human and spatial. But what causes this change? What fuels it?

The negative aspects of models: motors of change
Aging, and the consecutive time conflicts, form the motor (a very
traditional one) in the sector model: aging of housing in Hoyt's theory
puts the rich on the move; aging of the family head in the interpretation
of sectors made by factorial ecologists (the life cycle). In both cases, there
is also an implicit change in peoples' tastes and means.

Progressive *integration* into an alien culture is the mainspring which
causes the movement of the concentric rings of people and buildings.
More profoundly, this drive is made of the deep transformation of a man's
mind, of the relations between human beings in a family, of the position
of a man in society (social ties, job, consumption patterns), and of
conflicts between generations.

The third kind of motor is social *segregation*, turning conflict between
individuals of different race, status, etc into the homogeneous grouping of
them in single-type neighborhoods.

In all these models, change is fueled by conflict: time conflict,
generation conflict, racial and social conflict. Does it mean that change,
as conceived in these models, is real—that is, is dialectical and irreversible?

True change or quasi-change?
If change is built into these models, then it is in such a way that it
happens only at a given geographical scale, but not at any other; for
instance, in the life-cycle model, change is ontogenetic (individuals keep
moving) but not phylogenetic—a generation's realm is inscribed inside a
sector, and remains stable. In Hoyt's conception, rich families keep
moving (drawing along with them the whole town) not for love of change
but, on the contrary, because they do not want their houses to age and to
change, and they move further away in order to keep living in the same
new structures.

Integration into a new culture has a similar effect at a more general
level—generations are constantly on the move from the center to the
periphery, but the community as a whole remains the same. As in the
preceding case, it is to ensure the unification of the culture into the one
unique mold, the 'American way of life', that so many immigrant families
undergo such deep changes. As a result, everything should stop when all
families have become 'good American'. Here we have a transitional
process, and not a truly dialectical one.

Again, social segregation leads to the same pattern: households move
all over the city only in order to ensure stability of the neighborhoods.
What is inscribed in those models is clearly quasi-change, often of a cyclical
nature: the more recent 'wave theory', for instance, naturally develops
the sectorial model by assuming the rich come back to the city center
when distances to the suburbs have become excessive, hence the movement
turns in the opposite direction, and urban renewal can take place. These
rich should then, logically, move again to the periphery along a well-trodden

path as time passes. It is also interesting to note, in Burgess's theory, the keen interest for the hobo. Geographers do not seem to have attached any importance to this classification, but its place in the theory is clear: the hobo is the dropout who, left behind by social progress, returns to the city center where everything started; to conceive the model as a cyclical one might be to consider the situation too optimistically. Within the sectors containing different life cycles, individuals, as they age and become more lonely and poor, tend to return to the districts where they lived as young bachelors.

In all of the above models change is essentially *cyclical*, that is to say not actually true change at all. It can be infinitely reproduced. Nowhere is there a stopping point, a limit beyond which movement would naturally, as if it were following some inner logic, transform itself into something else. The basic processes in these theories are built to work forever. In actuality, they can be stopped only by a drying up of the immigrant flows, an event which, as we know, made them suddenly obsolete, but was neither forecast by the authors, nor noticed by their followers.

Real change is absent from existing urban theories; they include only a kind of 'stable change' which reminds one closely of Aristotle's example of the turning wheel, which is in movement but, at the same time, immobile, since its position in space and the relative location of its parts do not experience any change whatever. William Alonso (1964b) was sensitive to this aspect of urban modeling when he proposed a rent model which would definitely not be cyclical. The rich would not move because they want new buildings (nothing would then forbid them, after a certain period, to come back to the city center and to clear away its old structures and start again from scratch, as in urban renewal policies) but because they need increasingly wider pieces of land: if this were the case, urban renewal would be doomed to failure. In fact, rich people do come back now to settle in the city center, but they form a new and original group of rich bachelors who do not wish to marry anymore, at least for the time being. They are culturally very different from their wealthy parents, and this makes it impossible to test Alonso's ideas. But his criticism of the cyclical character of Hoyt's model is both clear and perceptive.

2.4.3 What to expect in Los Angeles?

Is it possible, from such a review of existing urban theories and the spatial models they produced, to try to predict the evolution of spatial forms in Los Angeles? Except for a seminal but simple study (Shevky and Williams, 1949), we still know very little about the city and its evolution since the war. It seems impossible, however, to base any prediction on the theories reviewed above, for two fundamental groups of reasons:
First, on the one hand, practically all the basic assumptions behind the theories do not hold anymore, and even less so in Los Angeles than in any other American metropolis. Not only did the migrant flows from abroad

which fed city growth dry up after 1931, but actually they never played a
noticeable role in the case of the south Californian metropolis; it has been
populated, as will be shown later, by wealthy city-dwellers from the East
and the Center of the USA, from authentic American stock—so much for
the concentric model. As for the sectorial model, the fact that the city
center is located inland and not on the shore seems to hinder the
formation of sectors along local amenities, which are here the mountain
slopes and the littoral; we should rather expect, according to Hoyt's ideas,
to observe the development of a center at Santa Monica, where slopes and
shore intersect, with sectors radiating away from it.

Second, and on the other hand, the growth conditions particular to Los
Angeles seem to make the appearance of regular spatial patterns highly
unlikely. The city is *too recent*, too new to exhibit sectorial or concentric
patterns; its most important period of growth is after 1931, the key year
in American demography, and the model assumptions did not hold any
longer when the city really began to explode. It developed so *fast* that it
is difficult to believe regular patterns had enough time to form. Population
densities are among the *lowest* in the world for an urban center of its
size—is it likely we shall find any center with the power to organize space
at such distance? Finally, the city is too big, both in population and in
space, for any spatial model to fit it even if we speak only, as has been
explained before, of Los Angeles *stricto sensu*: "... the smaller a city, the
closer it approximates the integrated model [that is, a combination of the
three models indicated above] postulated earlier" (Berry and Horton, 1970,
page 386). The paramount role played in Los Angeles by the private car
is another argument casting doubt that any model can be useful here:
"... the automobile has lessened the applicability of the concentric zone
and sector theories ..." (Murphy, 1974, page 305; the same idea is
repeated three times on the same page). And the same author concludes:
"... it would appear impossible for any such system of concentric zones as
that conceived by Burgess to be applicable now in the American city except
in an extremely general way ..." (Murphy, 1974, page 298).

Finally, global urban theories have too weak and too inconsistent a
content to allow one to make predictions, but this is made even more
difficult in Los Angeles. All urban literature on Los Angeles points in the
same direction: a spineless, disorganized, amorphous city, with no noticeable center and no regular spatial patterns, no historical influences and no
spatial memory; the only regularity we might expect to find in the city
space should take the form of a combination of random laws.

The emergence of Los Angeles: historical background

Although, by European standards, Los Angeles is a very new city in a new country, history plays a paramount role in explaining the present patterns and in determining recent trends in its housing and population. In this chapter I shall try to build, on the stage of American urban history, the scenery where this action takes place.

3.1 California comes to the fore
The changes that have taken place in Los Angeles during the study period result from a political, economic, and social evolution which took place on a much larger scale. Such a huge metropolis, located as it is at a strategic position on the active fringe of the most powerful nation in the world, is naturally influenced by the transformations in the whole American hemisphere. But in addition it is influenced by transformations in countries located on the far shore of the Pacific Ocean, and even in Europe. The growth in the city is a remote but definite effect of many complex factors: the decadence of the Chinese empire, the rise and the fall of Japan, the technical and scientific development of the Soviet Union and its first successes in space.

As far as the growth of Los Angeles is concerned, it is sufficient to divide United States growth in the middle of the twentieth century into three different periods. First, a time of doubt and, for many, of misery, from 1929 until 1941—as the traditional economy with the role of the independent entrepreneur, the laws of the market, and the predominance of the East Coast underwent a dramatic crisis. Then, a time of unheard-of prosperity as successive wars, hot or cold, in Europe, the Pacific, Korea, and Vietnam, fueled the economy. The important point is that, during this period, most American activities were directed to the west, to the Pacific ocean, and that California profited by them more than any other State. Last, a deep crisis starting with the early 1970s, partly as a consequence of the Vietnam War, which hurt the Western world, the United States, and particularly California. The period analyzed has very clear limits: it starts with the preparations for a new urban era, develops with the Californian dream, and ends as the people of Los Angeles awake to the disillusionment of the early 1970s (see Bowman, 1974; Dash, 1976; Kuehn, 1978).

3.1.1 The Great Depression and its consequences
United States policies during the First World War as well as its prosperity during the 1920s are basically associated with Europe.

The end of World War I and the consecutive redrawing of the map of Europe brought about a series of political crises, revolutions, and displacements of populations which fed the last huge flow of immigrants to enter the United States. These uprooted Europeans, coming mainly from Central Europe and the Balkans, settled down in the East Coast metropolises, or to a lesser degree, in the Midwest around Chicago and Milwaukee.

In a similar way, prosperity during the Roaring Twenties was largely connected with European factors: the growth of the market, the progress of industry, euphoria after victory and peace, and also inflation, beneficial at least at the beginning.

The industry of the Midwest (the car industry then settling down in Michigan) and the Northeast (New England, New Jersey), as well as the business companies and the banks in New York City, led the movement. To be sure, California participated in this prosperity, and the film industry, then setting up in Los Angeles, brought with it money and fame, but it still remained a fallout of eastern activity—most of the development was yet to come. Money, commodities, and ideas circulated mostly between New York and western Europe: the Yankees had the power and Paris was still the center of Western civilization.

By comparison, the other side of the American continent seemed to open onto an empty ocean. The Soviet Union floundered in the bloody conflicts of a painful birth, and did not take much interest in Asia. The Chinese empire sank into anarchy and widespread disorder—it was then too weak and too poor to become an interesting partner, and too wide and too unstable to be colonized and profitably exploited. Australia and New Zealand were too sparsely populated and, at a time of sea travel, far too remote from the industrial world to have any important weight. As for the Pacific coast of South America, at the time it was losing much of the economic interest it may have offered in the past—the chemical industry back East and in Europe threw onto the market competitive synthetic products.

Japan was the only partner worth considering, but it was still weak and remote. From any point of view, during the 1920s California was still a peripheral region. The Great Depression, by breaking down the prosperity in the East and transforming American society in depth, prepared the conditions for a radical change.

The Great Depression

Tradition has it that the Great Depression started on Black Friday, in October 1929. The first symptoms actually reach back to 1927, and the crisis progressed in two distinct phases (Sauvy, 1970): an American period from 1929 to 1931, when the United States sank into the crisis more deeply than did Europe, and an even worse relapse after 1931, as the British pound broke down under the strain (most raw materials were then quoted in pounds) and made the Depression worldwide. In the United States, the troughs in the economic curves were reached in 1932 (unemployment, prices, salaries, bankruptcies, ...). But more important than the crisis itself was the long period of stagnation which followed the shock, and lasted until at least 1940, since this had a most important moral impact, as I shall now describe. It was the social consequences that were of principal importance. These were:

(a) The breakdown of the patriarchal family. Unemployment and misery undermined the prestige of the head of the family. Each of its members, the wife, children, became more autonomous as they tried to fight on their own to make a living. At the same time, inactive people (young or retired) fell back onto the family, the only structure where they could find help and compassion. As a result, the family structure underwent a deep change: traces of patriarchal hierarchy, inherited from European migrants, tended to vanish. The well-structured family often turned into a quite amorphous group where centrifugal tendencies are strong and limited only by economic necessity.

(b) The widespread misery, combined with this breakdown of family authority, with the expansion of the private car, and with the fact that it was so easy to get a weapon, explained the increase of crime and violence, particularly among young people (as witnessed by the legend of Bonnie and Clyde). In 1932, thousands of young people drifted through the Union in stolen cars, all the more mobile in that they had lost their roots and kept running away from the police. Indirectly, through this development of crime, the Depression had strongly increased mobility.

(c) Concentration in land ownership, itself largely an effect of the crisis in the economy and the banking system, uprooted the poor farmer and forced him on the road to the West. Steinbeck has given a classical picture of the phenomenon (Steinbeck, 1939). The Promised Land reached finally by Steinbeck's farmers still exists today: it is a small agricultural community asleep in the Mojave desert, sixty miles from Los Angeles. A catastrophic drought in 1936 and consecutive soil erosion combined their effects with those of the economic Depression. All in all, millions of Americans left their homes and moved North and West: dispossessed farmers, ruined people from the lower middle-class, Okies[1]—many of them came to southern California during the 1930s. They were followed during the 1940s by industrial workers, not pushed away by misery, but attracted by the prosperity brought by the war. Although it changed both in nature and in form, the huge flow of migrants which started in 1930 did not stop for twenty years, and constituted one of the main factors which determined the growth of Los Angeles.

(d) Black families participated largely in these movements, all the more so as they were poorer and more oppressed. The great black drift from the South to the North, the Midwest, and the West was one of the most important urban phenomena in contemporary United States history, urban because these migrants settled down mainly in the big cities. Although the

[1] A migrant agricultural worker from Oklahoma.

movement started in the 1930s, it was during the war years that it became
particularly strong: the peak in the black flow occurred later than in the
white one. Consequences were paramount, especially in Los Angeles.
The black community, negligible before the Depression, became in the next
twenty years a very important part of the city and an instrumental factor
in its change (Brooks de Graaf, 1962; Williams, 1956).
(e) The links of all sorts which formed the structure of society before
1929 tended to dissolve; they were replaced, during our period of analysis,
by new ones. New Immigration Acts, between 1930 and 1933, severed
all the traditional migration flows from Europe, one of the bases of
American history since its origin. Instead, an inner network of migration
developed through the United States, one from which California was to
benefit more than any other state.
(f) Another constant of American society, the network of private
associations which linked individuals and households in religious, charitable,
social, and professional goals was also eroded and dissolved by the crisis.
In its stead appeared a new network, mainly public, of organisations and
agencies responsible for assisting families and helping them to get a home
or find a job. The old network had been made up of a large number of
small local cells, poorly linked together: it had been dangerous for an
individual to leave one of these helpful associations, because it was difficult
to find a similar one in another place, and still more difficult to be accepted
as a part of it. This obstacle to mobility disappeared with the crisis.
(g) There was one quite paradoxical effect of the Depression after 1929,
education experienced a considerable expansion. To avoid unemployment,
many young people remained in school or at the university as long as
possible. Many adults, who were idle against their will, used their free
time to register in technical courses in the hope of finding a job more
easily—the Roosevelt administration widely developed this kind of teaching.
As a result, social mobility, as well as industrial productivity increased
during the late 1930s: migrants coming to Los Angeles in 1940 to find a
job constituted, for the most part, well-qualified manpower ready to
contribute to the major war effort.
    So the consequences were multiple: the Depression tended to weaken
the industrial preponderance of the North and the East; to move a large
part of the national manpower away from the South; to increase strongly
geographical and social mobility; to dissolve family structures by speeding
up the transition from the patriarchal family of European immigrants to a
much smaller and looser family group, almost free of such hierarchy (which
soon appeared as characteristic of California); finally, to bring to the West
considerable manpower, mobile and hardworking, because it had suffered
so much from unemployment, and well-qualified. All the social conditions
for an economic boom in California, and particularly in Los Angeles, were
assembled in 1940. Only the economic spark was missing: the war in the
Pacific provided the flint and steel.

The New Deal

However, it was still a problem for the government to foster favorable economic conditions, and this was to be the main goal of President Roosevelt's 'New Deal'. It will be presented here only inasmuch as it bears on the fate of Los Angeles.

In a famous speech made in San Francisco (a meaningful choice) in 1932, Roosevelt explained that territorial expansion on the Frontier was over and that America should renounce the individualist methods of old: this was the dawn of a new era where government was going to intervene in economic matters. Beyond political rhetoric and Roosevelt's quite confused dreams of 'planning without socialism' which he was never to realize, lurked a supreme phenomenon probably unforeseen by the President: the end of small traditional capitalism, based on the activity of the individual entrepreneur, and the real beginning of the corporate era.

The New Deal began with a strong emphasis on planning. The government tried to break up monopolies and to act as a businessman— huge programs of public works were launched, partly to heal the wounds made by excessive and careless capitalist exploitation, partly to undertake the necessary tasks private enterprise was not interested in (replanting trees, controlling soil erosion, building low-cost housing, ...). Another aim of this public action was to take the place of private initiative at a time when it was failing in so many domains. Finally, the government also tried, against many private lobbies, to foster international commerce by lowering customs duties (a policy strongly advocated by Justices L Brandeis and F Frankfurter) —a large windfall for the ports, and particularly for Los Angeles.

It is now a matter of record that the opposition to his policy was so vocal and so powerful that Roosevelt had to lower his expectations and to satisfy himself with 'regulating' the economy—a limited action with a much narrower scope. The Depression and the New Deal nonetheless mark a major turning-point in the history of the United States; the predominance of industry of the Midwest, the services of the East Coast, and the agriculture of the South were badly shaken, once and for all. European immigration, the very basis for eastern preeminence was stopped, and the constant, if irregular, flow of cheap manpower dried up. Social and economic structures underwent drastic changes: by 1940, business remained very weak and the economy was still sick, but the United States was turning towards the new forms of life quite typical of the West Coast, and the new types of production for which California was particularly well prepared. World War II gave the necessary push.

3.1.2 War and Prosperity: 1940–1963

World War II

It is important for this study to note that the war started in the Pacific. Indeed, antagonism between Japan and the United States was basic and probably more important than the rejection of Nazism, an ideology which was not without followers in America. Had not Hitler been fool enough to declare war on the United States without any treaty forcing him to do so, and with no advantage to be expected, one might even wonder if America might not have waited much longer to wage war in Europe.

Roosevelt nevertheless tried, at different times, to disengage America from commiting itself too heavily in the Pacific. In spite of the invasion of Manchuria by Japan as early as September 1931, and although Russia, after a long eclipse, again began to throw her weight around in this region, the US government tried to keep out of the hornets' nest: in 1934, by granting independence to the Philippines, it abandoned any direct commitment to defend those islands. The White House observed with patient restraint the successive coups of the Japanese government: speeches devoid of precise threats were uttered when Japan, after the affair of the Marco Polo bridge, invaded China (summer 1937); a diplomatic note of protest was sent when Japanese artillery opened fire on an American gunboat on the Yang-Tse-kiang (December 1937). In contrast to this patience in the Pacific, Roosevelt took careful and difficult steps to prepare American opinion for a war in Europe. In all American history, danger and war had always come from Europe, or from Mexico with the complicity of a European nation. Of course, there were other reasons for Roosevelt's attitude but they are not relevant here. The interesting point is that such a dissymmetry in US policy showed clearly the secondary status still occupied by the West Coast in 1940: at that date, 72% of national industrial production came from the Northeast; by 1970, this production had dwindled to less than half of the total (*Newsweek*, March 21, 1977).

The attack on Pearl Harbor, on December 7, 1941, forced the United States to switch their priorities: the Pacific suddenly became the theater of war. The war effort generated was immense and attracted soldiers, workers, and industry to California's two main harbors. The whole US Army, in the summer of 1939, had only 174000 men enlisted, and by 1941 still no more than 1.4 million; but by 1945 the number had jumped to 8.3 million. The increase was even larger in the US Air Force and much more significant for Los Angeles, because the biggest aircraft factories were to be located on the West Coast, in or close to the city: Douglas at Santa Monica, Lockheed at Burbank (April 1942), and Boeing at Long Beach. The US Air Force had some 2000 operational aircraft in 1939, but more than 100000 in 1944. During the last year of the war, the country produced 50000 planes.

Government spending took a prodigious jump. In the heyday of the New Deal, it never went above $8 billion a year; during the war, it reached $100 billion. Even if we discard inflation, which was actually quite modest, the result was an enormous injection of capital into the war industries, which were so important to California. National wealth also made incredible progress: the GNP grew from $100 billion in 1940 to $213 billion in 1945. Unemployment virtually disappeared: 45 million employed in 1940, more than 64 million in 1945.

Private companies profited not only from the economic boom and the exceptional benefits generated by armament production. The fact that most of the burden of the new investment needed for such endeavor was borne by the federal government was a godsend. West Coast industry in particular, the youngest in the country, thrived with quite limited private funding. Nor was the moral benefit to private enterprise any less important: after being decried for ten years as responsible for the national crisis, businessmen now appeared as the saviours of the country and champions of freedom. As during the heydays of puritan ethics, profit and respectability again went hand in hand.

In California, racism used the opportunity to raise its head and engage in operations profitable to it. In January 1942, a delegation of West Coast States to Congress (in fact, California was preponderant) obtained the vote, through some alarming but baseless rumours, for a law leading to the arrest and concentration in camps of 100000 people of Japanese descent whether they were American citizens or not, and to the confiscation of their property. This oppressive behavior left all the more bitterness in the Californian and Los Angeles Japanese populations because it was perfectly groundless, and it remained a unique episode in the history of the United States, a country which had treated with much tolerance its German and Italian minorities (and even the Japanese in Hawaii), who had also remained perfectly loyal (Mason and McKinstry, 1969).

After the war, the reconversion of industry to peacetime production was easier than in 1919. There was no exorbitant increase in consumption or in credit like the boom experienced during the 1920s, which was such an important cause of the 1929 depression. One of the main reasons for such an harmonious recovery was the spatial dispersion of the American production system, which had widened the economic base of the country. Here again, growth in Californian industry has played a very important role. Increased mobility of manpower and even of whole families was another favorable factor: people had been made footloose during the Depression, and flows of workers had been attracted by employment in the war industries, in addition to the migrations of military personnel and their families (Milbank Memorial Fund, 1947).

Savings, accumulated during the war, were invested in industrial reconversion, thus avoiding dangerous inflationary pressures. Even demography contributed to the prosperity both as cause and effect. The Baby-Boom in 1946–1947 is celebrated but not surprising—it is a normal occurrence after a war. What was less spectacular, but more important, was that the national birth rate remained at a surprisingly high level after the boom. In this way, the number of consumers and producers was bound to grow for a generation, and continue to fuel economic progress as the country expressed its confidence in the future.

The Cold War and the American Committment in the Pacific
Until 1963 war, both hot and cold, had rather a favorable effect on the
economy.

The war in Korea (1950–1953) again widened the market open to
industry. Armament production increased, along with investment and
productivity, and this kept inflation at a moderate level and allowed a
regular increase in the standard of living. Military spending grew from 6%
of the GNP to 14% during the war, and fell back after 1953 to the still
quite high level of 9%. The reason for this maintained level was the
armament race with the Soviet Union (Clayton, 1962; Burton and
Dyckman, 1965). The real or imagined superiority of the Russians in
rocket engineering was one of the main anxieties of the Eisenhower era.
It led to a very expensive program of research and development which
particularly benefited California and Los Angeles (it is enough here to cite
the names of the Rand Corporation in Santa Monica, CalTech, and the Jet
Propulsion Laboratory at Pasadena).

The victory of John F Kennedy over Richard M Nixon for the Presidency
although the loser had started his career as a lawyer in Los Angeles, did
not hinder the progress of California in any way. The enthusiasm of the
man from Massachusetts rang out with a Californian sound with his slogan
of the 'New Frontier'. The West Coast remained a model for the whole
nation, and also a myth.

It is noteworthy that most external crises which confronted America
happened in the Pacific Ocean: the Chinese revolution triumphing in
1949, the Korean War (1950–1953), the Vietnamese victory at Dien-Bien-
Phu (May 1954) and the cry for help from the Christian Democrat French
government, the arrival of US 'advisers' in Vietnam as early as 1962, and
the subsequent build-up of American military power, ending finally in open
war. These major events forced the United States to remain in full force
in the Pacific and indeed to get bogged down there. The career of General
Douglas McArthur is a good illustration: his conflict with Roosevelt, who
was more interested in Europe while he advocated putting the main effort
in the Pacific, his service in Korea, his revocation by Truman who did not
want to go too far in the Far East, and his return to America as a glorious
victim—never had the Pacific Ocean played such a role in an American
life. Here was the place where China, Japan, and Russia were playing
their cards. In contrast, Africa was still easily dominated, and Europe was
relatively quiet because of the stalemate between East and West: the
airlift to Berlin, and the Suez expedition represented dangerous tensions,
but the United States had never had to intervene militarily (except in
Lebanon). There is an obvious change in the center of gravity of American
involvement between the years after World War I and those following the
second world conflict.

The deep transformations of American society
In the years following World War II one of the most obvious features in
the United States was general prosperity (table 3.1), readily evinced by the
increase in consumer loans (table 3.2). Their volume grew slowly until
1940, remained limited by government policy during the war, but then
jumped ahead strongly.

The major constituent in the creation of this situation was the
appearance of the modern corporation, and with it, simultaneously, a new
human type—the manager. During the period of the New Deal, and still
more with the mobilization of the economy for war, a new kind of inter-
changeable personnel began to occupy the key positions in government,
private enterprise, justice (particularly in positions dealing with the law of
the firm, the antitrust laws, and labor legislation), economic planning, and
politics. These managers were honest, efficient, and qualified. Usually,
they did not have any direct financial interest in the activities for which they
were responsible and, in contrast to the entrepreneurs of old, they looked
much less for individual profit and more for efficiency in management,
regularity in production, or power in administration.

The unions also underwent a change: they no longer spoke of subverting
the existing social system and they did not use violent action, except
against their competitors. During the McCarthy era (1950–1954), they
were much more vocal in their fight against Communism than were the
managers or businessmen in general, and they exhibited, as during the
Vietnam war, a bellicose and violent patriotism which placed them among
the more solid props of the existing order.

Because of its noncentral position and the late start to its development,
California had had much less experience than had the Northeast of the
small-scale capitalism of the individual entrepreneur. It was also famous,
at least in its southern half, for its relatively weak and badly organized
unions. Thus by dint of its location in the national territory and the
time of its industrial development, which coincided more or less with the
deep transformations in the nation described above, we have the
explanation of why it progressed so fast and took up a position in the
forefront. The modern corporation found itself less hindered in its growth

Table 3.1. Growth of US Gross National Product.

Year	1947	1950	1952	1956	1960	1966
Billions of current dollars	234.3	284.6	347	419.2	500	740

Table 3.2. Evolution of consumer credit.

Year	1930	1940	1945	1950	1955	1960
Billions of current dollars	7	9	6	21	39	55

Source: Glaab and Brown (1967).

here by customs, vested interests, and relics of the past than it did back
East. Finally, the race to the moon directed an enormous flow of money,
ideas, and qualified staff toward Southern California.

3.1.3 The end of the American dream: 1964-1970

At the end of the 1960s, after the murder of John F Kennedy in
November 1963, a most decisive change occurred.

The political fallback: from rebellion to repression (1964-1968)
Under Kennedy's presidency, and still more under Johnson's, the troubles
that were now shaking American society (Vietnam war, urban riots, etc)
could be concealed no longer, but hopefully they were to be solved
'scientifically' by efficient and powerful action. This was the time of the
'Great Society', with great ideas, great projects, great budgets. The racial
crisis in the Deep South, which spread to the North and the Midwest,
compelled changes in the law and still more in the attitudes toward
minorities.

The upheaval contributed to the explosion of an urban crisis, probably
more social than racial, with the historic riots in New York (Harlem,
1964), and then in Los Angeles (Watts, August 1965) (Sears and
McConahay, 1969; 1970). Black rioters from the ghetto did not attack
white neighborhoods but tried, inside the black districts, to destroy ("Burn,
baby, burn") a retail system which exploited them (by systematic looting
and burning of supermarkets and shops) and which was mainly the
property of whites living outside the ghetto, but which was managed by
Blacks. This is a typical example of the economic structure of a black
city, located inside a white metropolis (Cohen and Murphy, 1966). In
addition to these demonstrations, there was a protest against the ghetto's
lack of accessibility—people burnt the cars in the parking lots, obstructed
the freeways exits leading into the ghetto, demanded free rides on the
public transport system, and burnt the buses to back up their demands.

Finally, the Vietnam war, and the extension of the draft it implied, had
a particularly strong impact on California as a base for the action in the
Pacific, as one of the main centers for the war industry, and as a state
where the population was younger than in most other states of the Union.
In 1964, the Free Speech Movement shook the University of California at
Berkeley, and spread to most other US campuses, and even, although
belated and altered in many ways, to Germany, Japan, Czechoslovakia,
and France.

The democrat government acted as if the solution to these problems was
money. Federal grants to research institutions, and to public and private
universities increased enormously. This was the heyday of the research
grant, to which the huge flow of orders to the war industries added its
effect. California, and particularly the southern half, with its universities
among the best in the USA, its research institutes (like Rand at Santa
Monica), and its aerospace and electronic factories, gained the biggest

slice of this pie. Federal grants to local governments increased in a similar fashion (table 3.3). Between 1953 and 1962, the total volume of grants almost tripled; the most favored sectors were transport and housing, particularly urban housing where grants were multiplied by a factor of five.

The election of Richard M Nixon to the presidency marked the turning point. The purpose of government was no longer to be understanding and to spend money, but to repress and cut back public spending in order to try to stop the disastrous increase in taxes. America had sent a man to walk on the moon, but no longer knew anymore what to do with such an expensive acquisition. The budget for the aerospace industry was severely pruned. American forces were removed from Vietnam, and the military budget was trimmed. Just as it had benefited previously, now California was hit more severely than other states by such policy. Los Angeles was plunged into a deep crisis: migrant flow slowed down and stopped; many factories closed down, and there were massive layoffs of blue- and white-collar workers at Lockheed, Boeing, Douglas, and the Rand Corporation.

Inflation became dangerous. Many attributed it to the Johnson policy for financing the Vietnam war. Whatever its causes, its effects, among which was the sudden and enormous increase in oil prices, were disastrous for the economy. The very foundation of national behavior was shaken. Malthusian ideas, as always in time of economic crisis, spread again, and fast. Hollywood produced a whole series of 'catastrophe' films ('Poseidon Adventure', 'Towering Inferno', 'Earthquake', ...); characteristically, many such catastrophes happen in Los Angeles.

Table 3.3. Federal grants to local governments (in billions of current dollars).

	1953	1962	1967
Total	2857	8190	14647
Specific sector grants:			
Commerce and transport	528	2842	4308
Housing	68	354	878
Health and welfare	1810	3554	6615

Troubles ahead for California

'California: the Cornucopia of the World': even if this slogan was a publisher's bluff, the State was certainly the wealthiest in the Union, and Los Angeles County was its wealthiest part. Roosevelt's public-works policy had largely developed the availability of cheap water by the building of gigantic dams on the Colorado River, and by the development of irrigation. In the late 1960s, however, urban needs for water were in competition with the demand from industrial plants and agricultural production units; it was clear in 1970 that further growth in the use of water would have to be controlled and limited—a completely new concept for the West (Ostrom, 1953; Moskovitz, 1957; Humlum, 1969).

For a peripheral region like Southern California, with such an enormous
city as Los Angeles, transport was fundamental. In the past the railroads
had been the main factor of growth.   Among the projects of the New Deal,
the development of a modern road network occupied an important place.
The network was neglected, for obvious reasons of priority, during World
War II, but as early as 1944 the Federal Aid Highway Act provided for the
building of 40000 miles of modern road across the Union.   The decisive
step was taken in 1956, with the construction of the Interstate and Defence
Highway System—a complete network of highways with separated lanes—
which connected the West in particular with the rest of the country.
Beyond the powerful lobbies (the 'concrete lobby', and by oil companies
and car manufacturers) and the interests of defense, California reaped a
large share of the fruits of such endeavor.   Actually, this network was to
develop only slowly, and it was to take thirteen years to build the 41000
miles; by 1963, only one third was completed.   The effects of the highway program on Los Angeles tend to have been exaggerated, though the
project was a godsend for the states—the federal government actually
covered some 90% of the cost.   By 1970, this network, at least in the
big cities and in Los Angeles more than anywhere else, was saturated and
insufficient.   But it had contributed positively to the decrease of
population densities, to the spread of the city over a very wide area and
had made the building of a new *public* transport system extremely difficult
(Carlin and Wohl, 1968), if not impossible (see the publications of the
Los Angeles Metropolitan Transit Authority, 1954; 1959; 1960; and of
the South California Rapid Transit District, 1967; 1968).

During the period, urban crime also reached California cities, although
insecurity in the streets has never been as tragic in Los Angeles as it is in
New York or Chicago.   Most crimes are committed less frequently here;
only rape is committed more often, possibly because of the local weather,
daring fashions, and the beauty of Californian women.   But the situation
was inflated beyond reason by the media, and fear appeared during the
late 1960s among Los Angeles citizens, and became a political issue.

With the highest number of cars per household in the world, with
important industries located in a very narrow plain between the ocean and
a mountain range and frequently under a canopy of marine haze, Los
Angeles became 'Smog-City', a symbol of air pollution (Nakamura, 1973).

Finally, the major industries entered into crisis.   The aerospace industry
was looking for an objective, and the space-shuttle was proposed, by
President Nixon, partly to extend the space-race.   Nonetheless, activity
continued to slow down.   The big aircraft manufacturers found themselves
suffering simultaneously from a stagnation in the standard of living and a
consequent slow down in air traffic, from attacks by ecologists, from
much higher oil prices, and from the high cost of credit.   Near to
bankruptcy, Lockheed received a guarantee from the federal government

(an unheard-of procedure), only to sink again in an enormous scandal about bribes.

For the first time since its founding two centuries earlier, the population of Los Angeles was no longer increasing. By the early 1970s, after a period of extraordinary growth and immoderate hopes (Alonso, 1971), the time is ripe for a looking back at the city's history and an attempt at an evaluation (Hirsch and Hale, 1970; see the special issue published by *Planning* in March/April 1973).

3.2 Urban growth in the United States
In spite of being in a country where population growth has all been exceptionally rapid, and whose civilization is basically urban, Los Angeles, with these characteristics, still appears as a unique phenomenon. At this point therefore, it is necessary to draw a brief sketch of urban growth in the USA, in order to identify some general laws of urban evolution and to distinguish the particular originality of Los Angeles. The following analysis is based on Bogue's work (Bogue, 1953; 1959; Bogue and Harris, 1954).

3.2.1 Forms of urban growth in the United States: 1900–1950
The main characteristics
In 1900, 52 cities in the USA held 24 million people, or less than one third of the total population. By 1950, there were 162 large cities with 86 million inhabitants, or more than half the population of the country. During the first half of this century the number of Americans had been multiplied by a factor of 2, but the number of urbanites by 3.5.

Urban growth spread more and more over space. Up to 1910, cities had grown while still remaining compact. During and after World War I, the city centers became saturated; suburbs grew faster in a typical urban evolution which, from 1930 onwards extended to most middle-sized towns (table 3.4).

Table 3.4. Distribution of population in the US city for the 52 largest Standard Metropolitan Areas.

	Distribution (%) during:					
	1900	1910	1920	1930	1940	1950
Standard Metropolitan Area	31.7	34.4	37.0	40.3	40.2	41.6
Center	21.1	23.2	25.0	25.9	25.2	24.1
Periphery	10.6	11.2	12.0	14.4	15.0	17.6
urban	4.9	6.1	7.3	9.4	9.5	10.6
rural	5.7	5.1	4.7	5.0	5.5	7.0
Outside the SMA	68.3	65.6	63.0	59.7	59.8	58.4
urban	13.7	16.4	18.9	20.8	21.8	24.4
rural	54.6	49.2	44.0	38.9	38.0	34.0

Source: Bogue (1953, page 13).

Growth took on different forms in different regions. In the Northeast and the North Central (Midwest and Prairies), where the proportion of the population living in cities was already high, urban growth was slower than in the South and the West, where records were broken. On the Pacific Coast, cities grew mainly from the constant flow of American migrants moving westward. On the other hand, the South did not attract population from other regions—cities grew from the rural population leaving the countryside.

The size of a city plays an important role in its further growth: there is a threshold, around one million inhabitants, beyond which the city grows much more slowly. The bigger the city, the faster the growth of the periphery in comparison with the center. The most significant point, however, is that when the effect of size is eliminated (for instance, by freezing this variable through partial correlation), suburban growth seems more typical of the cities of the Northeast and North Central than it does of the urban settlements located in the South or West. Consequently, it would be wrong, or at least exaggerated, to compare the old cities of the Northeast with their densely occupied centers with those of the West, which have a different urban structure, more widely spread out and tending to be a simple collection of suburbs without a center. Peripheral development is really the consequence of saturation at the center rather than of any regional choice. The frequent cliché about spineless, amorphous western cities should really be attributed to a time-lag in their growth: suburbs developed around eastern cities between the two world wars; western cities, and particularly Los Angeles, only experienced a similar evolution after World War II.

Urban densities are low in the USA compared with Europe: 6000 inhabitants per square kilometer in the center, no more than 350 at the periphery.

Differential growth of American cities

Table 3.4 shows the distribution of population according to their place of residence. At the turn of the century 32% of the total population was concentrated in the big cities (SMA; or SMSA since 1960[2]); this had risen to 42% by 1950. However, the center of these big cities did not lose population: the proportion of people living there increased slowly from 1900 to 1930 (by up to 25%), and then decreased slightly. In 1950, more people were living in city centers than in 1900 (in relative and, of course, in absolute numbers). Again, the cliché about urbanites flying to the suburbs has to be qualified: even if urban centers have slowly tended to lose their relative importance (table 3.5), without doubt the number of people living there has continuously increased.

Nonetheless, it is still true that while urban centers grew by 14% from 1900 to 1950, peripheral growth jumped by 60%. Urbanized suburbs

[2] SMA, Standard Metropolitan Area; SMSA, Standard Metropolitan Statistical Area.

doubled the proportion of population housed there, a remarkable progress since it happened on the basis of an increasing urban population. The rural part of the periphery, whose relative population remained stable until 1940, doubled its share of the total population in ten years (1940–1950). Agricultural land became actively developed in suburbs not yet urbanized.

The growth of middle-sized and small towns was also exceptional: during this period their share of the population doubled, meaning that the sector had grown four times faster than that of the big cities. The countryside became depopulated: the proportion of more than half of the population living there in 1900, was reduced to only a third in 1950.

In the big cities each part experienced a different evolution (table 3.5): decline occurred at the center (although it still contained more than half of the SMA population in 1950), progress occured at the periphery, particularly in the urbanized part. The accompanying rural area followed a contrasting evolution: decline took place from 1900 to 1930 (farmers were pushed away by land speculation, land was developed too early with lots remaining vacant for a long time, as in Los Angeles). But between 1930 and 1950 the trend was reversed: the rural part of the suburbs received an increasing share of the urban population, with very low densities (the urban fringe).

The rates of growth for each urban area are important (table 3.6). Urban growth actually slowed down; it was much faster at the start (1900–1910). Paralyzed by the Depression, the growth rate fell to 7%. With the Second World War, it rose again, and remained quite stable after 1945, but at a level (18·6%) which was relatively low, almost half of the rate at the turn of the century.

Everywhere in the Union, the attractive power of the urban center was destroyed by the Depression. The phenomenon was so widespread and so clear that it can be explained only by the brutal stop to European immigration. Poor migrants from abroad settled first in the dilapidated hearts of the cities and then moved slowly out toward the periphery as people climbed the social scale. The very basis of the model built by the Chicago School vanished in 1931: this will be most important to remember

Table 3.5. Differential distribution of population inside large agglomerations for the 52 largest Standard Metropolitan Areas.

	Distribution (%) during:					
	1950	1940	1930	1920	1910	1900
Center	58	63	64	67	67	66
Periphery	42	37	36	33	33	34
urban	25	23	23	20	18	16
rural	17	14	12	13	15	18

(Total SMA = 100%.) Source: Bogue (1953, page 28).

when, in the last chapter of this book, we analyze the laws of growth in
Los Angeles. After 1930, and particularly around 1940, Blacks occupied
the hearts of the big cities, but they were contained there, even when their
income rose, by racial prejudice. At that moment urban centers lost their
role as starting point for a fluid social movement throughout the city.

The development of the periphery followed an opposite path, and after
1920 it grew faster than the center. Some would attribute this to the
recent impact of the automobile on urban form; its role has certainly
been important, but it will be shown below that its effect has been largely
exaggerated, even in Los Angeles.

The Depression brought about quite abnormal, certainly atypical,
evolution in the cities: the rural part of the suburbs grew twice as fast
as its urban counterpart, and small and middle-sized towns attracted
population more strongly than the large SMAs. Actually, the whole trend
toward urban concentration is momentarily broken in times of crisis.

Table 3.6. Relative growth of urban population 1900–1950 for the 52 largest
Standard Metropolitan Areas.

	Growth (%) during:					
	1900–10	1910–20	1920–30	1930–40	1940–50	1900–50
SMA	31.3	23.7	26.3	7.0	18.6	160.3
Center	33.1	23.9	20.4	4.1	9.6	126.4
Periphery	27.8	23.3	38.6	12.2	33.6	227.4
urban	49.7	37.3	49.7	8.6	26.4	322.2
rural	8.8	6.6	21.5	19.1	46.1	145.1
Outside SMA	16.3	10.3	10.2	7.4	11.7	69.5
urban	45.0	33.0	27.8	12.4	27.9	254.4
rural	9.1	2.8	2.6	4.7	2.4	23.3

Source: Bogue (1953, page 13).

3.2.2 Factors of urban growth

The size of an agglomeration does not play an important role in determining
its growth, except in the case of the large SMAs (more than one million
inhabitants) which tend to grow more slowly, at about 85% of the growth
rate of the smaller SMAs.

Regional factors played an important role which varied very little with
time; again the Depression determined a break in the evolution. Large
cities grew at a decreasing rate (table 3.7), which was related to the size
effect indicated above. In the Northeast and North Central growth,
which was strong before 1930, had been almost stopped by the Depression,
then started again between 1940 and 1950 at a rate reduced by half. On
the other hand, the South and West changed in a very different way.
Large cities in the Deep South grew only a little more slowly during the
Depression years, and then continued to develop with the same high rate.

In the West, urban growth was extremely fast (urban populations multiplied by a factor of six in fifty years!) but more erratic; growth was fastest at the beginning of this century.

The lower part of table 3.7 shows the relative share of the large cities in and growth of each region. Strong values in the Northeast and North Central are no surprise: urban development there was long established. The West and the South, however, followed separate tracks: whereas the South remained rural, the West definitely became urban (Scott, 1949). For fifty years, the huge migration westwards has been mainly a movement toward the metropolitan areas: "the closing of the Frontier did not stop the flow to the west, but simply redirected the main part to the edification of metropolitan areas" (Bogue, 1953, page 26).

Table 3.7. Regional aspects of urban population growth in the USA.

	Period					
	1900–10	1910–20	1920–30	1930–40	1940–50	1900–50
Growth rate in the 52 largest SMAs						
USA	31.3	23.7	26.3	7.0	18.6	160.3
Northeast	20.2	18.7	19.6	4.6	10.3	111.7
North Central	31.0	31.0	31.1	5.1	18.0	179.1
South	17.8	18.7	21.5	16.7	30.5	158.9
West	85.8	42.9	61.2	17.1	48.7	644.8
Proportion (%) of population growth taking place in the largest SMA						
USA	47.2	54.6	60.4	39.0	51.6	51.7
Northeast	84.8	89.2	88.1	76.7	79.0	84.8
North Central	57.4	64.8	76.7	48.9	64.7	64.9
South	8.7	14.1	15.2	17.8	26.1	16.7
West	36.3	44.3	62.7	42.6	49.6	48.2

Source: Bogue (1953, page 25).

3.2.3 Urban growth in the decade 1940–1950
In a later study, Bogue tried to identify the main growth factors by using multiple regression analysis (Bogue and Harris, 1954).

The main growth factors
Urban growth in the 125 largest SMAs is measured in two ways: by means of their growth rate, and by means of their absolute growth (table 3.8). Seven independent variables are used for the regression: several are very heterogeneous (with a high coefficient of variation), such as the 'size in 1940' or the 'past growth rate'; on the other hand, the SMAs are distributed quite evenly through space (giving a low coefficient for the variable 'distance to the nearest SMA', expressed as a logarithm).

The growth rate is a more useful measure than absolute growth: correlations with the independent variables are significant more often.

Absolute growth, basically, is a function of the city size at the beginning of the period ($r = 0.77$, that is, almost 60% of the variance in common); this is an excellent illustration of the perturbation introduced in an analysis by the regression effect described in chapter 1. All other correlations are low, except for the relation between present growth rate and past growth rate ($r = 0.68$), another example of the regression effect.

Three points must be underlined:

First. The importance of industry in a city is negatively correlated with its growth ($r = -0.48$; $r^2 = 0.23$). During the period covering the war (1940–1950), it is not possible to see the effect here of an eventual 'saturation' of the cities, rather we are seeing the priority development of a war industry in the SMA with little industry. Location of war production was particularly free of the usual constraints: investment was made by the Federal State; an up-rooted and particularly mobile manpower force was ready, after the Depression, to go anywhere for a job; and there was a certain disregard for transportation cost, or for any kind of cost, as long as the production goals could be reached. Cities poorly supplied with industry, but with important harbors, profited the most during the war years, and Los Angeles more than any other SMA (Hildebrand and Mace, 1950). Before and after the war, the growth of industry is again clearly related to urban growth ($r = 0.34$) (SCRC, 1964).

Second. The past growth of a city does not play an important role. The older SMAs grew a little more slowly ($r = -0.28$), and high center-densities were slightly negatively correlated with growth ($r = -0.18$, or only 3% of the variance is common). Only population evolution during the period

Table 3.8. Components of urban growth (1940–1950).

	Coefficient of variation $\sigma/\bar{x}$	Correlation with	
		growth rate 1940–50	absolute growth 1940–50
Dependent variables			
Growth rate (1940–50)	0.73	1.00	0.26
Absolute growth (1940–50)	0.73	0.26	1.00
Independent variables			
Size of the SMA, 1940	2.24	–	0.77
Population density of the SMA center, 1950	0.54	−0.18	0.40
Age of the SMA	0.35	−0.28	0.46
Degree of industrialization 1940	0.48	−0.48	–
Change in the industrialization rate (1939–1947)	0.61	0.34	–
Distance to the nearest SMA (logarithm)	0.17	0.39	–
SMA growth rate (1930–40)	1.08	0.68	0.18

Only correlations significant at the 5% level are indicated.
Source: Bogue and Harris (1954, page 31).

immediately prior to the period studied played any role, and that an important one: $r = 0.68$, as if the process was Markovian.
Third. The factor more relevant in geography, the distance to the nearest SMA, is not negligible ($r = 0.39$, or 15% of the variance). Since distance is measured on a logarithmic scale, Bogue's model introduces implicitly a gravity model and actually considers a kind of urban interaction.

All things considered, urban growth appears as a quite complicated and still largely unexplained phenomenon. All the factors introduced by Bogue as independent variables do not account for more than 55% of the total process: "other factors, omitted in this study, or non-linear relationships with the factors taken here into account, represent the other half of the variance" (Bogue and Harris, 1954, page 24). Still more impressive is the persistence of this urban growth: the best way to predict it is to assume it will not change! In chapter 7 I will try to analyze the deep mechanisms underlying the preservation of the urban forms in Los Angeles, in spite of such fast growth.

The regional factor
These general results obtained by Bogue are quite disappointing, largely because regional factors play a crucial role. In each region of the USA, large SMAs have both a common and an individual behavior (table 3.9). Large cities located on the Pacific Coast and in the Rockies experienced impressive growth, which made it all the more surprising that the Northeast and North Central were at that time the main industrial regions of the Union.

The regional effect is important: when added to the seven variables used before (and frozen through partial correlation), this effect accounts for 16% of new information (the total variance accounted for increases from 53% to 69%). With the addition of the regional variable, Bogue's multiple regression model produces a Fisher F value equal to 24.7, whereas the corresponding test value (at the 5% level, with 4 and 95 degrees of freedom) is only 2.48: the linear model fits the data well, thanks largely to the introduction of the regional factor.

In the West more than in any other region, past growth is by far the best predictor (table 3.10). Typically the correlation decreases with time: if half of the relative growth during 1940-1950 in the West is explained by the growth during the previous decade (1930-1940), only one quarter is explained by growth during the 1920-1930 period, and correlations with even more remote decades rapidly become not significant. No other

Table 3.9. Urban growth rate, 1940-1950. (Standardized, to take into account different sizes of SMA.)

Northeast	North Central	South	West
10.3	18.2	29.9	52.1

Source: Bogue (1953, page 27).

region in the United States is so strongly dependent on its immediate past growth: the usual clichés on the brutal and anarchic development of the Far West are once again unjustified.

Table 3.10. Regional factors of urban growth 1940–1950. Linear correlations between the growth rate of an SMA, 1940–1950, and various explicative variables, by region.

	USA	Northeast	North Central	South	West
Past growth (%)					
1930–40	0.69	0.54	0.38	0.60	0.73
1920–30	0.51	–	0.56	0.40	0.54
1900–10	0.49	–	–	–	–
Fertility					
Raw birth rate, 1939–40	0.22	–	–	–	–
Age of the SMA					
Number of years since the population exceeded 50000 inhabitants	−0.28	–	–	–	–
Industrial development					
% of workers in industry, 1940	−0.47	0.46	–	−0.48	–
% of change in industrial employment, 1939–47	0.34	–	–	0.45	–
Standard error	0.17	0.34	0.32	0.29	0.50

Only significant coefficients are indicated. Source: Bogue (1953, page 26).

Growth in the different parts of the US city

The peripheral rings (the suburbs) experienced a 40% growth between 1940 and 1950, while the centers of the SMAs increased by only 18%. Table 3.11 shows the correlations between this growth and various explanatory factors. Some of the correlations are surprising: size, age, and the growth rate during 1940–1950 of the SMA and of the suburbs are all practically orthogonal to the variable percentage of SMA population with a residence in the suburbs (1950), as if the relative size of the suburbs was completely independent of all these factors. One would have expected that the oldest, largest, and most slowly growing cities would have relatively larger suburbs; but this is not the case.

The 'regression effect' plays its role again: Bogue shows that the best predictor of the size of a suburb in 1950 is its size in 1940 ($r = 0.95$). The cities whose suburbs play an important role are not those surrounded by a ring of population living in a rural environment (low-density suburbs), but those encircled by satellites, that is, by an urban ring.

Since most of these explanatory variables are somehow intercorrelated, it is clearer to use the coefficients appearing in the multiple regression model which isolates the role of each particular variable by freezing all the others. These (β) coefficients measure what each variable contributes to the prediction of the growth rate after discarding all that they may have in common with the others—that is, after discarding the redundancy, or the double count of information. The relative growth of the suburbs then appears related to three basic factors:

the size of the SMA in 1940 ($\beta = -0.21$),
the density in the city center in 1950 ($\beta = 0.48$), and
the age of the SMA ($\beta = -0.60$).

High densities in the center correspond to a highly populated suburb: urban congestion leads to the growth of the periphery. Age is negatively related to the size of the periphery: there is a clear historical difference between the older cities, which are more centralized and compact, and the recent ones, which have relatively large suburbs. The private car has certainly played an instrumental role here, particularly so in Los Angeles, although other clues tend to show its effect has been overestimated.

Bogue notes that the size of suburbs in 1950 is not related to the growth rate of the SMA between 1940 and 1950. Thus the relative size appears to be the effect of a long historical evolution, quite insensitive to short-period fluctuations. This importance of the historical heritage, even in Los Angeles, will be strongly underlined again at the end of the book. Actually, growth of the peripheral rings probably corresponds to a redistribution of the population within the SMA, which is independent of its global growth.

Table 3.11. Changes in the role of the suburbs.

Variables	Linear correlation with % of	
	SMA population	suburban population
Dependent variables		
% of SMA population with a residence in the suburbs (1950)	1.00	−0.34
% of suburban population living in a rural area (1950)	−0.34	1.00
Independent variables		
Size of SMA (1940)	–	−0.44
Density at the center (1950)	0.24	−0.34
Age of the SMA	–	−0.52
Industrialization rate (1940)	0.25	−0.28
Changes in the industrialization rate (1939–47)	−0.32	–
Growth rate of the SMA (1940–50)	–	0.26
% of SMA population living in the suburbs (1940)	0.95	–
% of suburban population living in a rural area (1940)	−0.38	0.97
Growth rate of the suburbs (1930–40)	–	–

Only correlations significant at the 5% level are indicated. Source: Bogue and Harris (1954, page 34).

Once the other variables have been statistically frozen, the industrial activity is found to be independent of the size of the suburbs. The traditional population move to the periphery is not due to the possible nuisance of industries located inside the city.

Analysis of the growth of the peripheral ring leads to some interesting conclusions:

Growth of the ring and of the urban center during a given decade are practically independent; on the other hand, there is a clear relation ($\beta = 0.30$) between growth of the center during a decade and growth of the ring during the following period. There is here an historical structure to the phenomenon with a time-lag: the center grows first, then the ring.

Suburbs with a high growth rate during 1930–1940 also have high rates between 1940 and 1950: the growth of the periphery is a long-term process taking several decades.

Bogue's conclusions are based on a national study. They form the framework necessary for a detailed study of the change in Los Angeles over time. But it is still a fact that all these variables explain only a third of the variance: two-thirds of the phenomenon remain unexplained.

3.3 The birth and growth of Los Angeles: City and County till 1940

The growth of the USA and of its world role since the turn of the century readily explains California's soaring growth, and especially the boom experienced by the southern part of the State: irrigation, oil production, the importance of local amenities like the sea, the sun, and the magnificent scenery all contribute, although competition from the Bay Area and the San Joaquin Valley has sometimes hindered southern prosperity.

On the other hand, the growth of the third metropolis in America in the southwestern corner of the Union, close to the desert, and near a foreign border across which there are few economic activities, is not so easily explained. The best harbor sites on the West Coast are in the San Francisco Bay or, much more to the north, in Portland or Seattle. Los Angeles' harbors (Santa Monica, Venice, Long Beach, San Pedro) are quite mediocre and require very large and expensive dredging works. What is more, the city did not grow as a port but rather, from the beginning of the twentieth century, as a center for land development, a paradise for real estate developers. Even before it took the form of a suburb, Los Angeles had the function of a suburb. Fortunately, the beginnings of the city's story have been very well analyzed by Fogelson (Fogelson, 1967; see also Nadeau, 1960; Rand, 1967; Caughey, 1976; and Robinson, 1959; 1968).

3.3.1 Los Angeles: the 'fragmented metropolis'

The Spanish period

Spanish influence slowly extended northwards from Mexico along the
Pacific Coast at the end of the eighteenth century. Basically, it depended
on two organizations—the Church and the Army. From 1780 to 1830,
the Church tried systematically to destroy Indian civilizations. Indians
were placed in new centers, the 'missiones', and the royal army protected
this progression with fortified outposts along the coast ('presidios'), which
were supplied by sea—San Diego or San Francisco. Conquest and
evangelization, however, exacted a heavy toll from the natives through
forced work, new diseases, and, the most important factor by far,
dissolution of their religious, political, and family ties. A population of
130000 Indians living in Southern California in 1770, was reduced to
90000 by 1832 (Fogelson, 1967). The result was the ruin of a traditional
economy and a crisis for the supply of the presidios and missiones. The
Spanish crown was thus led, after a few decades, to found agricultural
centers—the 'pueblos'. Their population was made up of Mexican
immigrants, their purpose to produce food for the priests, the monks, and
the soldiers. In 1781 "el pueblo de Nuestra Senora la Reina de Los
Angeles" was one of the first founded. In English, this is the town of
Queen of the Angels. Each head of a new household drew a lot and
received a piece of land under the sun (a 'solar') to build his house (20
by 30 varas, one vara being approximately one yard), and four other pieces
to cultivate (200 by 300 varas each). Two were fields that could be
irrigated.

So in this way Los Angeles began as a planned agricultural center of
Mexican settlers producing foodstuffs. Irrigation, from the very earliest
years, played an important role. By 1835, it had become the largest
center in California, with more than 1000 inhabitants. From the very
beginning of the development of the West, Los Angeles and San Francisco
were in competition. The latter is a seaport and fortress on the most
beautiful bay of the whole coast, and is the heart of the Californian
communication network through the valleys of the San Joaquin and the
Sacramento. Los Angeles, on the other hand, is located away from the
sea on a vast plain, closed to the north and the east by mountains, and to
the southwest by the ocean, but it is the wealthy center of a large
agricultural basin.

In 1830, the government confiscated church land in order to allocate it
to a few rich families in Mexico. Land organization was thus deeply
disturbed. Cultivation was replaced by extensive cattle-rearing on huge
ranches, with the aid of local manpower. This was the era of powerful
and violent landlords, abusing the population working on their latifundia,
exciting widespread hatred and a thirst for revenge, as exemplified in the
myth of Zorro.

The introduction of capitalism

In 1846, war broke out between the United States and Mexico; after
their defeat, the Mexicans were forced to 'sell' the present states of New
Mexico, California, and Arizona for $15 million. Power, administration,
and the law changed radically and, as far as the Los Angeles basin was
concerned, they changed for the worst for a number of reasons as follows:

Northern California, a mining country with less agriculture and more
population than the southern part of the State, crushed it under property
taxes which spelt ruin to the ranchers.

The Indians were freed, but they also suffered acutely from the economic
crisis. Many lost their jobs and were forced to leave or face misery. Of
an Indian population of 85 000 in 1852, only 35 000 remained in 1860.

The Gold Rush of 1848, and even more of 1849, brought manpower
and wealth to Northern California, and increased the overshadowing of the
ruined South.

The huge estates in Southern California were progressively transferred
from Mexican rancheros to San Franciscan capitalists. The extensive
cattle raising, which had replaced the earlier crop production, was now in its
turn eliminated by modern food production for the new urban markets in
the north. The Mexican 'rancho' had been an autonomous unit: relations
between the landlord and his 'peones', who had lived and worked like
serfs, had been both distant, but also very direct and very personal. The
new anglo-saxon ranch was a capitalist unit producing for a remote market;
the labor force was free and worked for a wage; human relations were
reduced to a minimum. Between 1850 and 1880, Los Angeles was rapidly
integrated into the American economy. In thirty years, LA County grew
from 4000 to 34 000 inhabitants. The earlier Mexican rancheros had
produced most of what they needed on their latifundias. Their feudal
economy had not required any large urban structure, and Los Angeles had
remained a simple town (Reps, 1969). In contradistinction to this,
capitalist ranches depended on urban markets both for the sale of their
products and for the purchase of all the goods they were now too
specialized to produce for themselves. Los Angeles' growth as a true city
began with American rule—by 1885 its population stood at 20 000
inhabitants.

The railroad and competition with San Diego

Until the 1870s, Los Angeles easily overshadowed the surrounding cities
and harbors, indicating its predominance as an agricultural market. Its
only competitor was San Diego, the only good port with deep water south of
San Francisco. In 1869, Los Angeles was the social and political center
of Southern California, where the rich landlords lived and carried on
business. But San Diego remained the economic center, owing to its
harbor. Oddly enough, it was the very power of San Francisco that
favored Los Angeles: located too far to the south, San Diego had not

profited by the Gold Rush, and had not grown very fast. But it was the railroad, more than anything else, that sealed the fate of these cities between 1870 and 1876 (Swett, 1951). Twenty years earlier, bankers back East had chosen San Diego as the western terminal of the first trans-continental railroad, but the Civil War had killed the project. Talks about a new southern line started again in the early 1870s, but this time the San Francisco lobby stepped in. Most of the economic community of the city, as well as the interests behind its railway, the Central Pacific, feared the competition from the excellent San Diego harbor, and so favored the choice of Los Angeles, a city where landing was so difficult it could never become an important competitor. Lobbying worked in steps: in 1872, a new branch of the San Francisco railroad was built to Los Angeles, and finally, after bitter bargaining, the South Pacific Railway chose Los Angeles in 1876 as its terminal on the West Coast. This was a turning point in the urban history of California. San Diego never recovered from the loss of activity, until it became an important Naval base after World War II. Los Angeles, however, had to pay a heavy price: the South Pacific Railroad Company received as a free gift a brand new railway built for the municipality by Phineas Banning between the city and its harbor (Wilmington–San Pedro Railroad) (Banham, 1971).

The great migration and the first land boom (1880–1910)
In 1880, Los Angeles was still a small town of 11 183 inhabitants, many of local origin (LA County had 33 381 inhabitants). Three-quarters of the city-dwellers had been born in the USA, and more than half in California. Men and women were equal in number, as opposed to San Francisco, where men dominated having come from all over the globe, attracted by the gold mirage.

   This quiet equilibrium was radically broken by the building of a second transcontinental railroad, the Sante Fe. An ensuing tariff war with the South Pacific Company lowered fares to absurd levels. For a few days, it was possible to go from Kansas City to Los Angeles for $1.00! Large groups of American citizens came from the Midwest to buy land and to settle down in Los Angeles. Real estate speculation began as the main activity in the city and was to retain its importance for a long time. In a period of ten years, the population was multiplied by five to 50 400 inhabitants in 1890. Real estate investments were estimated at $7 million in 1880, and at $39 million in 1890. In 1888 the Sante Fe vice-president predicted, "People will keep coming here until this whole region becomes one of the most populated parts of the United States" (in Fogelson, 1967, page 67). In 1887, total real estate sales in the city were the third largest in the nation, after New York and Chicago. Land development became frantic. In two-and-a-half years (1887–1889) real estate developers created sixty new cities around Los Angeles as center, with enough land to house two million inhabitants, but as the boom petered out, only 3000 people

lived there. Two-thirds of those potential cities, projected in detail and
already allotted, disappeared for ever after the 1888 crash (Glaab and
Brown, 1967).

In spite of cyclical crises and the excess of land speculation, real estate
development persisted until at least 1920 as the main activity in the city.
From 1890 until 1920, the Los Angeles Chamber of Commerce played a
principal role in the process. It organized multiple exhibitions and fairs
throughout the whole country, everywhere showing oranges, grapes,
and vegetables produced in the south of the state, and spreading the
image of California as an earthly paradise, the "Land of Plenty, Cornucopia
of the World", Paradise lost and found again. During the period, no other
city in the United States was given so much publicity, and the migrants
kept flocking in.

In the late nineteenth century, migrants came mainly from Kansas or
Iowa: Los Angeles was at that time called 'the largest sandbeach in Iowa'.
From 1900 onwards, they came more from Chicago and from the heart of
the Midwest. More often they were city-dwellers rather than farmers and
this was partly owing to a progressive change in national morality, away
from the puritan work ethic toward a discovery of hedonism. Wealth was
more widely distributed, and it was now considered less as a proof of
success than as a means of obtaining the legitimate pleasures of life.
Advertizing also changed its slogans after 1900. To the potential buyer of
a piece of land in Los Angeles, it pledged the good life instead of monetary
profit, showing clearly that these newcomers had already made their profit
and were wealthy. US agriculture went through several periods of huge
prosperity (1904–1906; 1910–1913; and above all, during World War I),
and many farmers used the opportunity to sell their property back East and
to retire in Los Angeles.

A second boom on the real estate market: the 1920s
Land speculation reached incredible heights during the prosperous 'Roaring
Twenties'. Public imagination was excited by tales (often exaggerated) of
the many extraordinary profits made in real estate transactions during the
preceding years: by the sparkle of the movie industry and the name of
Hollywood (how many tourists come there just to glimpse the stars, and
how many girls just to become one of them?); and finally by the growth
of oil production, an activity where profits, and strikes, were spectacular
at the time.

Real estate developers, helped by local government and politicians,
founded in 1921 the 'All Year Club of South California'; its main goal
was to promote real estate development in Los Angeles and to launch
publicity campaigns to this effect. With a wider base and more flexibility,
this organization amplified the action of the LA Chamber of Commerce.
Slogans changed as the populations defined as the target changed. While
advertizing had placed emphasis on the Californian sunny skies and beautiful

weather for a long time (Winther, 1946), Los Angeles was now advertised as a summer resort for middle-class tourists. In this way, urban growth was established as a system here, with a positive feedback amplifying its own progress. Finally Los Angeles' own growth constituted the best argument to attract new migrants.

Origins of the population

Los Angeles is the only large American city to have been populated mainly by American citizens. This is an exceptional characteristic in comparison with New York or Chicago, where foreigners, either European or Asiatic, formed the essential basis of the population. Until 1885, while growth was still slow, newcomers to Los Angeles came mainly from the Northeast: Boston, New York, and the surrounding states. Between 1885 and 1895, the flow was made up of quite wealthy city-dwellers from Ohio, Indiana, and Illinois. During the next decade, the origin of the migrants moved away again from the old New England. They tended to be prosperous farmers from Iowa, Nebraska, Michigan, and Wisconsin. During and after World War I, migrations were even shorter—people came from Texas, Oklahoma, Utah, and Colorado (Fogelson, 1967).

Those migrants have slowly molded the spirit of the city. In general they were wealthy, stable, 'true' Americans; they got their money through hard work and they tended to be conservative. On the other hand, they accepted the loss of their roots to come to Eden in search of the 'Good Life' under a new sky, in a new environment, and they were not closed to innovation. Here already was the germ of the moral essence of Southern California, a puzzling mixture of extreme conservatism and extreme liberalism (moral as well as political); an anxious need for law and order, which paved the way to the career of a Nixon or a Reagan, and at the same time an almost limitless audacity in the search for new ways of life (Carr, 1935).

The urban functions of Los Angeles

Apart from the effect of its original role as an agricultural market until the middle of the nineteenth century, the growth of Los Angeles has been mainly the result of land speculation, which makes it an almost unique case in the urban history of Northern America. H S McKee wrote, in 1915: "What is most remarkable, in the case of Los Angeles, is that we are dealing here with a residential, not an industrial community. From the half-million people who live here, most of them did not come to do business, but just to reside in this city" (in Fogelson, 1967, page 108).

As a result, commerce and services played a preponderant role in Los Angeles activities, and this began to alarm local authorities as early as 1920. After World War I, the LA Chamber of Commerce tried to attract industrial plant by publicity directed at the big eastern corporations. Actually, industrial firms had settled in Los Angeles from 1915 onward, under two peculiar forms:

First. The movie industry, attracted initially by the sunny weather, was
destined to play an exceptional role. The first film was shot in a barn, at
the corner of Sunset Blvd and Gower St in 1910 (Banham, 1971, page 35).
Hollywood then grew at a rapid pace. In the image generated of the city,
provincial innocence was quickly replaced by glamour. In 1930, there
were fifty-two movie studios, some as big as a town, employing 15 000
people. The annual payroll reached $72 million and total turnover
exceeded $130 million. The contrast between the very modest beginnings
and the prosperity reached in a few years is totally striking. Charlie
Chaplin's first studio still exists at the corner of La Brea Ave and Sunset
Blvd. The slope of the avenue, going down from the Hollywood mountains
to the ocean, was the site for so many of the gags by the Keystone Cops,
running after their cars they had parked without brakes. During the
1960s, the movie industry declined in Los Angeles as fast as it had grown
up. More than in dollars on the payroll, its impact should be evaluated in
qualitative terms. In twenty years, this industry had attracted to Los
Angeles a large group of artists, writers, and intellectuals and conferred on
the city an artistic prestige which had taken other cities in the world
centuries to develop. "Hollywood brought to Los Angeles an unprecedented
and unrepeatable population of genius, neurosis, skill, charlatanry, beauty,
vice, talent and plain old eccentricity" (Banham, 1971, page 35; see also
West, 1939). The unheard-of rapidity in the development of this city,
promoted in less than a century from the situation of a small agricultural
market to the rank of one of the few cultural centers of the Western world,
almost equal to New York or Paris, and well ahead of Chicago, was due
principally to the indirect role of the movie industry.
Second. Oil production began just after World War I and grew fast. The
Los Angeles region accounted for 9% of the US and 5% of world
production in 1930. It was valued at more than $320 million and its
5000 workers received more than $11 million in annual wages. The city
profited directly since the oil was refined on the spot in no less than 32
plants (1930). This activity, after the Second World War, was to develop
into a large petrochemical industry located along the shore. Derricks were
built even inside the city, in Santa Monica, in front of Beverly Hills, and
in Venice. Some of them still stand today, but most have been replaced
by electric pumps which are living symbols, in their rhythmic movements,
of the city's affluence.

   In the 1920s, fortunately, various other kinds of industry came and
diversified the urban economy (Kidner, 1946; Neff and Weifenbach, 1949).
The big rubber companies, for instance, built plants on the West Coast and
chose Los Angeles, in spite of its inferior harbor, and not San Francisco
or Portland. The reason was quite simple: Los Angeles was equally well
located with respect to rubber plantations in Asia, cotton fields in the
Imperial Valley, and the tire market in Southern California (an almost
classical application of industrial location modeling).

Automobile plants also appeared, followed by related heavy industry: steel mills close to a harbor and receiving all their raw material by water, long before such a type of location became the rule.

Finally, there was the arrival of high-technology industry: aerospace firms, attracted during the war in the Pacific, have become the most important in the region. Boeing settled down at Long Beach, Douglas at Santa Monica, Lockheed a bit further away at Burbank. More recently, electronics has followed as a second wave.

Los Angeles' fortune and its causes

How are we to explain the prosperity of a city located so far away from the national centers of activity, devoid of a good harbor and without any industrial tradition, which had developed mainly as a resort center for retired people, whose main activity for years had been land speculation, but which has soared nonetheless to the third rank of cities, with the fastest rate of growth for centers of similar size in the Union?

Many businessmen have mentioned the absence of a strong union organization as a favorable factor (Fogelson, 1967, page 130). Unions, however, were as powerful in Northern California, and particularly in San Francisco, as in the East or in the Midwest. On the other hand, it is true that their power was limited in Los Angeles for quite a long time, although it increased somewhat between 1895 and 1905. Fogelson proposes two reasons for their weakness:

1. The rural origin of a proportion of the new settlers and the conservative attitude of most of them, even when they came from big cities, because they were from the cities of the Midwest or the Bible Belt. A related factor was the abundance of manpower in such a fast growing city which gave employers the upper hand.

2. The attitude of businessmen, merchants, and large real-estate developers who used this favorable situation to destroy any workers' social organization, to promote fast industrialization, and even to bar, when possible, any political control of their activities by local government. The 'Merchants and Manufacturers Association', a branch of the Chamber of Commerce representing local businessmen, played a considerable role in this fight against new-born unions, especially after 1915 (Louis and Perry, 1963; Stimson, 1955).

There is, however, another possible basis for this prosperity: the site of the city on the Pacific Coast made it an important outlet to the Orient as the USA became increasingly involved in military conflicts and economic development in that hemisphere. Progress in transport, first sea and then air, and the corresponding reductions in distance (as expressed in time or money) put Los Angeles closer to Tokyo or Taiwan than to New York.

Such favorable factors, however, also existed in San Francisco and Portland, they are not sufficient to explain the peculiar fortune of Los Angeles. Back in 1930, a British newsman looked for the sources of this prosperity and was not satisfied by the explanations of the Chamber of Commerce, which were the productivity of irrigated agriculture, sea traffic, and investments by big corporations from the East Coast. He thus concluded: "None of those reasons can adequately explain the growth of such a city. They seem rather to be the effects of this growth, produced by a puzzling accumulation of population ... . There is no plausible answer to the question: 'Why a city here? and Why such growth?'" (Markey, 1932, pages 226–227).

If the reasons for growth are not obvious, its factors are quite clear and may be listed as follows:

Transportation played a basic role: spatial development was slow in the time of the horse-drawn carriage, quite rapid with the electric streetcar (Lewis, 1951; Warner, 1962), and much faster with the automobile. Land development was directly dependent on the extension of the streetcar network. Real estate developers, and particularly the most important of them, Henry E Huntington, understood they could not sell land if it were not made accessible by a transportation line. On the other hand, extending the urban railways greatly increased the amount of land which could be brought onto the market. This systematic development of the streetcar system has been the main reason for the enormous urban spread in Los Angeles (Lewis, 1951).

The exceptional nature of the urban population, being made up of Americans born in the country, well-to-do and sufficiently qualified. These people came with a pretty good idea of what a 'good community' should be: a single house for each family built on a large plot, well away from the business center. They wanted residential suburbs, 'decent', homogeneous, clean and orderly, and finally, stable. They rejected the big city with its crowding, its physical and moral misery, its immorality, its disreputable mixture of languages, social groups, races, and origins.

Neighborhood homogeneity has been a constant goal for developers— Blacks and Orientals have been excluded from many new communities. A minimum price for a property has often been determined in order to group together families with similar income. Commercial and industrial activities have been excluded from most residential neighborhoods, foreshadowing the modern zoning laws. The main result has been the erection, in most middle-class districts, of single houses, "the foundation of this country's security".

The very rapid population turnover accelerated urban spread. This may seem paradoxical in a population looking for roots and security, but the point was to settle down in a well-determined and satisfying social environment rather than in a particular place. Here again, mobility was fomented by developers. A family moving means two transactions. People did not seem to be strongly attached as yet to such a new environment. The system itself explains the mobility: as new developments were constantly added at the periphery, old ones became relatively closer to the center, were overwhelmed by traffic and air pollution, and so declined rapidly.

The city center long remained predominant: according to a study made in January 1924, 1.2 million people (more than the total population, because of round trips) made a trip everyday to Downtown, that is, to the district limited by Temple, Figueroa, Pico, and Los Angeles Sts. But, surprisingly enough, the location of the city center changed and moved to the southwest, from Spring and Third (1885) to Sixth and Hill (1920).

The growth of Los Angeles has been strongly influenced by urban crises back East, and by a whole national ideology where the city is feared and hated. Los Angeles, as the 'good community', tried from the very start to define itself as a sort of counter-city, free from most urban diseases, from social conflicts and modern sins (White and White, 1962). The dialectics of urban evolution have changed this 'perfect' settlement into a super-metropolis charged with all the defects and all the sins it was supposed to be guarded against. The very pattern of the city makes this purpose obvious: the distribution of activities throughout the whole agglomeration was extraordinary, particularly after 1920. The relative importance of the suburbs as early as 1930, distinguished it radically from all other US cities: the population ratio of the center to the suburbs was, at that time, 16 in Pittsburgh and 23 in St Louis, but only 3 in Los Angeles.

3.3.2 The recent evolution of Greater Los Angeles

The Regional Planning Commission of Los Angeles County has published a *Quarterly Bulletin* (*QB*) for the past thirty years which is a gold mine of information. We will only use a few general indications here on the history of LA County corresponding approximately to the city *largo sensu*, although it extends partly over Ventura and Orange Counties (see also Arnold et al, 1960; Security First National Bank, 1965).

Population growth

After World War II, growth was rapid and varied very little, around 4% or 5% a year (Thompson, 1955; Foley et al, 1965), see table 3.12. Preceding decades experienced faster growth—rates were always higher before 1940, except for the Civil War period (1860–1870). However, if the growth of modern Los Angeles has created a strong public impression in spite of a reduction in its rate, it is because of the size of the absolute increase, the sheer weight of numbers of more people (table 3.13). Since 1940, population in the county has increased every year by more than 150000 persons.

Migration attracted by war industries was important, as was the number of soldiers who settled down in the city after being discharged. Of all American troops, 5% were drafted in California, but 9% were discharged in the State. Between April 1940 and September 1948, only 20% of the county's demographic increase was 'natural', that is, deriving from a difference between births and deaths—80% was due to migrations into

the county. The months following the Japanese capitulation were
particularly decisive—as many people came in the two years (1946–1947)
as during the preceding seven (1940–1946) (*QB* 28, 1948).

Some neighborhoods, where population growth was very fast during the
war, lost inhabitants between 1946 and 1948; some, because they were
very close to the armament factories (Adams or Baldwin Hills) and
controlled by the military authorities. Others, like Hollywood, Wilshire,
Downtown, because vacant dwellings had been commandeered, and occupied
ones had become more crowded; there were few new buildings in these
districts. In these cases, population increase was fragile, it arose and
disappeared again with the war.

During the 1960s, the county population increased by one million.
What is most interesting is that 70% of them were born in California (State
of California, 1964). Births exceed deaths by 700000, and more than
300000 people had left the county.

Population origin varies a good deal with the district of the city. In
low–middle class neighborhoods, east of Downtown, 70% of the

Table 3.12. County and City of Los Angeles. Population growth 1850–1970.

| Year | Population | | | |
	County	increase (%)	City	increase (%)
1970	7041980	165	2811801	113
1960	6038771	154	2479015	126
1950	4151687	149	1970358	131
1940	2785643	126	1504277	121
1930	2208492	235	1238048	214
1920	936455	186	576673	81
1910	504131	318	319198	312
1900	170298	168	102479	202
1890	101454	304	50395	450
1880	33381	219	11183	196
1870	15309	33	5728	129
1860	11333	323	4385	275
1850	3530	–	1610	–

Sources: US Bureau of the Census, 1970; *QB* 98, 1967.

Table 3.13. Los Angeles County; population increase per decade.

Decade	Absolute increase	Rate (%)	Decade	Absolute increase	Rate (%)
1960–70	1180595	19.5	1920–30	1272037	135.8
1950–60	1887084	45.5	1910–20	432324	85.8
1940–50	1366044	49.0	1900–10	333833	196.0
1930–40	577151	26.1			

Source: *QB* 108, 1970.

inhabitants were from California. On the other hand, in the wealthy districts on the mountain slopes people came mainly from the East: Beverly Hills (only 33% born in California), Hollywood (only 25%), Santa Monica (only 32%), and similar eastern origin in Culver City and Ladera Heights.

In 1960, only 12% of those born in California lived outside the State (847000 out of 7 million), a low proportion in comparison with other states, such as Michigan (17%), or New Jersey (20%). Most of the migrants who abandoned the State settled down on the Pacific north coast (9% in Oregon, 8·8% in Washington) or in Texas (8%): the influence of the aerospace industries is obvious.

Growth of the housing stock

During World War II and the few years after the conflict, Los Angeles suffered from an acute shortage of housing, particularly of conveniently located dwellings. The building industry virtually came to a stop. The few new housing units that were built were reserved for immigrants from other states converging toward Los Angeles, and were located close to the armament industries in peripheral locations (during the fourth quarter of 1945 alone, the number of housing units built for nonresidents was doubled; *QB* 18, 1946). Local authorities hoped that the newcomers working in the war industries would leave after the end of the conflict, but nothing of the sort happened. Many discharged soldiers settled down in Los Angeles, and the aerospace industry started hiring new workers for civilian production as early as October 1945. As a result, many new districts that had developed during the war did not lose population. This was particularly the case of the new communities where more than 80% of new construction was concentrated in the period 1943–1944. These dwellings were built as a ribbon behind the shoreline between Long Beach and Santa Monica, and also to the north, in Burbank (*QB* 15, 1945). The housing shortage persisted until 1949, in which year the county still had a deficit of more than 40000 dwelling units, or 3% of total existing units. The housing situation was improving, however, since the Security First National Bank had put the deficit in September 1948 at 70000 units (*QB* 32, 1949). Supply and demand on the housing market eventually reached equilibrium in 1950.

The arrival of equilibrium heralded a new beginning. People preferred to build single houses, and to own their own home. Between 1950 and the first years of the 1960s, the 'American dream' of a single home for each family tended to become a reality. Data clearly show a break around 1950 in the proportion of households owning their homes (table 3.14). This was, in fact, a national trend. The rate remained very stable, around 40%, from 1900 until World War II; it then increased to more than 50% in 1950, and reached 63% in 1960. Actually, in 1960, Los Angeles County lagged behind the nation in this trend. In 1970, the rate fell again as an economic crisis began to take shape, and the median age of dwellings went down as a result (table 3.15). It had been around 15 years in 1940, more than 21 years in 1950, less than 10 years in 1960 (a surprisingly low value, even taking into account the fast turnover typical of a West Coast city). After such a construction boom, the late sixties saw a decline in the construction rate, and the median age grew strongly again in 1970.

Table 3.14. Housing occupation status.

Year	LA County			USA
	owner-occupied	renter-occupied	owner-occupied rate (%)	owner-occupied rate (%)
1970	1 179 943	1 252 038	48.5	–
1960	1 097 491	914 164	54.6	63
1950	734 711	–	53.6	54
1940	357 000	–	40.0	40
1920	–	–	–	40
1900	–	–	–	34

Sources: *QB* 110 (1970); Robertson (1964).

Table 3.15. Los Angeles County, age of housing units.

Year	Total number of units	Years since completion		
		0–10	11–20	21 and more
1970	2 537 000			
%	100	24.1	31.1	44.8
1960	2 370 050			
%	100	41.0	20.0	38.8
1950	1 395 000			
%	100	33.5	19.7	46.1
1940	936 400			
%	100	24.7	46.1	29.2

Source: *QB* 120 (1973).

Table 3.16. Los Angeles County: evolution of housing types.

Year	Single-dwelling units		5-dwelling units and above	
	number	proportion (%)	number	proportion (%)
1970	1 692 400	66.6	849 176	33.4
1960	1 596 600	75.7	513 017	24.3
1950	1 108 600	76.8	334 114	23.2
1940	708 000	73.6		26.4

Source: *QB* 120 (1973).

From 1960 onwards, the nature of housing types changed. Multiple-
dwelling units became relatively much more important (table 3.16).
Whereas single houses had constantly formed three-quarters of all housing
from 1940 till 1960, in 1970 they constituted only two-thirds of it. This
was a substantial change with quite complex causes: disenchantment with
the suburbs, now too far away from the center in terms of time, because
the transportation network had often become saturated; downtown
renewal (for instance with the Bunker Hill complex); a large increase in
the number of bachelors, that is, people looking for apartments rather than
for houses; a slowing down of the city's demographic growth, and even a
slight decrease in recent years, the first since the Civil War. In 1958, for
the first time, the number of apartments built was larger than the number
of houses. In the 1970s the movement was accelerating—92% of housing
units built between 1970 and 1973 were apartments (*QB* 120, 1973).

Evolution of the urban administration

The basic trend in American cities in the past has been toward increasing
decentralization. The goal of most wealthy communities has been to
become autonomous in order to avoid losing their resources in the budget
of a big city, to control them in their own self-interest (to ensure, for
instance, 'good' schools for their children), and to preserve the economic,
social, and racial homogeneity of the community. The well-known result
of this is, of course, that the financial troubles of the center increase with
its population—its spending grows as the fiscal basis shrinks. Well-to-do
households try to avoid their fiscal obligations, while poor families, often
with many children and suffering from unemployment, are crowded in
the center. They need public services more than others, but cannot afford
them.

Such municipal secession has been rampant in Los Angeles because of
its weak urban structure and its spatial extension. Furthermore, the recent
and important growth of the city led naturally to the creation of new
municipalities on recently developed land. This administrative evolution
closely fits the social and economic history of the city (table 3.17).
During the period of prosperity (1920–1930), 26 new municipal bodies
appeared; 6 only were to survive. Between 1930 and 1940, during the

Table 3.17. Administrative organization of Los Angeles SMSA.

Year	Number of municipalities	Year	Number of municipalities
1970	77	1910	25
1960	68	1900	12
1950	45	1890	9
1940	45	1850–	
1930	44	1880	1
1920	38		

Source: *QB* 122 (1973).

Depression, 2 new cities only were created; one survives today. Their number did not change from 1930 to 1950, when municipal creation began again. In 1954, the Lakewood Plan fixed new conditions, much easier to meet, for creating a new municipal government (Crouch and Dinerman, 1963). The cost of building a brand new administration from scratch (building or renting offices, hiring municipal staff, acquiring equipment) was the main obstacle, particularly during the early years when tax revenue was still far from adequate. From 1954 on, the State of California subsidized the new city, and contributed to a large portion of the necessary investments, guaranteed the bonds the municipality might float on the market, and authorized County employees to staff the new municipal administration for some time. In 1973, there were 73 different municipalities in Los Angeles County, 90 having been created since 1850. The number of failures was thus quite low.

Developed during the twentieth century with a population of American stock, in form more recent and more residential than San Francisco, Los Angeles more than any other big city in North America (with perhaps the exception only of Vancouver, but in a different context) embodies in its history and its structure the hopes, the dreams, the contradictions, the successes and the failures, in short the myths, of modern American society. The city's site is an epitome of California, 'Sea, Sun and Sand', and its wealth, as well as its exceptional growth, justifies the slogan which attracted hundreds of thousands of migrants—'California is the Cornucopia of the World'.

The period of time extending from 1940 to 1970 forms a complete, well-closed development cycle, starting with the stagnation and the anxiety following the Depression, and ending with the crises lurking in the early 1970s; in between, a long period of sustained and exceptional prosperity. In this sense, the description and analysis of the evolution of Los Angeles take on the role of a very special example.

3.4 Los Angeles in 1940

In the center of a vast agricultural plain, which today is almost entirely developed, the city was founded as a rural market. It was also a stop on the north–south road going through the Bakersfield pass from the Fresno Basin, in the closed valley of the Rio Sacramento, to the coastal plain. Such a favorable situation on a main transportation axis has been the principal asset of the city, and its original function has not disappeared. The Los Angeles SMSA is still a major dairy and poultry center, thanks to large undeveloped tracts at its periphery and even in its center, as witness the flourishing 'Farmers' Market' held regularly in Wilshire Blvd.

The site is favorable to the development of a huge metropolis, but it also presents serious dangers. A vast sedimentary plain, filled with very recent sediments which are only poorly consolidated, it is cut at different levels by marine terraces. A few rocky hills stick out of the deposits: Baldwin Hills between Culver City and Hyde Park District, in the south Rolling Hills which fixed the whole shoreline and protects Long Beach harbor from the western winds. The sedimentary plain rises above the ocean level by only a few meters. In Wilmington, the altitude is actually negative—3 meters below sea level (Nelson and Clark, 1976, page 8). The shoreline is either sandy or, in some parts, formed of a small cliff no higher than 20 or 30 meters. The city is bounded north and northwest by the Santa Monica Mountains, a few hundred meters high. Deeply notched by gulches, dry most of the year, those rocky slopes reach from Santa Monica to Hollywood and Griffith Park, via Beverly Hills and Bel Air, and offer the most beautiful locations for living, particularly the deep canyons with their narrow and isolated ribbons of expensive houses.

Earthquakes, as in most of California, form the main natural hazard (Nelson and Clark, 1976, page 16). Since the disaster of 1934, which partly destroyed the city of Long Beach, modern buildings have been designed to resist and survive the shocks. The strong 1971 earthquake (magnitude 6·4 on the Richter scale) destroyed only a few buildings but still killed three hundred people. In fact the Santa Monica Mountains are limited by fresh faults, and the plain is a collapse basin (Graben). The most dangerous parts of the city are not the rocky hills, where shocks are strong but short, but rather the plain, where shock waves move back and forth, reflected by the hills. The recent sediments shake rather like a jelly in a glass.

Two other dangers threaten the city: floods, when violent Mediterranean-like rains swell the dry gulches quite suddenly, and also when earthquakes shake the foundations of the river dams; and fire at the end of each summer, not in the city itself but on the northern hills, where the most expensive homes are built (cf the Bel Air fire in 1963).

All in all, this flat and wide plain has offered a practically limitless space, particularly to the east, for city growth. Development constraints have not really been physical but rather human, due to socioeconomic as well as racial tensions, and to the unequal levels of land rent.

3.4.1 Urban structure in 1940
At the beginning of this study, population and dwellings in Los Angeles presented a classical spatial structure. A factorial analysis (principal components analysis with Varimax rotation) of the 1940 Census data indicates three main types of grouping: household type, socioeconomic level with the corresponding professional distribution, and ethnic relations.

Household types
Thirteen variables were chosen out of the 1940 Census (Income and Percentage of Singles are two variables which were not available in the 1940 Census). Almost half of the information (44.4% of the total variance)

collapsed on the first factor (table 3.18) which opposed two types of household:

(1) Houses (single-dwelling units) occupied by their owner, with a number of children, versus

(2) Apartments in large buildings, rented by older people.

In this second group one finds most of the vacant dwellings for rent or for sale.

These two types do not represent different social levels: the variables 'housing value', 'rent', as well as 'number of school years' (a good substitute for income) are practically uncorrelated with this factor. Discrimination is based on the age of the head of the household: young bachelors getting married, then having children and moving to a larger and more detached dwelling, mature people without children at home, old people with more limited income, returning to cheaper apartments in the city: the classical *Family* or *Life Cycle*, determining a clear distribution through space.

Old people in rented apartments are located in the old city center (Downtown) in a large zone surrounded by a transition ring. Three other smaller zones are typically located in Beverly Hills, Huntington Park, and Santa Monica, in each case around the city center. Old people renting apartments are definitely located in most central parts of the city, and this pattern is so regular that the area of these old-people districts is roughly proportional to the age of these early centers.

Two facts are noteworthy: around each early center we can observe very regular 'rings' where household types are less definite, and which represent the gradual transition to the opposite type and the spatial pattern is most regular all over the city. It is also necessary to recall that these family types are not correlated with social level, and that they exhibit population mobility: such a regular pattern can be explained only by frequent migrations by short distances along radial directions during family life, that is, toward or away from the city center. Young people move to the periphery as they build a home, and then come back to the center as they grow older.

Table 3.18. Household types in Los Angeles (1940). Loadings on factor 1 after Varimax rotation (44% of the variance).

Positive loadings	r	r^2	Orthogonal variables	r
Number of persons	0.894	0.79	Whites	−0.034
Houses (single-dwelling unit)	0.878		Blacks	0.032
Owner-occupied houses	0.861		Value	−0.084
Young persons	0.812		Rent	0.114
Negative loadings			Number of school years	−0.164
Apartments	−0.855	0.73		
Renter-occupied	−0.843			
Old persons	−0.831			
Vacant	−0.357	0.13		

The belt formed by young households with children is equally regular. Differences in scores are due to unequal development of peripheral districts in 1940. The result of such a multitude of small individual movements is the typical *concentric* pattern which has been observed in practically all US cities. It plays a principal role (half of the available information) and relates a housing type to a household type, showing a dynamic process at work.

Socioeconomic level and professional distribution
Although we do not know what family income was in 1940, we can use three substitutes: 'rent', 'housing value', and 'number of school years' (table 3.19). The second component concentrates approximately a quarter of the available information. Most variables are orthogonal to this axis and do not contribute more than a few percent. The only important negative loading corresponds to the percentage of young people (a quarter of the variance in common with the component). Such a factorial structure may be explained in two different ways: either less educated families tend to have more children, or families with many children usually stay away from expensive dwellings. Both explanations are likely but their meaning is different; the correlation circle enables us to decide which is preferred[3]. Figure 3.1 shows that if 'young persons' (J), 'old persons' (V), and 'number of school years' (S) are lined up with the origin, the point L (rent) is shifted to the side—rent is less related to the percentage of 'young people'. This confirms the first hypothesis, namely that better educated households tend to have fewer children.

Table 3.19. Social level in Los Angeles (1940). Loadings on factor 2 after Varimax rotation (25% of variance).

Positive loadings	r	r²	Orthogonal variables	r	r²
Rent	0.941	0.88	Whites	0.187	
Value	0.893		Blacks	−0.068	
Number of school years	0.865		Old persons	0.224	
			Owner-occupied houses	0.233	0.05
Negative loadings			Vacant	0.160	
Young persons	−0.509	0.26	Houses (single-	−0.109	
Renter-occupied houses	−0.301	0.09	dwelling unit)		
			Apartments	0.073	
			Number of persons	−0.099	

[3] In factorial space, scales are different along each principal component equal in fact to the root of the corresponding eigenvalue: 5.8 for the first component, and 3.2 for the second. Let us weight each factor by $(\lambda_i)^{-\frac{1}{2}}$, where λ_i is the eigenvalue corresponding to the ith factor. Then the cloud of points becomes a hypersphere, and all axes have the same scale. The first and second components form a plane intersecting the cloud as a circle. Variables are points on this circle; their relative position shows their relationships.

There is something disturbing in the position of this second component. Social level, however one measures it ('housing value', 'rent', 'education'), is not correlated with any other variable except 'family size'—better off people have fewer children. This is a common fact in the United States but a quite surprising one for Europeans accustomed to see in wealth one of the main factors of urban discrimination. Here in Los Angeles, 'housing tenure', 'type of dwelling' (apartment versus house), and 'crowding rate' have no relation with a family's social level (less than 5% in common with component 2). This is an urban society where social differences are narrowed down, or rather where the code expressing them is much wider than in Europe, made of more fluid elements like transportation mode (number and make of the automobiles used by the family), type of leisure, type of neighborhood, etc. This is a much more mobile urban structure, where social relationships are in perpetual and rapid evolution: in contrast to western Europe, family incomes may fluctuate quite widely over a few years as a consequence of changes in personal success or in national conjecture, households move every two or three years, buildings deteriorate in a few years and may be replaced by other dwellings attracting quite different social groups. Unlike European metropolises, and even perhaps the great American cities along the eastern seaboard, Los Angeles appears to grow so fast that the main variable groups (demographic structure, social level, types of housing) do not seem able to achieve a permanent reaction upon one another.

Factor scores on the second component form interesting spatial patterns (figure 3.2). As in most cities, the west is rich and the east is poor—a trivial distinction that remains rather mysterious in its ubiquity. Two triangular sectors diverge from the center: well-off households extend along Hollywood, Wilshire, and Sunset Blvds as far as Santa Monica. The poorer sector stretches from the north of Downtown to the south, along

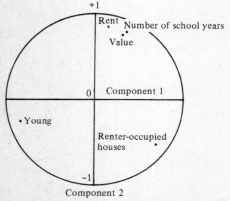

Figure 3.1. Circle of correlations in the plane defined by the two first components: population and housing in 1940 (before rotation).

Central Avenue and the Watts ghetto. Between these two extreme
branches, other sectors, narrower but more regular in shape, succeed one
another. Moving from east to west, first there is a sector less depressed
than along the ghetto axis, then a middle-class sector (centered around
Inglewood), two small sectors, rich and then poor from Ladera Heights to
the seashore, and a middle-income sector (from Culver City to Venice)
before reaching the wealthy western slopes, along Santa Monica Blvd.

Two characteristic exceptions exist to this regular pattern: the old
center in Santa Monica, made up of poor districts, limits the rich sector
before it reaches the sea. Conversely, most of the rest of the shoreline
is formed of middle-income to high-income neighborhoods.

The sectoral pattern, as described by Homer Hoyt in Chicago during the
1920s, is very clear. The well-defined sectors to the west and the east
contrast with the central ones, less well delimited: these were developed
and inhabited later, during and after World War II. In Santa Monica, an
old autonomous city swallowed up by Los Angeles during the 1930s, the
city center superimposes on the large metropolitan pattern a small sectoral
pattern of its own contained in a circle of some 3 km radius. As a result
one encounters, on moving northward along the shore: first, a prominently

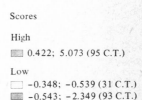

Scores

High
   0.422; 5.073 (95 C.T.)

Low
   −0.348; −0.539 (31 C.T.)
   −0.543; −2.349 (93 C.T.)

Figure 3.2. Los Angeles in 1940—socioeconomic level (factor 2, 24.5% of total
variance).

middle-class tract, then a poor one followed by a wealthier one, then another poor one, and finally, in the north, the wealthy neighborhoods of Sunset Blvd and Pacific Palissades.

Hoyt explained the radial pattern by the role of the main transportation axes diverging from Downtown on the one hand, and by local amenities like the Michigan shoreline in Chicago, which brings about the existence of long ribbons of agreeably located and expensive districts, on the other. Los Angeles exhibits such a spatial organization even more clearly—the two extreme sectors, which are also the more typical ones, follow two main axes: Central Avenue, in the east, and Santa Monica Blvd in the west. Slopes along the Santa Monica Mountains offer particularly well located sites, and this easily explains the high rents in this western sector. In 1940, the shoreline began to play the role of a local amenity and brought about, although in quite a confused way, the development of expensive neighborhoods along the ocean shore.

Santa Monica and Venice present a fascinating case. The global sectorial pattern centered on Los Angeles Downtown tended to push to the shore two poor sectors which should intersect the ocean at Venice and at El Segundo. This was in conflict, however, with the local amenity formed by the seashore—land along the shoreline tends to be expensive. The contradiction was to survive for several decades and leave scars on the urban landscape. In 1970, land neighboring El Segundo was occupied by Los Angeles International Airport, mainly because the price was kept low by the continuation, at this point of the shore, of a poor sector of the global sectorial pattern. Attracted, however, by the beach, a small neighborhood around Trask Avenue was included in the airport as an odd product of conflicting spatial patterns. The Venice seashore shows the results of this conflict even better. A part of the community is in crisis; old cottages with low rents, on a beautiful site in great demand, were occupied mostly in 1971 by hippies living quite miserably, the sons and daughters of well-off families—a surprisingly clear way of living the contradiction between the two spatial influences. The Venice southern shoreline, however, has been radically transformed by developers into a modern Marina, where small buildings, designed for well-paid bachelors, open directly onto yachts anchored in the small harbor, Marina del Rey.

What appears here is much more than a sectorial pattern of social groups: a complex dynamic process has been at work for several decades. Beyond the apparent confusion of household mobility and functional change, it is determining the urban landscape. Even the contradictions to the process exhibited by some districts of the city, where two patterns conflict, have important and peculiar special effects.

The average proportion of the seven main professional groups in the 1940 census tracts are given in table 3.20. For the sake of simplification a few small categories have been discarded, so the whole active population is not completely represented here, but relatively few households are lost (see the Introduction).   The percentages of the various groups do not differ very much between one another, which ensures a near maximum of information on the distribution of professionals.   Linear correlations between the groups (table 3.21) indicate to what degree they tend to live together in the same tracts, or whether they avoid one another—it is a measure of spatial segregation.   Two main groupings emerge: 'professionals', 'managers', and 'clerks' tend to share the same neighborhoods; they are clearly separated from the four other groups. 'Craftsmen' and 'operatives' live together (45% of the variance in common). 'Operatives' and 'laborers' mingle slightly, but since the absolute value of their (positive) correlation is smaller than the absolute value of all other correlations between other groups (which are negative), it is obvious that these two groups are brought together less in the same blocks by common affinities, than they are rejected equally by all other social groups.

Table 3.20. Los Angeles: proportion of professional groups in census tracts (1940).

Professionals	10.4%	Craftsmen	14.9%
Managers	12.5%	Operatives	19.0%
Clerical and	24.4%	Service workers	11.8%
sales workers		Laborers	7.0%

Table 3.21. Los Angeles: correlations between professional groups (1940).

	Professionals	Managers	Clerical and sales workers	Craftsmen	Operatives	Service workers
Managers	0.49	1.0				
Clerical and sales workers	0.53	0.36	1.0			
Craftsmen	−0.53	−0.47	−0.31	1.0		
Operatives	−0.71	−0.62	−0.58	0.67	1.0	
Service workers	−0.18	−0.42	−0.30	−0.27	−	1.0
Laborers	−0.43	−0.10	−0.65	−0.09	0.11	−

Nonsignificant correlations have been omitted.

Ethnic relations
The third factor (after rotation) contrasts the position of Whites and Blacks (table 3.22). Although social differences are represented on factor 2, orthogonal to, that is, uncorrelated with, this ethnic factor 3, Whites still have a slightly higher school level than the Blacks. It has often been suggested that the location of 'poor Whites' in black districts has confused the picture that one has tried to present of such districts. However, this third factor removes the effect of social differences very efficiently, and in the process isolates the poor Whites, but this does not cancel out educational inequalities. In other words, at equal income levels, the social position of

black households is built on a more insecure basis than that of white families, who have a much wider background.

This third (ethnic) factor is, by construction, orthogonal to the first two factors: ethnicity appears as uncorrelated with family type or social level. This observation, quite common in North American cities, has been used sometimes, though not from an unbiased point of view, to suggest that black households were not underprivileged groups. Actually, the logical interpretation is the reverse: among Blacks a wide variety of incomes exist, but widespread racism, either open or implicit, bars even the wealthy families from access to neighborhoods corresponding to their social level and confines them together in the same tracts. It is an unplanned but very effective way of avoiding social tension between different ethnic groups, by simply displacing the tension and moving it inside the black city where it is aggravated. This is plainly shown in the loadings of several variables ['value', 'rent', 'houses (single-dwelling)', 'apartments']; all are practically orthogonal to the ethnic factor. In this way, racial prejudices disrupt the inner dynamic of classical growth models (Burgess's or Hoyt's), which were formulated when city centers received poor but white immigrants. Nothing stopped their children, so long as they went up the social scale, from moving to better neighborhoods and mingling with the American bourgeoisie. The end of massive immigration from Europe in the 1930s, and the great drift of Blacks away from the South during World War II trapped colored people in the city centers, which became ghettos. The result was the appearance of a third pattern of urban growth represented by Harris and Ullman's multinuclei model.

In 1940, black districts extended along Vernon and Central (figure 3.3), near Downtown, with two separated nuclei. Watts, in the south was still a poor neighborhood in 1940, Blacks formed less than half of its population; the other inhabitants were poor whites, often of Greek or Italian origin, like Simon Rodia, the builder of the famous surrealist 'towers' made of broken plates and Coca Cola bottle caps. The other

Table 3.22. Ethnic distribution in Los Angeles (1940). Loadings on factor 3 after Varimax rotation (12% of the variance).

Positive loadings	r	r^2	Orthogonal variables	r	r^2
Whites	0.950	0.90	Young persons	−0.030	
Number of school years	0.214	0.05	Old persons	0.134	0.02
			Owner-occupied houses	0.131	
Negative loadings			Renter-occupied houses	−0.171	
Blacks	−0.963	0.92	Vacant	0.118	
			Houses (single-dwelling unit)	−0.034	
			Apartments	0.073	
			Value	0.044	
			Rent	0.070	
			Number of persons/room	−0.125	

nucleus, to the west, consisted of a few blocks around the University of Southern California. From these three embryos, a black ghetto was to diffuse, by jumping to contiguous blocks, until it occupied by 1970, a wide stretch of the city.

Other nuclei of different ethnicities remained more stable during the evolution of the city. Puerto Ricans and Chicanos from Mexico remained located in the south, in Gardena and particularly between Culver City and Marina del Rey, near the airport, in barracks built during the war, for armament industry workers (Fogel, 1967). Families of Oriental stock did not move from Downtown, just north of the large black ghetto: the Japanese in 'Little Tokyo', and the Chinese in Chinatown.

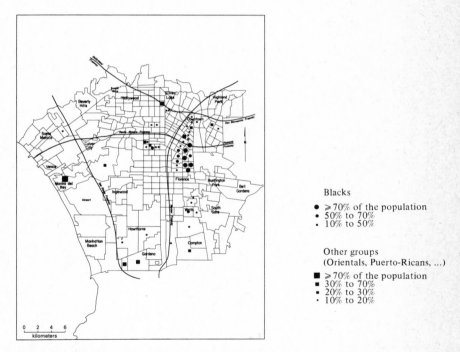

Blacks

● ⩾ 70% of the population
• 50% to 70%
· 10% to 50%

Other groups
(Orientals, Puerto-Ricans, ...)

■ ⩾ 70% of the population
▪ 30% to 70%
▪ 20% to 30%
· 10% to 20%

Figure 3.3. Los Angeles in 1940—ethnic distribution. (NB. Only populations classed as non-White are represented.)

Vacant housing
Uncorrelated with the three factors analyzed above, the spatial distribution of vacant dwellings differs from the preceding patterns (figure 3.4). It corresponds to the fourth component and represents approximately 6% of the total information (table 3.23). On average, 6% of the dwellings in a tract are vacant, with a quite small dispersion (the coefficient of variation is only 0.65): the vacancy rate is reasonably constant over the whole city.

Most vacant dwellings are apartments in multistorey buildings; owner-occupied houses have the lowest vacancy rates. On the whole, one would expect apartments for rent to present a higher occupancy turnover than houses occupied by their owners, but surprisingly enough this obvious fact explains only some 12% of the variance, most of the phenomenon does not have an easy interpretation. 'Rent' and 'value' (housing value) do not play any significant role, and neither do the ethnicity or the social level of the inhabitants as measured by the number of school years completed.

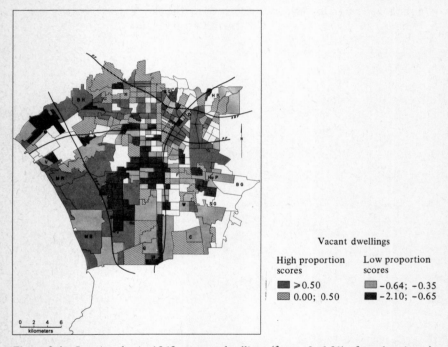

Figure 3.4. Los Angeles in 1940—vacant dwellings (factor 2, 6.3% of total variance).

Table 3.23. Vacant housing in Los Angeles (1940). Loadings on factor 4, after Varimax rotation (6% of the variance).

Positive loadings	r	r²	Orthogonal variables	r
Vacant	0.850	0.72	Value	0.123
Apartments	0.357	0.13	Rent	0.095
			Whites	0.016
Negative loadings			Blacks	−0.088
Owner-occupied houses	−0.316	0.10	Number of school years	−0.050
Houses (single-dwelling unit)	−0.312		Renter-occupied houses	0.124

The spatial distribution of vacancies therefore seems, by these means, to elude a logical explanation. Figure 3.4 shows, however, that this is not true: the quite regular arrangement of factor scores on the map gives the clue. Vacancy rates are particularly low between Hyde Park and the University of Southern California Campus, through Inglewood, south of Downtown. The city, on the contrary, is surrounded by a clearly defined ring of high-vacancy rates, particularly in the northeast, the north, the west, and the southwest along the ocean shore. Downtown forms an original case, with a few high rates contiguous to blocks of very low scores; such exceptional heterogeneity probably indicates a very high rate of turnover of housing, with a random spatial distribution of vacancies in a city center where rotation is rapid. On the other hand, the part of the ring of high rates extending from Hollywood to the ocean contains very different types of districts; their only common point is that they have all been recently developed, particularly the tracts on the slopes of the Santa Monica Mountains and those on the shore. The vacancy rates here mark an urbanization front, the limit of a kind of building wave which left behind in 1940, in the middle of the city, concentric rings of relatively old and already occupied housing, and at the periphery a larger proportion of new buildings which had not yet been occupied.

Such a diffusion process is of rather special interest. On the one hand, it accounts, in a purely spatial way, for a phenomenon (housing vacancy) which other variables were unable to explain—this is a typical case for which geographical mapping provides the solution. On the other hand, it indicates a turning point in the history of Los Angeles: we can observe, in 1940, the last steps in the complete occupation of the urban space. Further movements after this will only be redistribution processes inside a totally occupied space.

In this way, urban analysis demonstrates four different spatial patterns; three of these are classical and have been shown to exist in practically all American cities. They are:

1. a concentric structure around an urban center, or rather centers, corresponding to the distribution of family types;
2. radial sectors separating districts into poor and rich zones, the geometrical regularity being altered and reinforced at the same time by local physical amenities such as mountain slopes or seashore;
3. several nuclei where ethnic minorities congregate.

A fourth pattern plays an important role in Los Angeles, although it has not been given enough attention, namely

4. diffusion waves of residential buildings which in 1940 almost completely covered the city and began to be reflected by the obstacles presented by the mountains and the shore.

The first application of factor analysis to the urban environment demonstrated these structures in Los Angeles as early as 1949 (Shevky and Williams, 1949). One of the main criticisms directed against urban factorial ecology, born of this seminal study, is that it does implicitly assume the homogeneity of the basic cells, which are here the census tracts (Ciceri, 1974). The problem is very clear in the case of Los Angeles: the variable 'Blacks' correlates negatively with housing 'value' (−0.152) and 'rent' (−0.161), suggesting that Blacks are generally poor and look for cheap housing. Loadings on the fourth (ethnic) component, however, tell a different tale: housing 'value' (0.044) and 'rent' (0.070) are orthogonal to this component. The difference is due to the 'poor Whites' who live in black districts and are poorer than the average black household; loadings, that is projections onto the component, are similar to the coefficients of partial correlation; they restore the true relationship by eliminating spurious links.

Another criticism shows how artificial it is to break up into independent components natural or social phenomena which are always interrelated. Such an attack may be well founded; as a check, the preceding analysis was completed by an *oblique* rotation of the eigenvectors extracted. Axes keep the same interpretations but loadings are generally higher, showing a better fit of the factors to the groupings of local variables. Angles between rotated factors, however, remain close to 90°, and loadings change minimally. Factors are now slightly correlated: 'household type' and 'social level' $r = 0.126$; 'household type' and 'race', $r = -0.083$; 'social level' and 'race', $r = -0.267$. This is the highest and the most interesting correlation between structures, showing the tendency of black families to be poorer, but the link is still weak (only 7% of variance is common). All things considered, in this case, a classical analysis in principal components does not distort overmuch the true relations between variables.

3.4.2 Relations between social and housing structures

One of the main concerns of this research has been to study the adequacy of the balance between housing and households. Each of these is determined by a whole set of variables, and the problem is to analyze the various forms of relation between these two sets; for this we use Canonical Analysis[4].

Population has been defined here by six variables:

Whites	Young persons	Number of persons/room
Blacks	Old persons	Number of school years

and Housing by seven variables:

Owner-occupied houses	Houses (single-dwelling unit)
Renter-occupied houses	Apartments
Vacant	Value
Rent	

---

[4] Whereas usual linear correlation analysis measures the relation existing between two *variables*, Canonical Analysis demonstrates the relations existing between two *sets of variables*.

The analysis extracts six pairs (or doublets) of canonical factors and six eigenvalues (which are nothing more than the square of the correlation between the two factors forming each pair). Bartlett's test shows that three canonical pairs are enough to describe the relationship between the two sets of variables; the third one, however, exhibits a very small relation (only 22.7% of variance in common between Housing and Household). The first two pairs are the important ones (table 3.24).

The first doublet corresponds to a strong link between Population and Housing. For this particular relation these have 81% of the variance in common: households with children (0.745), the rather young, quite well-off (0.430), and mainly whites, although ethnicity plays only a limited role here (0.128 and −0.029). We are left with a typical description of families in the third stage of the family cycle (after the bachelors and the newly marrieds) and rather middle class (or upper-middle class). They occupy dwellings as 'owners' and not as 'renters' (0.810 and −0.812), and hence these are rarely apartments but usually houses (single-dwelling units) or flats in small buildings (as it is shown by the dissymmetry between 0.645 and −0.764). Housing cost is quite high; occupation is stable, and there are less vacant units than in other districts. A description of the typical young middle-class with means in good separated houses—the American dream of the time.

The other strong relationship (71% of the information in common) is quite different: families with a large number of children (0.914), very

Table 3.24. Canonical Analysis: Housing and Households in Los Angeles, 1940.

Canonical factors	Eigenvalues c_i	Canonical correlations, $c_i^{1/2}$	Canonical factors	Eigenvalues c_i	Canonical correlations, $c_i^{1/2}$
1	0.81182	0.901	3	0.22724	0.477
2	0.71471	0.845	4	0.03732	0.193
			5	0.00638	0.080
			6	0.00315	0.056

Loadings on canonical factors 1 and 2.

	1	2		1	2
Households			*Housing*		
Whites	0.128	−0.297	Owner-occupied houses	0.810	0.328
Blacks	−0.029	0.294	Renter-occupied houses	−0.812	−0.258
Young persons	0.368	0.914	Vacant	−0.313	−0.371
Old persons	−0.495	−0.601	Houses (single-dwelling unit)	0.645	0.684
Number of persons/room	0.745	0.578	Apartments	−0.764	−0.609
Number of school years	0.430	−0.809	Value	0.403	−0.754
			Rent	0.641	−0.738

young, with a low educational level and mostly black, although such districts contain poor whites as well. The basic characteristics, rather than ethnicity, are the low social level and the large number of children. These families also live in single houses rather than in apartments, but these dwellings differ strongly from the preceding type—capital value and rent are now very low. The demand for such low-cost housing is high; vacancies, as in the first case, are rare. Many of those poor households own their dwellings, but not so often as in the first case. Being tied down by children, the adults are forced to choose a well-defined type of housing and to rest content with it.

Interestingly enough, households without children, old people, and bachelors do not correlate with any important canonical factor. They are not tied to any particular type of housing and live in very different dwellings. Note also that in both canonical pairs with a strong internal relation, the vacancy rate is low. It demonstrates a bad adjustment of housing to households in the city.

3.5 Conclusion

In 1940, Los Angeles was already a well-organized city, exhibiting classical urban patterns. Downtown played a basic role; several older municipal centers included in the city during its rapid growth slightly disturbed its regular organization, by adding their own sectorial and concentric patterns (Santa Monica, Inglewood, Hollywood), but they did not destroy the general spatial order.

Three main types of human ecology stand out:

(a) young professionals with small families were living in quite expensive single houses which they owned;

(b) poorer families often black and with many children, but without professional qualification, inhabited shabby single houses;

(c) single people (young bachelors or old lonely people), mobile and moving frequently, tended to occupy apartments in larger buildings; their resources and social levels differed widely. This type was too heterogeneous to be linked with a particular type of housing.

It would be a mistake to describe Los Angeles as a suburbia developing without structure or order, a kind of invertebrate amorphous mass without center or poles. In 1940, it was as clearly and as strongly organized as any other American city of the same size. To see the automobile as the main cause for spatial growth and the main factor responsible for any alleged spatial disorder would be another mistake. The private car played an important role in Los Angeles from the late 1920s onward, but fifteen years later, the regularity and the simplicity of the city's spatial structure had not been altered in any way. Much more complex and much more powerful phenomena were going to determine the transformations of the city, the alteration of its population, and the changes in its housing.

4

Changes in the use of urban space

Los Angeles has been notable for the speed of its overall growth, due in part to the irregular growth of the population and to the transformation of the different characteristics of the city. These factors of change, which form the material presented in section 4.1, determine in turn the evolution of the various urban landscapes (section 4.2). Urban transportation also contributes (section 4.3) to an explanation of the spatial structure of a city which is so widespread and of such a low population density. The interplay between differences in townscapes and inequalities in accessibility has produced a complicated evolution in land rent (section 4.4).

4.1 The evolution of the population
Population growth has been irregular in time and space, and this has caused the continuous modification of the relative equilibrium between neighborhoods, while their social content changed even more significantly.

4.1.1 Demographic evolution
For thirty years the population has increased quite slowly in that part of the city analyzed here. The period of fastest growth was between 1940 and 1950; migration before and, above all, during the war was particularly strong (table 4.1). As a result, population density in the city increased by 55.9% over the period. Ethnic composition also changed a lot (figure 4.1). Although the absolute number of Whites increased during the war, it fell again afterwards (table 4.2). More than 100000 Whites left the city (as defined above) between 1960 and 1970. The significant development of the black population is attributable to their general migration to the cities, and also to a geometrical effect particular to this study. Since the limits of the urban region analyzed here are fixed, and since the metropolis has grown considerably in the period the spatial extent of the city in 1940 now corresponds to the central part of the SMSA as defined in 1970. Ethnic groups other than Blacks (Chicanos and Orientals) remained constant at around 2% of the population.

Table 4.1. The general growth of population and housing in Los Angeles (stricto sensu). (Source: US Bureau of Census.)

	Total population	Housing (number of dwellings)	Persons per dwelling
1970	2555021	1029697	2.48
1960	2352468	959348	2.45
1950	2128062	749409	2.84
1940	1638632	575331	2.85

The demographic structure of the population has changed in an important way. The young (less than 19-years old) and the old (over 65 years) have increased in absolute numbers as well as in percentages.

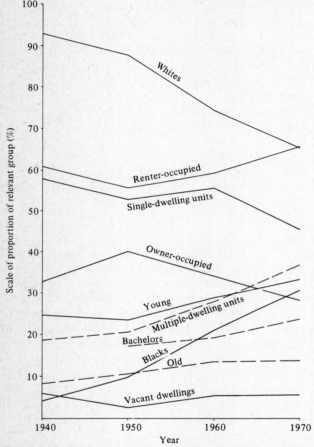

Figure 4.1. Changes in ethnic composition, population development, and housing development in Los Angeles, 1940–1970.

Table 4.2. Components of the population; absolute values. (Source: US Bureau of Census.)

	Whites	Blacks	Other ethnic groups	Young (<19)	Old (>65)	Adults (19–65)
1970	1 769 369	641 706	143 946	809 793	288 384	1 456 844
1960	1 863 326	403 926	85 216	739 859	267 921	1 344 688
1950	1 897 967	191 005	39 090	526 592	200 156	1 401 314
1940	1 538 412	66 889	33 331	396 374	135 646	1 106 612

The active population, crushed between those two groups, has declined from 67.5% to only 57% in 1970.

The homogeneity of the main variables through space is a very interesting indicator. It is measured here by the coefficient of variation, or c.v. (= standard deviation/mean). The diffusion of the black population across the city is marked by a regular decline in its c.v. Simultaneously the heterogeneity of the distribution of Whites through space increases, and this corresponds to a quite complicated phenomenon: it seems spatial segregation increases for the Whites while it decreases for the Blacks. Actually, if the proportion of Blacks within each census tract changed by the same rate in the whole city, the c.v. for Whites would remain constant. If there was no racial segregation, both communities would account for the same proportion of population in each tract, and their c.v's would be zero. The location of Blacks becomes more homogeneous because they occupy an increasing number of tracts, but the two populations do not mix any better. Whites leave those tracts to concentrate in a decreasing number of blocks, and are thus less homogeneously distributed in the urban space.

The three decades between 1940 and 1970 correspond to three different types of spatial organization:

The period during World War II and immediately afterwards shows how an urban structure can be radically transformed by huge external flows of migrants. These newcomers, mainly adults, do not have the time or the opportunity to distribute themselves harmoniously through the city. They settle down in groups in certain districts, which disrupts spatial organization and increases social segregation.

Spatial equilibrium is recovered during the second decade (1950–1960) through huge intraurban migrations, as social groups redistribute themselves across urban space. Spatial segregation remains a very difficult phenomenon to grasp. Although the variables 'number of school years' completed and 'income' are strongly correlated, the first becomes more homogeneous while the second is more heterogeneously distributed over space. Also, there is an increasing segregation of old people, while the young are distributed more and more evenly. The c.v.s for Whites and Blacks also vary in opposite directions. The figures are correct, but the concept itself is decidedly complex.

The relationship between ethnicity and income is particularly interesting (table 4.3). In general, Whites are always wealthier than Blacks. This advantage, however, can be attributed either to the better qualifications of Whites, or to racial prejudices reserving the best jobs for Whites. Suppose we fix the variable 'number of school years'. With the same educational level, Whites still have a higher income level than Blacks and this differential increases from 1950 (0.256) to 1970 (0.329); the zero-order correlation coefficient gives opposite results. Here, racial prejudice plays a basic role (see also Case, 1972).

The stability of several variables over time is indicated in table 4.4. Three periods clearly emerge. The location of family types did not change very much during the war, in spite of the significant migration of people and the functional changes. New workers and new industries managed to settle down in the fissures of a still loosely organized city, without altering it too much. The redistribution through space of men and activities occurred only during the second decade, after 1950 when these movements became very important. A new equilibrium was slowly forming during the 1960s.

The Blacks progressed across the city from 1940 to 1970 by moving slowly from one contiguous block to the next (Van Arsdol et al, 1971).

Table 4.3. Correlations for social level and its links with other variables.

	Income	NSYC[a]		Income	NSYC[a]
1970			1950		
Whites	0.35	0.13	Whites	0.42	0.40
Blacks	−0.32	−0.12	Blacks	−0.37	−0.36
Young	−0.26	−0.45	Young	0.20	−0.42
Old	0.10	0.20	Old	−0.27	0.29
NSY	0.54	1.0	NSY	0.56	1.0
1960			1940		
Whites	0.34	0.33	Whites	Data	0.35
Blacks	−0.30	−0.34	Blacks	missing	−0.25
Young	*	−0.39	Young		−0.58
Old	−0.17	0.25	Old		0.29
NSY	0.49	1.0	NSY		1.0

* Nonsignificant correlation.
[a] NSY ≡ Number of school years (completed).

Table 4.4. Population stability: autocorrelation (percentage of variance common to two successive censuses; r^2 is the coefficient of determination).

Variable	r^2 (%)		
	1940–1950	1950–1960	1960–1970
Whites	67.1	54.2	72.9
Blacks	73.9	57.3	73.9
Young	81.5	65.5	68.2
Old	66.4	46.5	48.1
Bachelors	–	72.1	57.1
Income	–	57.9	57.1
Number of persons/ room	72.8	70.2	75.0
Number of school years completed	68.1	61.5	66.7

Figure 4.2 represents the residuals after regression of the variable 'percentage of Blacks' on itself for the three intercensal periods; in this way, inequalities in the variable at the beginning of each period are eliminated. It is an almost perfect example of diffusion by contiguity. Obstacles have channeled the direction of this black diffusion wave. Downtown has constantly played this role, dividing the black movement into two flows: one toward the north–northeast, the other turning northwest, then west, along Hollywood Blvd. Why was Downtown such an obstacle? Probably because of the concentration at this point of an Oriental population (Chinatown, Little Tokyo) which substituted its racism for white racism, obviously with more success. Also, the unique functions of Downtown, with its huge stock of offices, contributed to the formation of a barrier. The main diffusion axis was first directed to the west (1940–1950, then 1950–1960). It then turned south and met another axis, oriented to the northwest, coming from Watts. Interestingly enough, the district located between the main ghetto and the smaller one in Watts has never really been occupied by Blacks in spite of the speed of their progression. The fact that this district forms an autonomous municipality (Florence) probably explains its ability to persist as a white neighborhood.

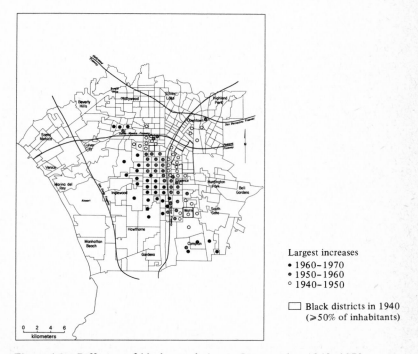

Largest increases
- 1960–1970
- 1950–1960
○ 1940–1950

☐ Black districts in 1940
(⩾50% of inhabitants)

Figure 4.2. Diffusion of black population in Los Angeles, 1940–1970.

The clarity of the black diffusion process provides some important observations:

(a) Diffusion by contiguity indicates a difficult process, slowed down by strong resistance, and based on the sum of individual efforts.

(b) The role of municipal autonomy is very important. Neighborhoods that were able to resist the black progression, diverting the flow without being affected were almost always independent municipalities (except for the unique instance of Downtown), which throws a crude light on the efficiency of so many illegal but successful methods of racial segregation.

(c) Black expansion mainly went to the south, clearly exhibiting the latent sectoral structure. The orientation, however, of other diffusion axes perpendicular to these sectors shows that land rent, usually differentiated sectorally, did not play the main role in channeling black movements.

(d) From a detailed examination of figure 4.2 it appears that pressure has been exercized by Blacks. They tried to move away in many different directions, but could succeed only where a barrier broke down. In many cases, spatial progression came to a stop early, for instance toward Downtown and Hollywood.

4.1.2 The socioprofessional evolution

Within the seven major professional categories, the number of adults of working age has doubled in thirty years (table 4.5), a clear indication of the important increase in population density. Clerks and Salesworkers form the most important group, followed by Operatives and Professionals.

The evolution over time of some of these groups presents several interesting features (figure 4.3). The number of Clerks, for instance, declined strongly in 1950. Had they followed the general pattern, they would have increased by 80000. In the same census, the number of Service workers increased enormously—in excess of 75000 people. Other curves (Laborers, Operatives, and Craftsmen) present erratic profiles.

Table 4.5. Evolution of major professional categories (absolute values). (Source: US Bureau of Census.)

	1940	1950	1960	1970
Professionals	68803	102079	141113	169856
Managers	77387	103021	91280	82399
Clerks, Salesworkers	161846	149356	271253	394840
Craftsmen	88041	80950	123095	164287
Operatives	110093	125964	185415	179739
Service workers	69753	157317	89182	123710
Laborers	30370	81790	38392	42798
Total of the seven categories	606293	800477	939730	1157629

Actually, the way in which people are classified has probably changed slightly from one census to the next, although the official definitions have remained the same. Caution is needed in the interpretation of the curves. Since the area studied here does not include the whole SMSA, it is safer to observe the changes of manpower in percentages.

Professionals form the most stable group (figure 4.4), increasing slowly but regularly over time. Managers decline, which indicates a movement of this group away from the city, toward the suburbs. Almost half of the active population is constituted by Employees (44%), Clerks, Sales, and Service workers, that is lower middle-class, and a third consists of industrial workers (in 1970, Craftsmen + Laborers + Operatives = 35.5%). As a result the population quite clearly appears to be divided between opposing groups. A majority of employees work in business; a small but stable group of wealthy people play a leading role in the economy; whilst the small, heterogeneous group of industrial workers decreases over time.

These socioprofessional groups are distributed quite unequally over space (figure 4.5). Laborers are quite concentrated. They are the poorest workers, and those who suffer the most from social segregation. The wealthiest groups (Professionals and Managers) however, are also very

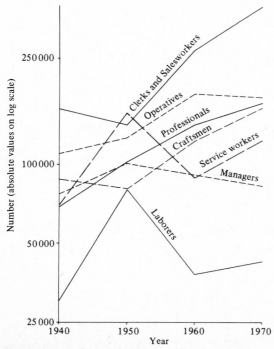

Figure 4.3. Employment by category (totals) in Los Angeles, 1940–1970.

concentrated; the concept of 'rich ghettos' is certainly meaningful in Los Angeles. The city, as delimited above, is mainly populated by the lower middle-class group of employees. On this pervasive background some isolated groups stand out: industrial workers on the one side, business leaders on the other.

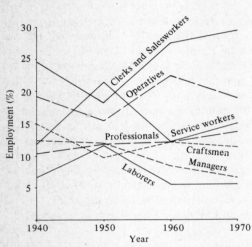

Figure 4.4. Employment by category (percentage) in Los Angeles, 1940–1970.

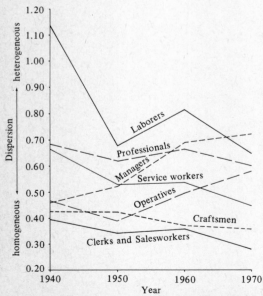

Figure 4.5. Changes in dispersion of employment in Los Angeles, 1940–1970.

Social segregation contributes to the organization of urban space in a very ordered fashion. The wealthiest groups (Professionals and Managers) lead the way; the poorest ones concentrate themselves by locating in the 'fissures' appearing in the social fabric of the city. The leading business categories group themselves together from 1940 onwards, whereas the poorer groups wait until 1960 to begin a process of concentration. The active population is clearly divided into two distinct sets, between which some intermediate categories (Employees and Craftsmen) hesitate to choose their location. The spatial grouping of distinct categories in the same census tracts is, of course, a function of their income (table 4.6), but still more of their way of life. In 1970, for instance, the average weekly wage of the employees was $121, which was much lower than the corresponding wages for Craftsmen of $157. Employees, however, lived close to the Professionals ($181) and Managers ($190), whereas Craftsmen avoided these neighborhoods (table 4.6).

Residential segregation between the two major groups of white-collar and blue-collar workers has clearly worsened with the years (table 4.7). Negative correlations between the two groups increase in absolute value between 1940 and 1970 (table 4.7); meanwhile, correlations between social categories within each of the two groups regularly increase. The two social groups become increasingly homogeneous, and separate themselves more and more. The city is actually breaking into two fragments.

The stability of the various groups is most interesting (table 4.8). The wealthiest groups remained in the same neighborhoods until the last decade, then, between 1960 and 1970, they began to move. Employees are also very stable. On the other hand, industrial workers and Service workers were extremely mobile until 1960. Between 1940 and 1950, Laborers and Service workers had almost completely abandoned the districts in which they had lived. Conversely, from 1960 onward they were extremely stable. During the 1960s, all groups seem to have been frozen. The social typology of the neighborhoods was fixed. One reason

Table 4.6. Distribution of income, sex, and race by social category (1970). (Source: US Bureau of Census, 1970.)

	Weekly wages ($)	Women (%)	Blacks (%)
Professionals	181	40.2	5.4
Managers	190	16.7	2.7
Clerks, Salesworkers	121	64.0	6.3
Craftsmen	157	5.0	6.4
Operatives	115	39.2	12.9
Service workers	87	55.7	17.3
Laborers	110	8.3	20.1

Table 4.7. Linear correlations for the spatial relationships between social categories.

		P	M	CS	C	O	SW
1940	M	0.487	1.000				
	CS	0.531	0.363	1.000			
	C	−0.527	−0.472	−0.309	1.000		
	O	−0.712	−0.623	−0.585	0.671	1.000	
	SW	−0.178	−0.419	−0.303	−0.267	0.018	1.000
	L	−0.429	−0.104	−0.653	−0.088	0.111	0.040
1950	M	0.565	1.000				
	CS	0.434	0.296	1.000			
	C	0.379	0.578	0.449	1.000		
	O	−0.540	−0.354	−0.268	−0.170	1.000	
	SW	−0.706	−0.641	−0.620	−0.644	0.444	1.000
	L	−0.385	−0.525	−0.372	−0.471	−0.131	0.384
1960	M	0.476	1.000				
	CS	0.364	0.540	1.000			
	C	−0.377	−0.372	−0.213	1.000		
	O	−0.717	−0.704	−0.775	0.365	1.000	
	SW	−0.464	−0.515	−0.502	−0.175	0.346	1.000
	L	−0.576	−0.549	−0.769	0.040	0.688	0.562
1970	M	0.684	1.000				
	CS	0.514	0.508	1.000			
	C	−0.446	−0.445	−0.181	1.000		
	O	−0.700	−0.615	−0.745	0.325	1.000	
	SW	−0.471	−0.494	−0.404	−0.059	0.156	1.000
	L	−0.584	−0.518	−0.533	0.157	0.433	0.429

Key: P—Professionals   O—Operatives
      M—Managers   SW—Service workers
      CS—Clerks, Salesworkers   L—Laborers
      C—Craftsmen

Table 4.8. Stability of social categories (autocorrelation; percentage of variance, r^2, common to two successive censuses).

Variable	r^2 (%)		
	1940-1950	1950-1960	1960-1970
Professionals	85	85	73
Managers	71	71	74
Clerks, Salesworkers	62	56	73
Craftsmen	4	2	60
Operatives	41	28	77
Service workers	9	19	69
Laborers	6	31	48

for this might be the economic crisis, but there is a more interesting explanation. A sort of crystallization of social relations (cf. figure 6.1, page 173) produced a clear spatial opposition between the two groups, which naturally immobilizes their locations.

One of the most famous clichés in American urban geography is that of the flight of the upper middle-class away from the city to the suburbs. This is not really the case in Los Angeles. The wealthy neighborhoods extending along the shore and along the mountain slopes from Santa Monica to Griffith Park, West Los Angeles, Beverly Hills and Hollywood, have not been abandoned by the well-to-do families who lived there in 1940. On the contrary, the city, far from tending to a kind of social homogeneity, has become increasingly split into two parts, one quite poor while the other was never so rich. Typically, the lower middle-class and the poor move frequently, while the rich remain settled in their residences, at least as a group. Of course, this stability might very well conceal an important mobility in individuals.

In order to locate social change among the census tracts, we need a measure of social change. Each of the four censuses provides a vector of percentages which indicates the relative importance of the major social groups located in each census tract. The problem is to compare the vectors. One could measure the distance between the four vectors of each tract using the chi-square statistic (Lancaster, 1969), and indices have been proposed for such purposes (Duncan et al, 1961). These measures, however, are based on assumptions about the mathematical structure of the data which are not always met, and rarely verified. Also, expressing the social content of a tract in percentages is much more convenient, but introduces a new constraint—the sum of the data is fixed and we lose one degree of freedom. For these reasons it is much safer to use a measure of deviation between two frequency (that is, percentage) distributions taken from Information Theory (Goldman, 1953; Marchand, 1972). No initial hypothesis is needed about the data, and percentages may logically be treated as the probability of extracting a person of a given social group from a census tract if we took a random sample.

The measure used here evaluates the *differential information* conveyed by a message whose content is compared with the previous knowledge we had. Let X be a set of mutually exclusive events; let p_i and q_i be two probability distributions defined on X: q_i is the probability that event i happens *before* any message reaches us; p_i is its probability *after* we receive the message. The difference in information contained in the message (in other words, the amount of surprise we experience after reading the message) is given by H, where

$$H = \sum_i p_i \lg \frac{q_i}{p_i} \; .$$

If the event was certain before the message came ($q_i = 1$), H is nothing but the usual entropy measure. Otherwise, H measures the amount of change that happened as the message came and time passed. This is exactly what we want to measure in this situation. Let q_i be the percentage of social group i in a tract at time t, and p_i be the percentage of the same group at the next census (time $t + 1$). H measures, then, the distortion experienced in a census tract as its social content changes over time. The results for the three intercensal periods have been mapped (figures 4.6, 4.7, and 4.8). The unit is the *dit*, the quantity of information conveyed by a message indicating which decision has been taken among ten equally probable decisions. This unit is particularly convenient with the use of decimal logarithms. The three maps use the same thresholds (0.1 and 0.04 dits) and thus are comparable.

During the first decade (figure 4.6), social transformations occurred in two types of districts: (1) the north–south axis from Downtown to Compton through Watts and Florence; (2) a ring of eccentric districts, which were suburbs during this period: south of Hollywood along the Santa Monica Freeway, the seashore (Marina del Rey, Manhattan Beach), the south (Gardena, Compton), and the southeast (Huntington Park, Bell Gardens, and South Gate). Two structures are superimposed here:

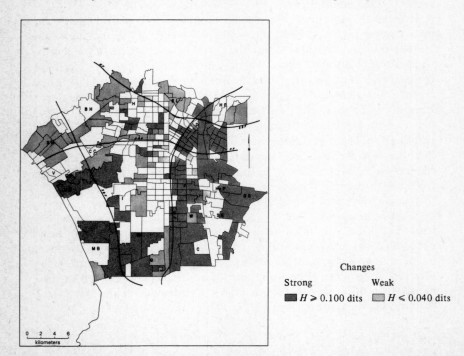

Figure 4.6. Changes in socioprofessional category in Los Angeles, 1940–1950.

a sectoral one, usually corresponding to social status, and a concentric
one, representing the classical life cycle. The ring of districts with large
changes corresponds to the urban frontier in 1940, along which the city
was growing and encroaching onto rural land (see figure 3.4). The most
important changes happened: (a) in the poorest districts particularly
affected by the construction of war industry, and the return to peacetime
production; and (b) in the most recently developed districts. The
stability of the well-to-do neighborhoods is remarkable.

Between 1950 and 1960 (figure 4.7) changes are less numerous. There
is less stability in the arc of wealthy districts to the west. This is a period
of prosperity, and changes of social category are more frequent for the
well-to-do families.

The last period is the quietest (figure 4.8). Most tracts are extremely
stable. Downtown again experiences important social changes, as does
Watts with its famous urban riots. Districts around Culver City, Palms,
and Marina del Rey have experienced important transformations for nearly
thirty years.

The population of American cities is supposed to be very mobile and
socially very volatile. The case of Los Angeles somewhat corrects these
clichés. If it is true that families move frequently (Rossi, 1980), then

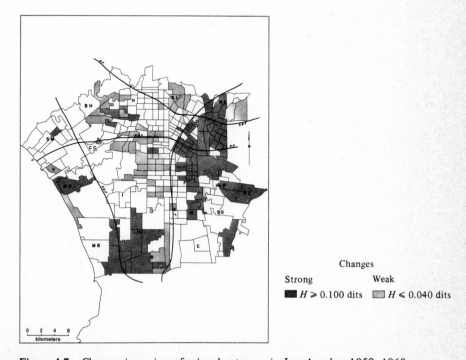

Figure 4.7. Changes in socioprofessional category in Los Angeles, 1950-1960.

the socioeconomic composition of most neighborhoods is remarkably stable once they have reached their equilibrium. In contrast to the huge metropolises of the East Coast, Los Angeles did not experience the typical and rapid decline of the city center, precipitously abandoned by the middle class and invaded by poor unemployed families. The trend exists, but it is a slow one which has not really changed the social map of the city in thirty years, years which were otherwise full of important events. Rich districts have the most stable socioprofessional composition, in complete contrast to classical urban theories.

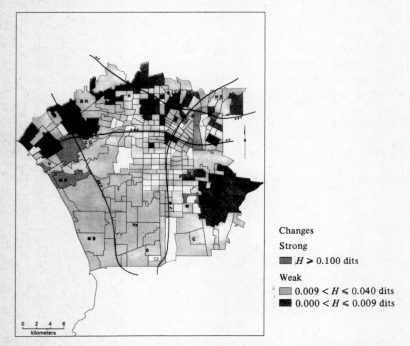

Figure 4.8. Changes in socioprofessional category in Los Angeles, 1960–1970.

4.2 Evolution of the townscapes

The urban landscapes which are juxtaposed to form Los Angeles, sometimes vertically, appear clearly and distinctly only to those who have lived in this immense city. The first contact, after leaving the airport, gives the visitor the false impression of a crushing uniformity. And indeed, in order to know Los Angeles well, one needs to have worked there and to have commuted through the city, particularly during rush-hours. Banham notes quite rightly that *movement* is the local language in which landscapes are expressed. Mobility replaces monumentality; one must learn to drive in order to read Los Angeles (Banham, 1971). The following pages draw on Banham's book freely.

4.2.1 The main types of landscape
Los Angeles is built in a sedimentary basin limited by faults and opening
onto the ocean. The distinction between the center, the rim, and the
shore also corresponds to differences in social groups and family structure.

The uniformity of the central plain
The mountains that surround Los Angeles are young and are still lifted
today during the quite frequent earthquakes. The mediterranean climate
creates drastic slope erosion, and the wide basin has been filled up with
recent and soft sediments. Variations in the climate and the sea level
have led to the formation of low terraces deeply cut by dry rivers, like
the Los Angeles River, and by innumerable gulches. The resulting slopes
are short but steep. The iron grid of the street network is blindly superimposed on such a relief, in the traditional Spanish fashion. Some
rectangular blocks of rock, limited by faults, have been thrown up and
loom above the surface of the plain, like Baldwin Hills, between Culver
City and Inglewood. Some faults or superficial folds are oil traps, and
these explain the presence of many derricks or electric pumps amid the
dwellings.

The central plain is a dangerous place to live, although flash floods in
the rivers and gulches have now been controlled by several dams. The
softness of the deposits amplifies terrestial waves, which are multiplied by
reflection and resonance and produce greater destruction than the short,
sharp tremors in the rocky hills. After the 1971 earthquake, which
particularly devastated the San Fernando Valley, geologists emphasized
the danger of building on these plains where the earth shakes like 'jelly in
a glass'.

The townscape of the plain is the only part of Los Angeles which
compares with other big American cities, particularly those in the Northeast. Here the city has no other specific originality than its mediterranean
climate, the mark of which shows in the palm trees lining many streets and
in the very large number of houses with a tiny swimming pool behind
them. Yet even these latter are not typical. In the USA, swimming pools
are a status symbol rather than items of sporting equipment, and they can
be found under much harsher climates (Chicago and Boston) where they
are useless for most of the year. Only tiny nuances, small quantitative
differences distinguish these neighborhoods from the Bronx, or Skokie in
the northern suburb of Chicago. Basically, the townscape remains 'all-
American'.

The plain's townscape occupies the triangle between Santa Monica
Freeway, the Harbor Freeway, and San Diego Freeway, but the limits are
not clear-cut. Baldwin Hills to the immediate southeast of Culver City
presents a different aspect, and in many places the townscape goes beyond
the three freeways. Several neighborhoods differ from the more general
type. Some are poor, even miserable, like the black ghetto around the

University of Southern California campus, or Watts. Some, like Inglewood, have better architecture, wealthier houses, and shaded streets. Driving south on Western Avenue one encounters the same low buildings along hundreds of blocks, all with similar flanks, backing onto unasphalted streets full of garbage cans. The street fronts of the buildings, however, present incredible efforts of imaginative architecture to distinguish themselves from their neighbors and appear different. Stucco and plaster ornaments, woodless wood on stoneless stone, pseudogothic frontages by the side of a pseudo-Maya frieze, light pink or dark blue contrasting with white and brown painting. Every decorative detail expresses the dialectic between the personalized frontage and the common frame, mass production and originality, home sweet home and the industrial product.

Good sites: slopes and beaches
The sunny slopes, above the pollution, looking over the city, and tens of kilometers of beaches, with blue water and surf, are the local amenities restricted to the rich but which make Los Angeles one of the most beautiful cities in North America. The southern slopes of the Santa Monica Mountains limit the city to the north and northwest. As early as the end of the 19th century, land developers tried to build on these hills (Sunset City and Morocco), but they were located too far from the center and were too inaccessible and so they failed. Only the arrival of the electric streetcar at the mountain foot in 1895 allowed the development of the slopes.

These hills, limited by fresh faults and deeply eroded, offer three different types of site:
The canyon or the glen (Brown Canyon, Beverly Glen, Laurel Canyon, ...) Along a deeply excavated ravine winds a narrow road up the mountain. A string of houses make use of the smallest terraces, burying their back in the mountain, though more often than not they cannot avoid obstructing the valley bottom, forcing the road to make sharp deviations. Cars are parked on lots half dug into the rock or located on frightening slopes; gardens hang above the roofs. Sights vary with each turn of the road. Houses with baroque forms are isolated, quiet, and peaceful. It is like living in a desert only ten minutes drive from the nightlife in Westwood Village.
The Roost Higher up the mountain, clear of the deep-cut valleys, are locations with exceptional views of the city and the ocean. Famous architects have found the opportunity to show their skills here. Owing to the steep slope, houses are built on piles (Smith House, West Los Angeles, 1955). The 'chemosphere' (Hollywood Hills, 1960) is a large disk standing on a unique pile of concrete at a tangent to the slope. Such structures are extreme cases, remarkable but very expensive. They are typical, however, of thousands of cheaper dwellings similarly located on the hundred square kilometers of slopes limiting the city to the north.

The Staircases The enormous power of modern equipment makes it possible today for the grading of a hill to be achieved at relatively low cost. Instead of adapting construction to the slope, one removes it by cutting out huge terraces on which cheap and standardized houses can be built. Much of the site beauty disappears in the process, soil stability is imperiled and the danger of erosion and landslides is increased. In spite of this destruction, however, the site is open to relatively low-income families as a dialectical form of democratization.

Banham notes a strong correlation between household income and the altitude of a home. This is a general phenomenon which has also been observed in Europe as well as in South America, on the hills surrounding Caracas, for example. There is a push–pull phenomenon, with high-income families competing for the up-slope sites which offer the best views and the quieter environment. On the other hand, altitude increases building and transportation costs. The result is social and architectural zoning downwards from the top of the hill. Large isolated houses, built with daring techniques by famous architects as unique masterpieces, give way to smaller and smaller houses that are built closer together. A line of apartment towers at the foot of the hill, along the main boulevard (Sunset Blvd or Santa Monica Blvd) finally merge into the plain dwellings.

The shore (Banham's "surfurbia") offers a different organization. Building densities and prices are also stratified, but in a horizontal and not vertical fashion. The pattern follows two directions: from the beach to the interior, prices decline sharply. Along the shore, from north to south, they vary widely depending on the neighborhood history. Pacific Palissades at the northern edge of Los Angeles, close to Santa Monica, is a plush district in which mansions with large bay-windows opening onto the beach and ocean are found. Moving along the shoreline, to the south, one sees a decrease in the size and price of houses as one comes closer to Los Angeles International Airport, a very significant source of air and noise pollution. Venice is an ancient fishing town with small woodframe houses, most of them old and quite dilapidated. This is the hippie and popular section of the beach. Next to it, Marina del Rey is quite the opposite. It is a new luxury community built on old piers with two-storey buildings along the waterfront; sailing boats and chris-craft boats are anchored beside the automobile parking lots. Its very mobile population is made up of young and rich 'swinging singles'. This expression, quite common in the United States nowadays, means persons who are "sophisticated, ultrafashionable, uninhibited especially in the pursuit of pleasure" according to Webster's dictionary. In fact, they are young professionals of both sexes who shun, at least for a few years, marriage and the constitution of a family.

A similar pattern of social stratification and architectural landscaping occurs both on the hills, from the top to the bottom, and on the shore, from the beach to the interior. The populations, however, are quite different, although with similar incomes. Proprietors and business owners live more often on the beach, professionals in the hills.

In the rearview mirror: the freeways
Banham rightly emphasizes the important role of movement, particularly automobile traffic, as a basic element of Los Angeles' townscape. One must observe this city "in a rearview mirror", to identify its constituents. *The commercial ribbons* (linear downtowns). Berry has chronicled the development, in all big American cities since the 1950s, of commercial axes along a boulevard which compete with the traditional CBD (Berry and Horton, 1970). Los Angeles is quite different, however, as this trend appeared much earlier than anywhere else. The most famous case, the commercial axis along Wilshire Blvd (The Miracle Mile), developed in the early twenties before the success of the automobile, thanks to the electric streetcars. On the other hand, these ribbons play a paramount role today in the commercial life of the city, exceeding not only the old CBD, but also the modern suburban commercial centers which occupy such a prominent place in most other North American cities. The Los Angeles commercial network appears as an original system, based on a number of famous commercial axes (Hollywood Blvd, Santa Monica Blvd, Wilshire Blvd, ...) which successfully compete with suburban supermarkets, that are located too far away in such an enormous agglomeration, and with a Downtown which has not played an important role for decades, probably for the same reason. The very size of the urban sprawl, so typical of Los Angeles, has largely determined this original organization. Banham notes that it is impossible today to identify the old central plaza with any precision. It has been moved and rebuilt many times after being devastated by earthquakes, floods, and commercial competition. Not only its exact location, but also the layout of the streets converging on it have been lost. From this viewpoint, Los Angeles is very similar to most of the other cities of the Pacific coast having been rebuilt in two or three different locations after physical or economic disasters: compare Los Angeles with Guatemala City (as distinct from Antigua Guatemala) and Managua, Salvador. "Most of downtown is now little more than a badly planned and badly run suburban shopping center for those who cannot afford cars ..." (Banham, 1971, page 208). The commercial ribbons, with their parking lots and towers dedicated to business (both small, speciality shops as well as huge luxury department stores like Manin) form the commercial urban framework. Even public facilities, so typical of the center, have emigrated: the famous County Art Museum is located on Wilshire Blvd, six miles from the Civic Center.
The freeways More than any other architectural form, freeways appear and truly are the very attribute of Los Angeles, because it is impossible to move around the city without using them, or to look anywhere without

seeing them. On average the area dedicated to traffic in large American cities occupies between one quarter and one third of the total area (freeways, streets, and parking lots). In Los Angeles, this proportion rises to one half. The automobile alone uses as much land as all other human activities put together, which, rather than the high frequency of one-family houses, explains the low demographic density.

The freeways often elevated to the second- or third-floor level, form an original townscape. With eight or ten lanes in both directions, they provide a traffic fluidity almost unique in the world. The Pasadena Express was the first one to be built, through the Elysian Park. It is dangerous and charming. Narrow and winding through the trees, it is a true 'parkway' in the full meaning of the word. Unfortunately modern cars are bigger and faster than those of the 'thirties, and modern freeways are more efficient and less bucolic.

They play a double role in the landscape. They are a definite nuisance for the neighborhoods that they pass through. They obstruct the horizon, pollute the atmosphere with noise and fumes, and split neighborhoods into two separate parts in spite of the occasional above- or underground passageways crossing them. Land rent usually drops along a new expressway. However, blocks located further away but close to an access ramp profit from their increased accessibility to the rest of the city, and their land rent goes up. The result is an increase in population density around the ramps, and an inexhaustible source of conflicts in choosing freeway locations. Their routes are closely determined by the social map of the city. They serve well-to-do neighborhoods by connecting mainly rich suburbs with downtown office buildings, passing through poor districts. Of course, this is not always possible. There was an uproar when planners proposed a new expressway linking San Fernando Valley with the city through Beverly Hills, and they were forced to give up the project. The phenomenon is dynamic and complex because there is a feedback. Being poor, a neighborhood is chosen for the location of an expressway, but this depresses the land rent and drives away the more fortunate households. Simultaneously, districts which have been made more accessible thrive and prosper. Freeway development is closely related to urban dynamics (Brodsly, 1982).

4.2.2 Architecture in Los Angeles

Urban development in Los Angeles has occurred too fast and too continuously to favor any one unique type of construction, like the wooden-framed houses with bay windows in San Francisco, which date back to the rebuilding of the city after the great earthquake and the fire of 1906. Los Angeles has never gone through such a catastrophe, even in the 1930s when Long Beach was badly shaken by a strong tremor. Various architectural trends have mingled, revealing the spirit of the place (Rubin, 1977).

Architectural trends
Basically, one can distinguish the interplay of four principal trends: the opening to nature; the Spanish Colonial Revival style; fantastic architecture; and movement and light.

The opening to nature More than in any other city, the separation between the inside and the outside of the house has tended to vanish. Huge windows or doors leading to a garden or having a panoramic view; inner yards with greenery; plants and trees growing in a room and climbing through a hole in the roof; openwork walls letting through light and air, penthouses on the top of towers with hanging gardens; wood and rough stones used widely in the decoration of interior rooms; so many parts of the decor express this interplay. And there is more to it than a trivial geographic determinism; it is true that rooms are open partly because the weather is sunny and mild, but this explanation does not go far enough. There is also the drive back to nature which has always haunted American city dwellers and which was precisely what attracted them to Los Angeles from the huge 'man-made' cities of the East and Midwest. They came from Boston, Chicago, New York to live in a 'clean' (a word heavy with connotation in the USA) city, in a strong symbiosis with nature which they could not get any more in their suburbs back East. In this sense Los Angeles can be described as an immense suburb, not at all because this metropolis lacks any centralized urban structure or any activity typical of a huge city, but because its layout and its buildings represent one of the strongest efforts in North America to mingle with nature and to let it enter into every room. The effort has certainly failed, but this does not weaken the dream.

Such a trend is particularly clear in many of the mansions in rich neighborhoods, or in the apartments on the top of luxury towers in Westwood Village or along Santa Monica or Sunset Blvds. It can also be found in poorer districts in what Banham calls "the californian bungalow". Created by the Greene brothers in 1906–1908, it is a low, ground-level house with a jutting out, almost flat, roof, wooden walls, balconies, verandas, wide fireplaces, and wood beams whose function is not, as in Europe, to recall the past and to recreate a certain legitimacy, but to express the wilderness from where they came. This style, notes Banham, is so attractive in southeast California that it is now widely used in restaurants under the name of "Gourmet Ranch-House style".

The Spanish Colonial Revival style recalls the influence of Latin America and, through it, of the Old World. It is not a direct inheritance from Colonial times, but rather a re-creation just before the First World War, largely under the influence of Irving Gill. It is a style where people look for legitimacy and tradition, the needed link to the past. Mexico is but a pretext. The connection that is established in this way is not with California's Spanish occupation but with Europe. Witness the extraordinary attraction for medieval paraphernalia strangely mixed with this neocolonial style. There is probably no other city in the world where flaming torches (using gas), heavy wooden doors with enormous nails, wrought iron decorations, chains, swords, and armor exist in such quantities. Spanish Jesuits and Lady Macbeth are married without hesitation to express the past.

If bad taste and money sometimes produce monsters which provoke hilarity among Europeans and restore their self-confidence, the neo-colonial style has influenced great architects and had favorable effects. Frank Lloyd Wright is a typical case. He was a man of the Midwest, born in Michigan, famous first in Pennsylvania for his 'Fallingwater' house. He developed his typical style mainly in Los Angeles, however, from 1916 onward (for example, 'Hollyhock House' for Aline Barnsdall, on Olive Hill).

His style, with its long horizontal lines, rhythmic vertical windows, narrow and elongated, wide balconies jutting out from the main building, and long stucco friezes, corresponds strongly to the desire to mix with nature, as well as to the influence of Latin America. It is characteristic that he built his first parallelepipedic houses, with long blind walls and sculptured friezes, in Los Angeles: 'Hollyhock House' quoted above; the house built in 1924 for Charles Ennis, one of his most celebrated constructions; and his early project, significantly named 'Cement Block House' built in 1921. All three are strongly reminiscent of the Maya Temples in Central America. Even in 1941 he used the same Maya or Aztec style for the interior decoration of 'Sisistan', a house drawn for John Nesbitt. Such a synthesis between Middle American architecture and North American techniques could only have developed in Los Angeles. Later he spread it throughout the world. In a project for a textile factory in Ahmedabad, India (1946), he again covered the large blind frontage wall with a similar pseudo-Maya decoration. He may also have learned in Los Angeles how to use those large glazed walls opening directly onto nature (for example, the 1937 'All Steel' houses project developed in Los Angeles, and, also the extraordinary 'H.H. Play Resort View' complex he built in Hollywood for Huntington in 1947).

Dream and anarchy: fantastic architecture A mystical and libertarian spirit pervades Los Angeles, as opposed to the liberal and rationalist mind of Boston or New York. It explains the realization in stone or metal, but more often in plaster, stucco, or plastic, of eerie constructions a Yankee could never conceive. Symbols and allegories dominate. The Brown Derby, a restaurant, *is* an immense derby hat that has been built—one enters through a door that opens in the hat ribbon. Only appearance counts. Oil derricks, still erected today in the middle of residential blocks in Santa Monica, are covered with plastic sheets and transformed into dutch windmills, medieval towers, or high narrow buildings with false windows. Dreams become reality. It took Simon Rodia twenty years to erect soldered metal towers decorated with ceramic fragments, bits of broken plates, and Coca-Cola caps. His Watts Towers do not fill any other purpose than the expression of a general dream, and have rightly become one of the most famous monuments in the city.

Behind this love for fantastic ornamentation and the effort to make dreams real, lurks the hidden but powerful influence of the cinema industry. One of the main activities of Los Angeles for the last sixty years, the immense Hollywood studios through their size and fame have transformed the tastes of the inhabitants and increasingly made them consider their city as a huge stage set for a film. Disneyland, the biggest dream city in the world, could not have been built anywhere but in the southern suburbs of Los Angeles. This was the first municipality in the world to propose in 1970 the replacement of the shrubs between the freeway lanes, which were dying from pollution, with brand-new spotless plastic washable shrubs, but this was going too far, even for Angelenos, and the project failed.

Movement and light Both of these manifestations play the role of architectural objects in Los Angeles and form the most original trait of this townscape. Freeways are a whole landscape by themselves. The lines and curves of the interchanges, the elegance and the complexity of their network is particularly impressive and beautiful from the hill tops or the penthouses, that is, from the luxury residences. They pollute the poorer neighborhoods they cross, but they appear as art objects of great beauty to the rich who can admire them from far away. Add to them the traffic movements, the varied colors of the cars, their white and red lights at night and 'op art' and 'cinematic art' are born largely in Los Angeles.

The multitude of lighted billboards covers the city with a huge decorative net, flashing and changing colors in the night. Here again the rich, from their privileged sites, contemplate it at its best.

Architecture and function: types of building
The various building types derive from two distinct forms: the single-family house and the large, multidwelling construction or office tower. Since the late 1960s people have dwelt increasingly in high-rise buildings; cheap ones for retired people, expensive ones for young well-paid bachelors. The contrasts between these two building types can be combined with a geometric opposition in land-use modes (figure 4.9). Briefly, the center can be identified with a point (0-dimension), the main axes (linear downtown) to lines (1-dimension), and the homogeneous neighborhoods in the plain to areas (2-dimensions); while the most luxurious mansions on the hilltops or the expensive penthouses in the residential towers with their terraces and their gardens use space in 3-dimensions. This model is an approximation; it tends only to show how land use is less and less constrained as the dimensions of occupation grow.

The *single-family house* changes from one social class to another, and also through time:

The cottage—small, simple and in general a beach resort. Many districts along the shore are built in this way (Venice, Naples, Manhattan Beach).

The mansion—huge and generally surrounded by a garden or a park. The fashion leaders were the movie stars, in Bel Air and Beverly Hills: this community became famous when Douglas Fairbanks and Mary Pickford moved in. Since World War II, the apparent life-style of the stars has changed. The point is not to show off anymore and to shock, but to hide luxury, to play the role of concerned parents in a well-groomed garden behind a hedge.

The Californian bungalow—the downgraded form of the traditional wooden house for middle-class incomes. This is by far the most common single-dwelling unit.

Dingbats—an evolved form of the californian bungalow appears along the main axes or at the important crossroads where better accessibility increases occupation density. The building is longer, with one or two stories, and contains several apartments. It is of a light construction

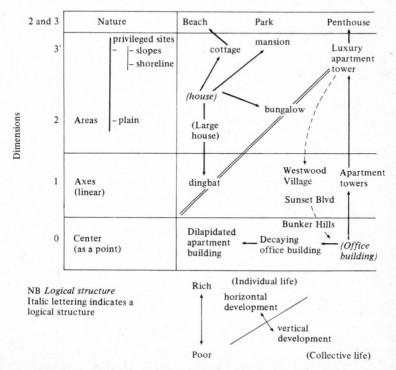

Figure 4.9. Human ecology in Los Angeles: the genetic evolution of links between architecture, functions, and location.

with a steel frame, plaster walls, exterior iron staircases, balconies which form the corridors serving the apartments, and a ground floor parking lot where children play. These shapeless constructions, built cheaply for rent, are appropriately termed 'dingbats' by Banham. The increasing population density of Los Angeles has led to the wide multiplication of these apartment complexes.

High-rise buildings are, in general, dedicated to offices and built in the center, where land prices are the highest. In 1970, residential towers corresponded to the two extremities of the social spectrum. They were either old, dilapidated, dangerous, and unhealthy buildings where marginal people (winos and junkies) or very poor families (chicanos and Blacks) lived, or new luxurious housing complexes which, because land prices and rents were high, increasingly attracted 'swinging singles', the unattached young professionals who wanted to locate close to the entertainment districts (for instance, the four towers of Bunker Hill with solarium, swimming pool, commercial center, and private security).

Expensive housing has partly migrated from downtown to the suburbs with the upper and middle classes. The extension of buildings upward, that is, the development of residential towers, parallels this movement. Gardens and terraces on penthouses are a reflection of the suburban garden, while allowing people to enjoy a more central location. The attraction of commercial axes or freeway access has increased population density and contributed to tower development along these boulevards. The most typical cases are Westwood Village, close to the University of California at Los Angeles (UCLA), which has become one of the main centers of night life during the period; and Sunset Strip, whose fame is of longer standing, with its nightclubs, rock and jazz clubs, and strip-tease. The last step in this logical evolution is for people with means to return downtown, as happened at Bunker Hill.

4.2.3 The transformation of housing

Consecutive censuses give very detailed data on the age of the buildings for every census tract, and one might thus hope to write a short land history of Los Angeles. Unfortunately, these data are extracted from 20% or 25% sample surveys. The proportions they indicate fluctuate widely, so that many an increase or decrease in percentage may not be significant. On this point census information is disappointing. Fortunately, we can use the detailed studies published by the Real Estate Research Program of the School of Business Administration at UCLA in the late 1960s. They make it possible to analyze the rhythm and the impact of building removals on the land market: the evolution of housing types can then be described.

The age of the buildings

Census figures are quite incoherent: it is impossible that, in the same area, the number of housing units built before 1940 increased from 510000 in 1950 to 523 000 in 1960. The same discrepancy exists for the number of units built between 1940 and 1950: they are said to be 241 000 in 1950, 191 000 in 1960, but 230 000 in 1970. Such data scarcely make sense. Since there are some 1 million units in the city, there is a high probability (95%) that the true values fluctuate between plus or minus 4%, that is, some 40 000 units above or below the indicated figures. The differences indicated in the censuses are not significant.

It is also quite difficult to map the age of buildings. Every block contains units built at different periods. Clark and Nelson (1976, page 10), however, using the average building-age, present an interesting map. A huge crescent stretching from Hollywood to Downtown, then south to Watts, contains most of the buildings erected before 1940. The rich neighborhoods on the slopes of the Santa Monica Mountains, from Hollywood to the ocean, date back generally to World War II, with the upper parts of these hills and their tops occupied during the 1950s. All of the interior plain, between the mountains and the shore, was developed more recently. The interesting point is that Los Angeles has not grown like an 'oil slick' by regular progress at the edge, but by the coalescence of distinct centers (Downtown, Hollywood, Santa Monica, Watts) which grew separately. Here again, data are deficient. It is hard to believe that the middle-part of the city, which appears empty on the map, was still undeveloped in 1970.

An attempt to explain land-use history
Fortunately, research undertaken at UCLA by Mittelbach and his associates during the 1960s provides useful information (Mittelbach, 1963; Mittelbach et al, 1970).

During World War II and the economic recovery which followed, housing policy was erratic and quite contradictory. On one hand, several hundreds of thousands of people, attracted directly or indirectly by military activities, had to be housed somehow. On the other hand, there was rent control, a rationing of building materials, and a lack of capital and man-power. During this period the housing inventory expanded rapidly to meet these demands by the conversion of existing buildings rather than by the construction of new units. The subdivision of single-dwelling houses into two or three apartments, the transformation of offices or lofts and sometimes of warehouses, and the construction of temporary buildings increased the number of people housed in every unit.

Families accepted smaller living spaces. Such transformations are difficult to locate but produce strong geographical changes. In a period of scarcity, population movements tend to stop (see the analysis of socio-professional relationships, section 6.1.2) while land-use turnover increases. In times of plenty, when the housing stock expands, households tend to migrate and land use is quite stable. In just this way the war decade prepared for the changes characteristic of the 1950s; first, by accumulating a large population in unsatisfactory housing who moved and produced a new equilibrium as soon as the tension caused by scarcity and rent control was relieved, and second, by transforming neighborhood functions and housing forms, which led to a redistribution of urban roles.

The period after the war and reconstruction (that is, roughly after 1948) offers a contradictory image of change and stability at the same time. Statements from the survey indicate that after a short absence, visitors did not "recognize the city any more". During the 1950s and 1960s, highways cut through the city and opened up new corridors. At each access ramp increased accessibility determined a higher density. Individual houses were replaced by apartment buildings three or four-stories high (dingbats), and these were in turn replaced by high-rise apartment towers. This explains the impression so often described in the press or the literature of the time of an effervescent city in perpetual turmoil.

This view is largely exaggerated and partly false. Demolition was limited, with annual figures of some 8700 units in the whole county, 5900 in the SMSA, and probably no more than 2000 in the city as delimited in this study; that is less than two housing units destroyed each year per thousand units.

In the SMSA, 3.9% of the dwellings were destroyed in the 1950s, 4.1% in the 1960s. The annual demolition rate seems to have fluctuated widely from 0.2% in 1960 to 0.5% in 1963. Basically, the housing inventory remained remarkably stable: 90% of the housing units existing in 1950 were still occupied in 1960, 2% had been converted to another type of occupation and 8% had been demolished.

Even if this turnover is slightly higher than for other US cities, the exaggeration is obvious. Most new buildings are particularly conspicuous, being erected along the main commercial boulevards or at the freeway exits. They form a superficial screen concealing the stability of 90% of the city. In 1959 new buildings (erected since 1940) numbered 850000, or 38% of the total, while the old buildings amounted to 1372000, or 62% of the total housing stock in the SMSA (US Bureau of the Census, 1960). In other words, 90% of the old buildings still remained, but they formed only 62% of the total. The difference between those two proportions explain the contradictory statements on turmoil and stability of housing in Los Angeles. The figures relate to the whole SMSA, though in the city itself new buildings were less frequent.

Four important factors play a role in this housing turnover:
1. *Housing decay*, through lack of maintenance, vandalism, and abandonment is *not* significantly correlated with demolition and rebuilding. Mittelbach explains this paradoxical lack of dependence by the fact that most dilapidated units are grouped in a few Downtown districts. The normal elimination of these old buildings cannot be distinguished from the speculative demolition in other neighborhoods of buildings in good

standing to make way for the construction of higher and more profitable apartment towers. Statistical data are not detailed enough (in particular, census tracts are too large) to allow the researcher to separate these different types of demolition. It is possible, however, to criticize a theory which exists implicitly in many urban studies (Mittelbach et al, 1970, page 17). Too often it is assumed that housing units have a predetermined life span and must be eliminated and replaced when they are worn out, like a car or an electric light bulb. Smith has strongly criticized this belief: "Housing units are demolished for a variety of reasons unrelated with their age; we could almost say they have no economical life span" (W F Smith, 1966). This would seem obvious to Europeans accustomed to living in buildings dating back to the eighteenth or even the sixteenth century, and it is certainly true in Los Angeles. Although more volatile than European cities, Los Angeles' land structure is quite stable and, when it changes, follows complex rules very different from a simple obsolescence process.

2. *Housing demolitions* are closely related to the development of new residential buildings (on average each demolition corresponds to the erection of eighteen new units). They are not related, however, to new office buildings. No competition appears between modernization or change in housing density and the extension of business and service activities. Zoning laws completely separate these two different land uses. Except Downtown, where offices may have encroached on residential blocks, housing and work occupy two distinct parts of the urban space and do not conflict.

3. *Demolition rate* increases regularly with time, even if we freeze the number of residential buildings through a partial correlation (they increase also and would influence the analysis). The meaning is clear: new units need more land. This may be the result of the increasing standard of living—modern households require more area—but the growing need for parking is probably the best explanation. For the last twenty years in Los Angeles the car has been trespassing more and more on man's territory.

4. *Housing suitability*. Housing units built between 1940 and 1970 fit the needs of the middle class particularly well, especially in terms of their size and price. Groups at the two extremities of the social scale, poor families with many children or quite affluent households, have to satisfy themselves with older residences; flats turned into slums, or large mansions dating back to the 1930s, which, for their cost, could not be built today. Except for the few very rich, the middle class sets the standards in Los Angeles.

4.3 Changes in accessibility: transportation in Los Angeles
In such a widely sprawling city, transport plays a basic role. The automobile, however, as a factor of spatial development, has been largely overemphasized. Various transportation systems have operated successively, and the main city-extension anticipated the model T Ford.

4.3.1 The origins

Until 1885, the main transportation axes were only fragments of a wider regional network, which tended to become continental. The 'Camino Real' forms the main axis of Spanish California, from Mexico to San Francisco. It crosses Los Angeles east to west, from the 'pueblo', located roughly at today's Downtown, to the asphalt wells at La Brea. It corresponds very closely to today's Wilshire Blvd. Then it turned north into the San Fernando Valley. The general layout of modern Los Angeles still closely follows this pattern. Downtown streets are slightly oblique (northwest–southeast) like the main avenues. The famous lieutenant Ord's map, drawn in the middle of the nineteenth century, shows clearly the gridiron plan typical of colonial cities which perpetuates the original street orientations laid down by the first colonists.

At the end of the nineteenth century, a second network started with the railroad from Downtown to Wilmington and Long Beach harbor in the south. Built by Phineas Banning in 1869, it became municipal property. It was offered as a gift to the powerful Southern Pacific Railroad Company in 1874, in exchange for letting its new railroad from San Francisco to the Mexican border go through Los Angeles, so anxious was the city to integrate itself into the general network.

4.3.2 Huntington and the electric streetcar: the P.E.R.

Thanks to this relationship with the continental rail network, a large influx of population from 1885 onward increased the size of the city. However, a new problem appeared—that of land speculation. In order to be put on the market, land had to be developed and, particularly, made accessible. Land development, Los Angeles's main activity until the 1930s and the most important factor in its growth, depended directly on the growth of local transport.

If, in the large cities on the East Coast, transportation development determined urban extension (Warner, 1962), then the process was even more typical of Los Angeles. There, the transportation system had to anticipate the population, which meant it required original means of financing the investments. Private transport companies extracted guarantees from the municipality which would, anywhere else, appear exorbitant, such as financial guarantees for their bonds and loans, the guarantee of a minimum profit, and a monopoly on definite routes. New lines increase accessibility and therefore increase or rather create land value, and the companies wanted their share. The small ones demanded subsidies from the local landlords. The big ones, working the other way around, bought the land, then built the rail lines and put the land back on the market in small parcels. Soon these enterprises profited much more from developing land than from their transportation interests.

Competition between land developers led to competition between transportation tariffs. After the beginning of World War I, the transportation industry was often in the red. As soon as a district was sold out or when a crisis depressed the land market, the entrepreneur got rid of his transportation company (usually by selling it to the municipality which had no choice but to operate it at a loss) and created another one further away after buying cheap agricultural land for development.

The best example of such an entrepreneur is Henry Edmunds Huntington. He created the Pacific Electric Railways in 1900, which allowed him to become the most important land-developer in Los Angeles. Painted in a celebrated red color and using a standard gauge, his streetcars served the whole city. In 1925 the network totaled more than 1100 miles, and gave a permanent form to the city. Then a deadly competitor appeared—the automobile, which was going to ruin the streetcars. But it would take a surprisingly long time before the red trains disappeared from the streets. Huntington generally had kept the property or at least the right of way over the land on which his lines were built. This enabled his streetcars to avoid the traffic jams which began to plague the automobile as early as the 1930s (witness the old Hollywood movies often filmed in the streets). Actually, the last red carriages disappeared only in 1961, but their role in Los Angeles had vanished during World War II, and most of Los Angeles was developed by that time.

4.3.3 The age of the automobile

At the end of the 1920s the automobile inventory in Los Angeles exploded: 20000 vehicles in 1910, 110000 in 1920, 800000 in 1930 (Fogelson, 1967, chapter 4). Between 1936 and 1956 it multiplied threefold (Meyer et al, 1965, page 75). The growth of Los Angeles did not originate from the use of the private car, but its role today is paramount (Rae, 1971). Among the many impacts of such a phenomenon, four are particularly important:

First The very low urban density, original even in the USA and *a fortiori* in the world, has not been created by the car, but has been preserved and extended by it. Land speculation is the explanation for the extensive land use. A private car in every household has mitigated its inconvenience. Today the inhabitants are locked into this transportation system, and cannot escape using it, even when they do not want to drive. The urban structure is such that everybody must own a car in order to survive; advertisements offering jobs demand that the applicant drives his own car. In this way a closed system has developed with two facets: housing sprawl and very low population densities on one hand, and a complete reliance on the private car on the other. With the automobile one can enjoy the dispersion of the population through the environment, but this dispersion forces people to drive. Public transport is inconvenient and always in the red. This evolution was not, of course, spontaneous. The various lobbies (the automobile industry, the oil companies, and the concrete lobby for building the freeways) were instrumental in choosing

such an extreme solution for people. It seems the city has burned its
bridges and cannot detach itself from the car. This feeling, even if rarely
expressed, may explain why so many visitors feel a sense of anxiety
when they discover life in Los Angeles.

Second Neighborhood types have changed. Watts, for instance, once an
important rail and streetcar crossroad, has been abandoned by the freeway
network—Simon Rodia's towers look out upon deserted tracks. This
abandonment has contributed to the social and architectural decline of
Watts and to the formation of a ghetto. On the other hand, along the
main boulevards, teeming with automobile traffic, the modern types of
commercial centers (Linear Downtowns) have appeared after the opening,
in 1928, of the 'Miracle Mile' on Wilshire. Car traffic has dialectically
fostered pedestrian zones, like the Farmer's Market on Grove and Third,
south of Hollywood. Typically their architecture has changed. In 1950,
pedestrians used the ground floor, while cars were parked on the roof of a
building, which seemed an audacious solution at the time (for example,
in Westchester). In the late 1960s in Century City, a plush commercial
center built between Beverly Hills and Santa Monica, the pattern was
reversed: the ground floor became a huge parking lot, and the shops and
their customers were located on its roof in order to be better protected
from the noise and fumes.

Third Unfortunately, the ease of travelling by car has led to the
development of eccentric neighborhoods, far away from commercial
centers. From these rich ghettos, every shopping trip is an expedition.
At the dawn of the automobile era Beverly Hills was built the opposite
way. A whole ranch (rancho Rodeo de las Aguas) was divided up by
Wilbur Cook, who was invited from New York for this task. It became an
autonomous municipality in 1914, and was made famous when the first
movie-star came to live there. Large green areas with trees, lawns, and
shrubs separate residential blocks and commercial zones: nature and
business activity are mixed with housing.

Fourth The enormous increase in automobile traffic has saturated the
street network, and the need for urban freeways has placed the
responsibility for transport upon the public authorities again, as in the
time of the electric streetcar. But the arguments have changed. Because
freeways are extremely expensive their supporters argue they serve everybody and not only a few privileged families, and this justifies that they be
financed with public taxes or municipal bonds. In this dialectical way
the private car, supposed to exhibit the triumph of individualism, is
becoming the major burden on the collective authorities, and the main
source of profit for lobbying corporations.

4.3.4 Accessibility and urban sprawl
Accessibility is closely related to land rent but also, in a more subtle way,
to land speculation (Holden, 1963).

The gridiron plan helps land development but hinders accessibility.
A nineteenth century engineer working for a San Gabriel Valley developer
notes: "The main advantage [of this plan] is that parcelling is much easier
and cheaper and lots sell much better than if they were cut along curved
lines" (in Fogelson, 1967, page 139).   Land was divided into rectangles
that were twice as long as they were wide.   The area (approximately
500 m²) was just enough for a modest house with a small piece of grass
in the front and a narrow backyard.   The streets between blocks were only
partly asphalted and many of them remain today as backstreets for garbage
collection.   The result is a dense but low-quality network of uniform
streets.   Few large avenues were included in the gridiron pattern.   This is
the best network for developing land but the worst for accommodating
traffic—the need for urban freeways is largely the consequence of such a
mode of land development.   They have been superimposed on the chess-
board plan, with scant regard to the surface streets.   A street has two
basic functions: to delimit blocks and to be used for traffic.   In Los
Angeles, both functions have been separated in time and in space.   Land
speculators have largely used the surface network while the big automobile lobbies have built the freeways.

Both interests are complementary.   Better accessibility increases land rent.
Conversely, the automobile traffic uses a large proportion of city land
(Los Angeles County, 1973; Niedercorn and Hearle, 1963); 60% of Downtown is given over to the car, whereas in most American cities the proportion
is only 40%.   Freeways use only 2% or 3%, and surface streets 35%, as in
other big cities (table 4.9).   The difference appears in parking area: 24%
instead of 12% on average (Smith et al, 1963, page 59).   This reduces the
amount of land directly available to people to 40% of the city and
increases land costs proportionately.   Building a very expensive network
superimposed on the normal one, and abandoning more than half of the
area of their city is the price Angelenos had to pay to travel in private
cars.   It may have been worth it (McElhiney, 1960).   Time distances
decreased significantly between 1936 and 1957, while the number of cars
multiplied threefold (table 4.10) (ACSC, 1957).   Except for the Pasadena
Parkway all of the freeways were built during the 1950s; little progress
has been made since then.   Los Angeles is now at a turning point, and
must look for new equipment able to solve today's traffic problems as

Table 4.9. The proportion of land given over to the automobile in American city
centers. (Source: Smith et al, 1963, page 59.)

CBD	Year	Streets (%)	Parking (%)	Total (%)
Los Angeles	1960	35.0	24.0	59.0
Chicago	1956	31.0	9.0	40.7
Detroit	1953	38.5	11.0	49.5
Minneapolis	1958	34.6	13.7	48.3

the freeways did twenty-five years ago. A Rapid Transit System seems to be the answer, but it would be the worst possible answer in such a low-density environment. The number of cars per household is the largest in the world (table 4.11), but the city's rate of ownership should be compared with the rate of similar big cities. In Los Angeles 22% of the households have no car at all, and 78% have one or more (4% own three cars or more). In New York City (Manhattan) the proportions are reversed: 20% own one or more cars, 80% have none (*QB* 77, 1962). The major originality of Los Angeles is in accommodating the automobile so well, while all the other metropolises try to drive it away.

Table 4.10. Travel time by car in Los Angeles in minutes (outside peak hours). (Source: Meyer et al, 1965, page 76.)

From Downtown (Broadway and 7th) to	1936	1957	1960
South Pasadena	26	15	14
Hollywood	23	17	16
Bell	25	22	20

Table 4.11. Relative number of households owning one or more cars. (Source: *QB* 77, 1962.)

	Number of cars per household (%)			
	1	2	3 or more	0
USA	56.9	19.0	2.5	21.5
California	53.3	26.9	4.0	15.8
Los Angeles				
County	51.8	27.4	4.1	16.7
City	49.2	24.4	4.1	22.3
New York Center				
(Manhattan)	18.2	0.9	0.6	80.3

4.4 The land question and its evolution

The successive censuses offer data on land rent, housing, and tenure types (see also Arthur D Little, 1963). Autoregression models (cf. section 2.2.1) describe the stability or the evolution of these characteristics very clearly.

4.4.1 Stability in land occupation

Land variables are much more stable than population variables. Only the housing vacancy rate is erratic and difficult to forecast. Two groups of variables that are particularly constant are the type of housing (single-family dwellings versus apartments) and the type of tenure (owner-occupied or rented housing).

The type of housing was very constant through the 1940s. The scarcity of housing during the war (there was then a shortage of 40000 dwellings, or 3% of the total) forced families to use existing buildings and to adapt their needs. Along the shore at Hermosa Beach, Redondo Beach, and Manhattan Beach many beach cottages used only as summer resorts were sold or rented for permanent residence (*QB*, 32, 33, 1949). Conversely, during the 1960s, the type of tenure was more stable than the type of housing. The wave of new construction enabled families to choose a residence according to their needs. Single-dwelling houses did not change much, but the low apartment buildings (dingbats) were demolished and replaced by high apartment towers.

Interestingly enough, land rent varies more widely over time than the type of housing. The market price of a house or an apartment depends on its intrinsic qualities (size, type of material, and builder's workmanship) but also on two external factors: accessibility (a function of transportation development) and neighborhood quality, a most important concept rather difficult to grasp (clean and safe streets, neighbors' social status and ethnic similarity, etc). These two factors, varying through time, explain the lower stability of land prices. Rents fluctuate even more widely. It is through rent that capital prices are influenced by local transformations and changes.

During the 1940s and 1960s two different markets coexisted. Rent discrepancies between different parts of the city were equalized much faster than land price differences. The rent market was much more fluid and fitted fluctuations in the global economy and in the city structure well. The capital land market felt the repercussions later. Urban districts are quite specialized by housing type. Price variations are very restrained in the case of single-family houses, which are mostly in well-to-do neighborhoods; fluctuations are much worse for apartment buildings. Land structure not only reflects differences in housing qualities, but also unequal levels of protection against market insecurity.

4.4.2 Types of housing: houses versus apartments

Housing is basically divided into these two types. Both present very different forms. The single-family house includes the small wooden home at ground level, with four rooms, as well as the luxurious mansion in Bel Air. Social differences may be important, but there is a common characteristic: each dwelling is closed in on itself and isolated from its neighbors. One encounters a similar diversity among apartment buildings, from dilapidated dwellings in the ghetto to the luxurious towers along Wilshire Blvd, but the juxtaposition of housing units multiplies contacts and frictions.

Since the turn of the century, American society has generated the myth of the individual house as a symbol of freedom and human development. This is an indirect glorification of a certain type of human relationship (the nuclear family), of demographic structure (two or three children), and

of economic prosperity, since such housing is expensive and closely
follows the fluctuations in the mortgage market and the lending rate.

The proportion of houses in the housing inventory mirrors these
factors. In 1940, houses represented more than half of the dwellings in
Los Angeles County, and apartments only a quarter (see table 4.12).
New construction almost stopped during the war, but experienced a boom
after 1945. Between 1940 and 1950 the proportion of single-family
houses increased rapidly, particularly in the suburbs. In the county the
number of houses doubled. This progress continued undeterred until
1960, which marked the peak of single-family dwellings. Half of all the
housing in the city and two-thirds in the county was of this type. But
by 1960, huge apartment towers were already increasing their share.
The intermediate type of huge mansions subdivided into a few apartments
(2 to 4) was vanishing. Representing only a transition form, these old
buildings were quickly demolished and replaced by more profitable
towers. The market tended toward polarization between two extreme
forms.

This long evolution toward the single-family house was broken in the
late 1960s, probably by the economic crisis, but also by a change in
mental attitude.

Apartment towers took over the lead. In 1970 the city, for the first
time since the war, saw the absolute number of single-family houses
decline while the proportion of apartments increased from 28% to 37%.
This new priority given to collective housing is a major phenomenon.

Table 4.12.   The evolution of housing types. (Sources: *QB* 108, 1970; US Bureau
of Census.)

Census year	Number (%) of		Percentage of owner-occupied homes
	houses	apartments	
	Los Angeles County		
1970	1521534 (59.1)	845155 (32.8)	48.5
1960	1401581 (66.4)	513017 (24.3)	54.6
1950	942611 (65.3)	334114 (23.2)	53.6
1940	606356 (63.0)	253531 (26.4)	40.0
	Los Angeles City		
1970	478510 (46.5)	383162 (37.2)	33.3
1960	534964 (55.8)	269318 (28.1)	40.6
1950	408246 (54.5)	154037 (20.6)	45.0
1940	311812 (54.2)	128348 (22.3)	33.7

Unemployment, general anxiety in American society during the Vietnam war, and increasing building costs are obvious reasons for this change in emphasis. But there are deeper ones. Mores and habits are changing. Increasingly, many young adults remain unmarried and prefer apartments in modern towers. They enjoy a good income and can afford to live there. They refuse to be tied down by a family or a mortgage, they want to move easily and frequently and to mix with other similar singles. The isolation of the family house, once its main asset, has become for the young middle class a heavy liability. Demographic changes have also played a role. Even after the postwar baby-boom peaked, the birthrate remained relatively high for the fifteen years between 1950 and 1965. The large number of children per family made the suburban house that much more attractive. In the mid-1960s the birthrate plunged and the need for space disappeared in many families. Simultaneously, marriage ties broke down and more permissive groups looked for more fluid housing arrangements.

The relationships between the single-family house (denoted SH) and the apartment (denoted A) are summarized in table 4.13, which shows the various values taken by the coefficient of determination (r^2) over time; it measures the proportion of variance the two variables have in common. The relative importance of houses expressed as a percentage remains constant over time, with a slightly lower stability between 1950 and 1960 when new dwellings were being built everywhere. For the apartment, the coefficient declines regularly. Their distribution across census tracts changes more and more as time goes on. This represents a spatial diffusion of this type of dwelling throughout the city. The diffusion is regular and begins with the first decade, which is of paramount importance. The new priority given to collective housing, which has such important consequences today, is much older than most authors think, and can be

Table 4.13. Relationships between housing types through time.

Type of relationship	Coefficient of determination (r^2)			
	1940	1950	1960	1970
Continuity				
SH		0.876	0.776	0.819
A		0.878	0.834	0.712
Opposition				
SH versus A	0.785	0.767	0.845	0.645
(r negative)				
Forecasting				
SH → A		0.677	0.637	0.601
(r negative)				
A → SH		0.719	0.714	0.721

SH ≡ Single-family houses; A ≡ apartments.

traced back to the 1940s. This is not so surprising, because a process based on the transformation of moral structures and habits is always a slow and sluggish process.

The separation of houses and apartments in space is very strong. It weakened somewhat after the war ($r^2 = 0.767$), then increased to a maximum in 1960. This is the time when houses and apartments were the least mixed in the city; when they were grouped in different areas. The low value in 1970 ($r^2 = 0.645$) is that more noteworthy. The late 1960s again mark a break in the evolution. Residential apartment buildings were no longer restricted to the city center or to a few commercial axes, but had largely diffused throughout the city.

By knowing the development of one housing type at a certain moment, is it possible to predict the development of the other type ten years later? The forecasting power of each housing type differs a lot. Knowledge of the percentage of houses in a tract does not permit a good prediction of the future proportion of apartments, and this low ability (cf table 4.13, bottom row) decreases with time. Conversely, if one knows the proportion of apartments in a tract, one can forecast the percentage of houses at the next census quite well, and this power remains the same throughout the thirty years. Houses form a large urban fabric that is slowly being encroached upon by apartment buildings. Once these buildings are erected they are never again replaced by houses; on the contrary, they tend to attract other apartment buildings and to accelerate the process. The evolution is dissymmetrical and cumulative, and it would be useful to analyze it as a function of the social level of a tract.

This has been done by means of a factorial analysis of intercensal changes (a factorial analysis of residuals after autoregression of each variable on itself, with a Varimax rotation—see table 4.14). During the war, houses developed at the expense of apartments, and competition between the two types was very strong (-0.879 and 0.867). The evolution took quite surprising forms. Changes in housing type are weakly related to increases in rent. Actually rent increases with the proportion of apartments, as well as with the inhabitants' social level (number of school years). Changes in housing type are practically unrelated to occupation type ('renter-occupied' or 'owner-occupied' variables have less than 10% of their variance in common with the process as represented by the factor). Such a strange evolution corresponds to the peculiar war-time conditions: rent control until 1947, houses temporarily subdivided into a few apartments, and lack of new construction leading to a housing shortage.

Change is more apparent during the 1950s. Where there is a development of apartment buildings, there are simultaneous increases in the average income, the proportion of renter-occupied dwellings, the social level, and the proportion of bachelors. As seen before, upper-middle-class bachelors began to choose their place in the urban structure, particularly along the Linear Downtowns: Hollywood Blvd, Sunset Strip, Santa Monica and Wilshire Blvds. These young professionals often owned their apartments (hence a weak loading for 'renter-occupied').

The last period is more complex. New apartments were built increasingly for renting, and were more expensive. The process, however, is losing its social significance; it has little, if anything, to do with change of income or social level ('Income' and 'Number of school years' are practically orthogonal to the factor).

Contrasts between both types of housing were to be expected, because together they represented most dwellings, their total being close to 100%. The intermediate type (large mansions subdivided into three or four dwellings) remains an exception. Each decade produced an original aspect of the evolution: war conditions deprived housing changes of most of their social meaning. The 1950s were mainly characterized by the appearance and multiplication of white collar bachelors or divorced persons, living in apartments along the main commercial axes, attracted by night life and free from family encumbrances. This new group has been generally neglected in urban studies, perhaps because it is so different from the traditional image. The famous ecological analysis of Los Angeles in 1948 (Shevky and Williams, 1949) does not mention it, although my analysis shows that this new urban form was appearing at the time of their study. The phenomenon received public attention much later, in the 1970s (see the frontpage picture and article in *Newsweek*, 15 March, 1972).

Table 4.14. The evolution of housing types (factorial analysis of residues from regression; loadings after varimax rotation).

1940–1950, factor 5 (14% of variance)		1950–1960, factor 1 (14% of variance)	
Houses	−0.879	Houses	−0.892
Apartments	0.867	Apartments	0.907
Owner-occupied	−0.320	Income	0.331
Renter-occupied	0.140	Renter-occupied	0.314
Persons/room	−0.129	Singles	0.252
Number of school-years	0.285	Persons/room	−0.204
		Number of school-years	0.278

1960–1970, factor 1 (18% of variance)	
Houses	0.760
Apartments	−0.853
Owner-occupied	0.853
Renter-occupied	−0.670
Young	0.243
Rent	−0.229
Persons/room	0.325
Number of school-years	0.107

During the 1960s, the process changed again. New apartment buildings were now built to be rented, and at higher prices. They were not located as often as in the past in well-to-do neighborhoods, and their development was practically independent of increase in income level; it was even slightly correlated with a *low* social level (negative correlation with 'Number of school years'). Apartment towers in the 1950s constituted a type of housing chosen by the most original and dynamic part of the privileged classes, certainly for their easy access to entertainment. During the 1960s these towers were built more for land speculation than for accommodation, in a wide and blind movement that invaded the whole city and penetrated into most neighborhoods. The goal now was less to satisfy the needs of a new way of life than to extend as widely as possible a profitable kind of investment.

Figures 4.10 and 4.11 show the spatial evolution of these types of housing. The number of apartments multiplied between 1950 and 1960 in Downtown, Hollywood, Sunset and Santa Monica Blvds and Westwood Village, close to restaurants, bars, clubs, and movie theaters. They were developed mainly to house the 'swinging singles'. Conversely, during the 1940s and also the 1960s, the spatial extension of apartments was much

Largest increase
• 1960–1970
◉ 1950–1960
○ 1940–1950

0 2 4 6
kilometers

Figure 4.10. Growth of multiple-dwelling units (apartments) in Los Angeles, 1940–1970.

more concentric, corresponding to a diffusion process in a wave pattern
around the population center (oscillating slowly around the Santa Monica
and Harbor Freeways intersection).   During the war, extension was slow and
the wave did not reach more than 6 km from the center.   In the latter
years, however, the circles were much wider: some are as large as 12 km
in radius, and somewhat elongated to the west along the Santa Monica
Freeway toward Hollywood and Beverly Hills.   The southern part of the
city was not involved in this apartment development.

On the other hand, single-family houses have grown throughout the
city in a much less ordered pattern: as a ring around the center (1950–
1960), to the south (1960–1970), along the arc of wealthy neighborhoods
and to the west and northwest during the war.

The various parts of the city follow three types of evolution:
Downtown and the population center, slightly to the south, experienced
violent change.   Houses grew strongly between 1940 and 1960, and
apartments from 1950 to 1970, with an intermediary period during the
middle decade.   Change was so radical that some blocks, exhibiting the
fastest growth of one type during a period, still led during the next
period, in spite of much faster growth of the other type of housing.

Largest increase
● 1960–1970
• 1950–1960
○ 1940–1950

Figure 4.11. Growth of single-family dwelling units in Los Angeles, 1940–1970.

Several of the wealthy neighborhoods (Hollywood, Santa Monica, and Marina del Rey) exhibited a very regular growth pattern with extensive construction of houses during the war and of apartments thereafter. The most noticeable trait here is not the upsurge but the continuity of the growth process.

The southern half of the city, particularly the shoreline south of Marina del Rey, changed very slowly.

4.4.3 The accession to landed property

The increase in the proportion of landowners occupying their own property is a very important social phenomenon. Again the process took different forms as time progressed. During the 1950s it was typical of quite wealthy families, but it involved houses and apartments equally, which was quite original. The later decades offer examples of more traditional choice. Owners tend to occupy houses, while apartments are usually rented. The choice is determined by family size and not really by income or social level. Except in Beverly Hills and Downtown, owner-occupation of both types of housing is closely related to accessibility, but very little to land value or to family income.

The contrast is clear. During the 1950s, to own one's own dwelling (whatever its nature) was an upper-class privilege. During the last decade, ownership depended on the way of life and the family size. Again, the well-to-do swinging singles radically altered the traditional clichés. As a consequence, a very strange diffusion movement appears that is concentric, but *centripetal* (figure 4.12). From 1940 to 1970 the ring, or rather the ellipse, corresponding on the map to the main growth in the proportion of 'owner-occupied dwellings' (as represented by scores on corresponding factors) tended to contract. In the last years the increase was strong in the blocks immediately surrounding Downtown. Although centrifugal movements on a concentric pattern are the rule in most American cities, counter movements slowly converging back onto the center are rare and little documented. Land use in the heart of the city is slowly becoming frozen, as owners occupy their property instead of letting it to produce income. This could be a little-known form of urban aging, but Los Angeles is too dynamic and too recent a city to present advanced forms of decrepitude. An alternative explanation seems more likely, namely that the city structure is becoming increasingly homogeneous with time, so that differences between the center and the fringes gradually vanish and Downtown slowly becomes similar to a large suburban agglomeration. This does not mean that the city loses its structure and turns into an amorphous mess, but rather into a multinodal organization. There remains one noteworthy fact: in this case the periphery determines the evolution of the center.

Largest increase in
owner-occupied dwellings
● 1960–1970 (factor 1)
● 1950–1960 (factor 4)
° 1940–1950 (factor 1)

Figure 4.12. Changes in home-ownership in Los Angeles, 1940–1970.

4.4.4 Land rent: market value and rent

Land rent, as measured by the rent paid by tenants and by the capital
value, is related to other variables in ways which contradict some
traditional clichés (table 4.15). Rent is not strongly related to value.
The relationship is stronger in time of crisis, as in 1940 or 1970 (then, both
have 77% and 64%, respectively, of their variance in common). During
more prosperous periods (1950 and 1960), value and rent have only 48%
of their variance in common. The occupants are no doubt more mobile
and the other components of rent (prestige, fashion, neighborhood
quality, etc) play a more important role.

Family structure is strongly related to capital value but, surprisingly
enough, remains quite independent from rent. Until 1970 the number of
children in a family had practically nothing to do with the amount of rent
paid.

Still more surprising is the relationship with the type of tenure. The
value of a dwelling is practically independent of the manner in which it
is occupied, either by a tenant or by its owner. On the other hand, rent
is always higher in blocks where many of the dwellings are occupied by
their owners. Since owner occupation does not imply higher capital
value, the best explanation is probably neighborhood quality. In a block
where many inhabitants own their dwelling, the environment is regarded
as safer, cleaner, and nicer.

Table 4.15. Relations between land rent and other variables. (Correlations between raw data). C is capital value, R is rent.

| | 1940 | | 1950 | | 1960 | | 1970 | |
	C	R	C	R	C	R	C	R
Whites	0.20	0.25	0.27	0.27	0.44	0.35	0.53	0.43
Blacks	−0.16	−0.16	−0.25	−0.22	−0.44	−0.30	−0.50	−0.38
Young	−0.55	−0.37	−0.53	−0.17	−0.52	−0.15	−0.70	−0.40
Old	0.29	−0.08	0.38	−0.03	0.43	0.07	0.53	0.16
Singles	–	–	0.33	−0.13	0.33	−0.15	0.31	0.02
Owner-occupied	0.02	0.25	−0.02	0.35	−0.07	0.35	−0.05	0.20
Renter-occupied	−0.09	−0.32	0.02	−0.37	0.08	−0.32	−0.08	−0.20
Houses	−0.29	−0.06	−0.28	0.14	−0.47	−0.02	−0.43	−0.12
Apartments	0.30	−0.01	0.34	−0.06	0.46	−0.05	0.48	0.14
Capital value	1.00	0.88	1.00	0.67	1.00	0.69	1.00	0.80
Number of school years	0.65	0.73	0.62	0.65	0.64	0.67	0.62	0.69
Income	–	–	0.42	0.67	0.39	0.69	0.60	0.73

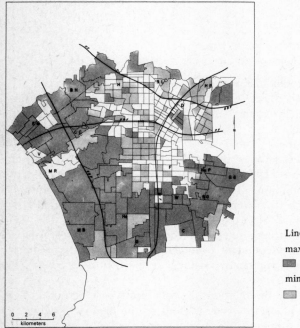

Linear regression residuals

maximum

▬ 22.90; 0.39 (93 C.T.)

minimum

▭ −2.77; −31.90 (93 C.T.)

Figure 4.13. Changes in land rent in Los Angeles, 1940–1950. (Analysis of residuals, 50% of total variance.)

The choice between apartment or house is not, for a tenant, a matter of money, as rent is practically never correlated with the type of housing.

Income is more related to rent than to capital value. Most owners take a long mortgage (twenty to twenty-five years), which allows even the lower middle-class to buy a home. The owner is then 'locked-into' his mortgage. Conversely, rent can be easily fitted to the income level.

The spatial distribution of land rent explains these relations further. Changes in rent during the first decade (figure 4.13) clearly follow a concentric pattern, quite similar to the spatial pattern of the life cycle. If we assume the same initial rent everywhere in 1940 (through partial correlation), then the largest increases are distributed in blocks forming a circle from the northwest (Hollywood) through Beverly Hills, Santa Monica, and the shoreline, to Manhattan Beach, Hawthorne and Inglewood to Bell and Maywood in the southeast. A few blocks, isolated in the north and northeast, approximately close the circle. Districts with stagnating or decreasing rent are not in the center but also form a ring inside the former one. The center rents remain stable, while a wave of higher rents seems to have moved concentrically away from the center, leaving behind a ring of depressed rent values. This pattern should be related to the diffusion of population away from the city center.

Capital values changed during the 1940s but followed a different pattern. Quite regular sectors radiate around the city center, with strong increases along the Hollywood and Santa Monica slopes (Homer Hoyts's 'local amenity' factor), and in a second sector orientated south from Downtown to Culver City and further east, to Watts and South Gate. Downtown itself experienced a land boom. Contrasts between the hills and the shoreline are clear. The prices on the slopes increased whereas they remained depressed along the beach, which was still quite inaccessible and occupied by armament industries.

Figure 4.14 locates the main increases in land values during the thirty years (scores on the corresponding factors). Again the pattern is that of a wide crescent to the west of the population center, inside which the upward pressure on prices has switched from one block to another during the period. The best districts, on the mountain slopes, have experienced a regular expansion during the period, as if the speculative wave had bumped into the hills and stopped there for good. During the 1960s the littoral shows the largest land-value increases. Outside this ring, several blocks downtown show high increases due to competition from office buildings. Higher land-rent values also diffused throughout the city during these thirty years as concentric waves, impinging against natural obstacles (the hills or the seashore). To the west and south, the waves have been reflected back toward the center. In Beverly Hills, Hollywood, and behind Manhattan Beach the process is clear, with high values during the 1960s appearing on the inside of the ring. Such a diffusion process with its obstacles and reflections has been observed in other cities.

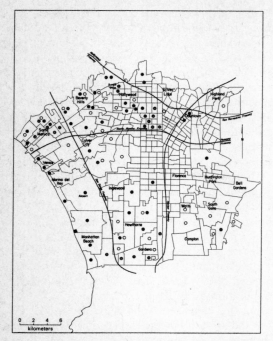

Largest increase in
land value

• 1960–1970 (factor 2)
• 1950–1960 (factor 3)
○ 1940–1950 (factor 4)

0 2 4 6
kilometers

Figure 4.14. Increases in land values in Los Angeles, 1940–1970.

4.4.5 Vacant dwellings

The proportion of vacant dwellings for sale or for rent in a block is by
far the most erratic and unpredictable variable. It is higher in districts
where there is a high proportion of apartments for rent. There is also an
interesting correlation, which increases over time, between the vacancy
rate and the proportion of bachelors. Until 1950, vacant dwellings
were usually located in wealthy neighborhoods, but in 1960 and 1970,
they were more frequently found in the poor ones. This is the
simultaneous effect of a growing general prosperity and of the persistence
of local pockets of poverty in the ghettos, where miserable families
crowd into some buildings while others next door remain empty. This
interpretation is corroborated by the correlation between rent and
vacancy rates. In 1960 and 1970, vacancies were high when rent was
low, whereas in 1940 and 1950, the relationship was exactly reversed.

The vacancy rate is correlated very weakly with rent and capital value.
Actually it is not a socioeconomic variable, but an effect of a certain
type of housing (the apartment building) and occupation (by a tenant),
plus a strong random component which makes forecasting very difficult.

Each decade presents a different picture of change in the vacancy rate:
During the war, vacancy (which was very low everywhere) increased with
land values, as the social level of the inhabitants decreased. The arrival

of unskilled manpower in dwellings which were often provisionally expropriated by the government, or in any case controlled, explains this strange evolution.

The rate increased during the 1950s in neighborhoods left by old people and rich families, but where land values still increased. Downtown is the best example. Better accessibility pushed up prices, but at the same time rich households moved to the urban fringe, leaving empty dwellings behind (figure 4.15).

The evolution followed a different path after 1960. The black population expanded and Whites tried to leave hastily, pushing up the vacancy rate at least temporarily.

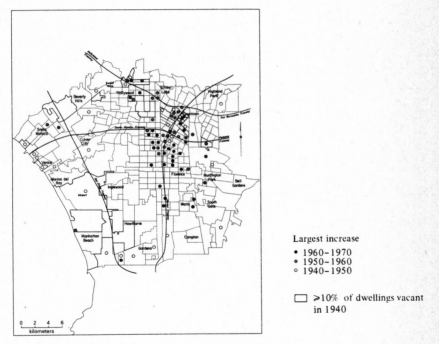

Largest increase
- 1960–1970
- 1950–1960
- 1940–1950

☐ ⩾10% of dwellings vacant in 1940

Figure 4.15. Vacant dwellings in Los Angeles, 1940-1970.

4.4.6 Conclusions

Several misapprehensions should be expunged when considering the question of land in Los Angeles.

First To contrast the single-dwelling house on the urban fringe inhabited by a wealthy family to Downtown apartments populated by poor and lonely bachelors or old people is unjustified. Apartment towers were developed throughout the whole city. They often contain expensive apartments owned by well-to-do couples or singles. The expansion of this 'swinging singles' group is not very recent. It can be traced back to the 1950s, and has become one of the most important, although little discussed, urban phenomena.

Second One does not build a house mainly for housing nor an apartment only as an investment. The actual distinction between these two different functions is blurred and almost impossible to make. Housing types are practically independent of rent and capital values.

Third If most land changes exhibit a concentric pattern, as wave diffusion proceeds from the center, some interesting processes effect an opposite movement toward the center. They have not often been described in the urban literature, although important problems of autocorrelation appear as a consequence (see chapter 6: Modes of change).

Last The inhabitants' socioeconomic level, as measured by average income or the number of school years completed, appears to be quite independent of land variables. Conversely, two factors do seem to play a paramount role in determining housing phenomena: changes in accessibility, and changes in family structure. Choosing the type of housing (either a house or an apartment) and the type of tenure (to own or to rent) is basically a functional decision, depending on one's way of life, on whether there are children and how many, and on how far it is to the workplace, rather than on ethnicity or income. So it is plain that the functional value of housing is fundamental, which poses a basic question: how does housing fit human needs?

The adaptation of housing to human needs[†]

In Los Angeles, as in many other great cities of the world, population and housing have basically changed in two ways. First, we can identify concentric waves of diffusion moving through the urban space at varying speeds, waves of building and change that are often related to new forms of transportation. Second, there are clear sectoral alignments, areas characterized by different types of inhabitants who change from one time period to another. These rather fundamental differences in spatial structure, evolutionary rhythms, and urban relations pose some difficult questions of human dynamics in urban areas. For example, how do residences adjust over time to the requirements and resources of their inhabitants? What forms do such adjustment take, and how do they evolve?

As we examine the historical development of any urban area, we face essentially three questions:
1. How were the needs of everyday life (for example, housing and work) satisfied? The main criteria here seem to be such things as dwelling size and type, as well as the degree of accessibility to work.
2. What were the relationships between housing costs and the ability of households to raise funds for housing? This question focuses mainly on the structure of mortgage financing.
3. How did the population accommodate itself to an evolving pattern of residences and changing family requirements? In many cities, certain evolutionary changes have been 'out of phase': these sorts of problems have been particularly marked in ghetto areas, as the population expanded at the same time that the buildings became more dilapidated. The marked contrast between housing characteristics and actual family needs is part of a larger problem—the overall evolution of spatial structure in the city.

In fact, each of these questions refers to an even more basic concept: namely, what is the *value* of a dwelling for its inhabitants? How does a dwelling evolve through time, and how are various residential qualities distributed over the urban space? In the context of this chapter, the very ambiguity of the concept of *value* is useful, since it is a term that covers a complex reality which may be analyzed at a variety of different levels. An important trend in modern French Social Science tends to distinguish four different kinds of values: in addition to the classical categories of *Use* and *Exchange* values, it considers also the *Sign* and the *Symbolic* values (Baudrillard, 1972). Using Baudrillard's categories in the course of this analysis does not imply the acceptance of his thesis nor the exact adherence to his definitions. Actually the meanings of his concepts have

† Parts of this chapter have been published, in a slightly different form, in Marchand (1982).

been substantially changed in this text. Nevertheless, his classification is a convenient one for a fruitful analysis of urban values. First, the nature and the dialectical structure of these four kinds of values, as applied to dwellings and neighborhoods in Los Angeles, are presented in section 5.1. In the following sections I analyze, in turn, the evolution of each one of these four values in the metropolis.

5.1 The different values of a dwelling
5.1.1 The new concepts of value
Baudrillard defines four types of value which may well be different for the same dwelling (table 5.1):

Use Value. This is the classical concept, representing the usefulness of an object in everyday life. As far as a single dwelling goes, its use value varies according to the needs of the inhabitants. For example, the large apartments in the center of Paris ("Le Marais"), which were luxurious in the seventeenth century but became dilapidated during the nineteenth century, were increasingly occupied by poorer families with many children. These people had no use for monumental doors or high ceilings, but suffered from the small number of bathrooms and other sorts of facilities. The use value of these apartments tended to decrease with time —a characteristic process in the central areas of many cities.

Exchange Value. This appears through equating different dwellings which have the same commodity or monetary value expressed in the housing market. It normally depends on the state of the market, on the equilibrium conditions holding between supply and demand, and on numerous factors which are quite independent of the dwelling itself: for example the degree of accessibility, the quality of the neighborhood, the prestige of the area, and so on.

Sign Value. This arises in urban areas from a direct transcription of concepts that are essentially linguistic. Every residence—its location, style, use of space, and so on—bears witness to the social position of the owner or the tenant. A major goal is to differentiate one person from another, often by using a kind of social language written in stone or concrete. Here, the role of the sign value is diametrically opposed to the role of the exchange value. Instead of establishing an equivalence between different objects, sign value tries to create and express differences between objects that are actually perceived as *too* similar. The best example might be the plaster frontages, so common in Los Angeles, which outwardly offer the most varied forms and colors, but in fact conceal miles and miles of similar wooden frames (Banham, 1971). In a sense, architectural details are the *vocabulary* of this language, while the spatial organization of the buildings, the gardens, the fences, the trees, the parking lots, and so on form its *syntax*.

Symbol Value. This concept concerns what we might call the deeper Freudian categories as they relate to architectural forms. We can think of these as acting unconsciously on the human mind to explain why some

Table 5.1. The major sources of housing value[a].

Value	Basic principle	Role	Nature	Domain of realization
Use	uniqueness of the home (*The One*)	fulfilling a function	a purely *concrete thing*	in everyday life
Exchange	equivalence of homes (*The Many*)	as money	a purely *abstract thing*	on the land market
Sign	communication between *many* people	as language	a purely *concrete idea*	in social relations
Symbol	an *individual's* unconscious life	as satisfaction of one's unconscious drives	a purely *abstract idea*	in individual affective life

	Logic	Dialectical realization		Example: A garden as a ...
Use	Qualitative	the object is used, that is, it is consumed and destroyed (in this case, as the dwelling is occupied and so is not useful for others)		children's playground
Exchange	Quantitative	the dwelling is transformed into something else, that is, money, which is itself nothing but potential objects (and dwellings) into which this amount of money will transform		local advantage increasing the market price
Sign	Differentiation	the dwelling describes its occupant, but only in order to separate him, to differentiate him from other city-dwellers		witness to an occupant's social position in relation to others
Symbol	Ambivalent (the noncontradiction principle does not apply here)	the unconscious effect of the symbol is prelogical and ambivalent; that is, it is made up of contradictory drives (love and hate, desire and disgust, attraction and repulsion, simultaneously)		evocation of a wilderness, attracting and frightening at the same time

[a] Inspired by Baudrillard (1972), but largely modified.

people are mysteriously attracted to some places and buildings, while they may be completely indifferent, or even repulsed, by others. Feelings are often ambivalent and contradictory, as they so often are in the Freudian context, because they are essentially prelogical. They do not obey the principle of noncontradiction—as Kevin Lynch demonstrated implicitly in his work on the perception of the urban landscape, particularly in Los Angeles (Lynch, 1960). Bachelard (1957) has also insisted upon the usefulness of such an approach, with many convincing examples chosen from European literary texts.

The first two values above might be labeled *classical*, and they tend to feed the normal sort of polemic that has been going on in economics for the last 150 years. But the last two appear to hold much more promise, although they have not been widely used in urban analysis. The townscape of Los Angeles appears as a particularly appropriate subject for an analysis based on these latter categories. Of course, it can be argued that the exchange value somehow synthesizes and represents all these other concepts of value. However, it seems more reasonable to integrate these four concepts in the notion of price. I shall not try here to analyze the relationship between price and value: this old problem has little bearing on this particular study.

5.1.2 The dialectics of value

The four basic categories of value, together with what we might call their 'inner mechanisms', are related in dialectical ways. The dialectical approach focuses upon the development of compatible and opposing relations among the three logical values, while the fourth one (symbolic value) contains a built-in dialectic of its own—since it is, in fact, prelogical. As is characteristic of an analysis of this sort, each value realizes itself by destroying itself, thus exhibiting its true dialectical nature.

Exchange value is a purely *quantitative* concept, based on the possibility of expressing any object in terms of something different from itself (whether it be cattle, coffee, silver, gold, or any other form of money) by establishing an equivalence between the two things. We say that an object is worth so many currency units, and that these express in turn the worth of another object. The relation is reflexive, symmetrical, and transitive: it is precisely an equivalence relation. At the same time, it negates any qualitative difference between objects, which are now perceived as though they had no particularities of their own. Thus exchange value, emphasizing the purely quantitative aspect, is the very negation of the idea of quality and qualitative difference.

Use value forms the exact antithesis of exchange value. It is based on all the individual peculiarities of an object as it is compared and contrasted with another. From the viewpoint of use value, all objects, whether commodities or services, are unique and can never be equivalent. The concept here is entirely *qualitative*.

Sign value is more complex: by expressing in an architectural language the wealth, taste, and upbringing of a landlord or the occupant of a building, sign value 'tells' us about social quality (in the use of the building) as expressed by money quantity (measured by its exchange value). As such, sign value is nothing but the *synthesis* between use and exchange value, as it retains both of these elements in dialectical opposition, and transcends them into a new equilibrium. Money (that is, income) is expressed by the sheer size, or the number and the kind of decorative elements on a house (to focus on one or two examples only), but it is not simply a display of money. Taste, whatever judgment we may pass on it, modifies and contradicts the sheer weight of money. In the same way that poverty may sometimes try to conceal itself by exaggerating stucco decor, so wealth might be delicately concealed in architectural understatement. When an owner 'says' something in terms of the size, shape, and style of his house, it is through the complicated and dialectical interplay between the brutal quantity of dollars invested in it, and the quality of taste which uses such financial raw material, molding it into an expression of the best quality—the word "best" referring, of course, to the inner personal judgment of the particular person.

In this way, sign value simultaneously *integrates*, *combines*, and *negates* both exchange and use values. In fact, these two elementary values have no real meaning if they are separated from each other. For example, in most of Western society how could we assess the exchange value of a dwelling on the market divorced from any reference to its use capabilities? Conversely, what is the point of discussing the use of a certain type of building without indicating either its profitability or the kind of occupant who will be able to afford it? Sign value integrates both of these basic concepts, and for this reason it is probably much closer to the actual market price.

Symbolic value stays outside of this dialectical trinity. It is a prelogical form of thinking, taking its cue from the working of the Freudian Id, and not from the conscious Ego. Typically it is ambivalent, like those unconscious impulses which unite in the same drives, the feelings of love and hate, desire and disgust, presence and absence. Its very nature is dialectical. While the three preceding values interact in the conscious mind, symbolic value constitutes their global negation—even as it is simultaneously embedded in each of them. It is present in exchange value, as it contributes to the determination of the price one is willing to pay by adding attractive or repulsive constituents to the decision process. It is present in use value, since it adds a whole galaxy of feelings to the practical aspects of a dwelling and makes it, in this way, agreeable, comfortable, or unlivable. Finally, it is present in sign value, since it imbues nearly all signs (of wealth, success, culture, and taste) with unconscious 'connotations' which radically change the meaning of an architectural message. By its presence in sign value, language is altered into myth: for example, the use of phallic decoration as expressions of power and domination, seen in the huge chimneys sticking out of roofs of so many Beverly Hills mansions, when the inhabitants think they only want to say "Home Sweet Home"! Sign value embodies and unites exchange and use value in a contradictory way; symbolic value is the negation of all three. The final relationship boils down to the contradictory connection between *language* (sign) and *myth* (symbol), both of them similar in the sense that they express ideas, but both very different and opposite in the way they express them.

As we approach the analysis of an urban area within this framework, it should come as no surprise that we recognize first the opposition between the One and the Many, a very old dialectical relation that leads us straight back to Plato's *Parmenides* (table 5.2). Use and symbol values have meaning only for the *individual*: an object (particularly a house or an apartment) fulfills quite different and distinct functions for each person, while symbols arouse unconscious impulses of an infinitely varied nature in each of us, often related to the most intimate memories of our early years. Thus, the values of these categories change not only from one person to another, but also for a particular individual at various stages of his or her life.

The *use value* depends on the most concrete apprehension of a *thing*: for example, how do the material qualities of an apartment—its size, form, inner layout and arrangement—fit our particular needs? In contrast, the *symbolic value* relies on the abstract effects of *ideas*—the images, memories, and desires they generate—and its domain lies at a deeper level of our psyche, so remote from the world of action that we cannot investigate it at will or act upon it, but so important that it determines each of our acts.

Table 5.2. Dialectical relations between values.

Cross-relations	Thing	Idea
Concrete	Use	Sign
Abstract	Exchange	Symbol
Main diagonal		*The individual life*
Values of opposite natures with similar roles	Use	
		(One)
		Symbol
Secondary diagonal		*The collective life*
Values of opposite roles with similar natures		Sign
		(Many)
	Exchange	

Both of these values are completely opposed in their form and in their domain, and yet, at the same time, they are completely similar inasmuch as each one determines the behavior of an individual—in a sense, one acting from the outside, while the other works from the inside.

The thing that these two opposed values have in common is that they are both defined for a particular individual, and at the same time define that person in turn. In marked contrast, *exchange value* and *sign value* have meaning only for a collection of people. Both of these values serve to relate an object (and the person behind the object) to another: a commodity like a house is related to another commodity like a sum of money by indicating their equivalence, or exchange, value. Similarly, an architectural or urban form (for example, a form of decoration or layout) is related to another form by demonstrating the value of their difference or sign value. Both of these are similar on different levels, even as they play opposite roles in the same collective or social context.

We know from Hegel that the One and the Many have no meaning when they are artificially separated from one another, and that they actually merge incessantly as each disappears into its opposite to create *change*—which is their actual form of existence. This logical dynamic suggests an interesting relation between a dwelling's *use* and its *symbolic* value: the experiences we have had of our home spaces generate the bases for the symbols which affect us. Conversely, these symbols from the unconscious shape our perception of space, and determine how we actually use our dwellings. This continuous and complicated dialectic over the course of people's lives is expressed in the concept of *neighborhood*, a piece of urban space defined by its inhabitants who present a certain degree of unity and share a number of similarities. However, the concept of neighborhood begins to take on a collective form, which then feeds back to influence the individuals who make it up, molding their tastes, their feelings, and their behavior—particularly the way they bring up their children. Thus the neighborhood should not only be considered as the sum of the individuals making it up, but also as a collective form acting on the individuals, so ensuring the social reproduction of the group itself. Its dynamic character is obvious: it is a necessary framework (necessary, at least, in this urban society) for individual and collective change.

Each value represents some potential for a particular object, a potential for being used for something, for being exchanged against something else, for expressing some social message to the onlooker and finally, for arousing feelings in him or her. These potentialities are realized in a dialectical way, by a process of self-negation that turns an object into something else, so changing its nature and its purpose in turn (table 5.1).

Use and exchange values undergo a quite clear process of negation. In using an object, we actually consume and destroy it. In the case of a dwelling, this can take two forms. On the one hand, the dwelling needs regular maintenance, repainting, and so on; on the other, it represents a potential home for anyone, but once an occupant has actually settled down it cannot be used by anyone else. Dialectical transformation is still more obvious in the case of exchange value; the physical structure of the dwelling has to be transformed into an opposite form of commodity namely money, in order for its value to be realized.

In a similar way, a dwelling describes, through the public message of its sign value, the social position of its occupant in a message visible to all other inhabitants, only in order to distinguish that person from all other city dwellers. The point here is not to decide if this value is high or low, or even if the message is clearly understood, but to clarify the *way* in which it actually works.

Symbolic value follows a rather different and original process, not being subject to the principle of noncontradiction, but rather to a powerful and prelogical mechanism of association of ideas as in dreams or cases of *lapsus linguae*. Symbols express contradictory feelings which have not been clarified and sorted out, but coexist together, albeit in opposition, within the symbolic object.

It is quite possible that further analysis along these lines may lead urban planners and sociologists to refine these concepts of value, or even redefine them. Nevertheless, as they have been outlined by Baudrillard and redefined here, they seem to offer a most useful and interesting platform for urban analysis. By their nature, their evolution, and their internal relationships, they are totally dialectical (that is, dynamic), constituting the very categories through which a city changes.

5.2 The housing use-value: its evolution in Los Angeles
The use value of a dwelling may be defined as its ability to satisfy its occupants' housing needs for shelter, protection, convenience, and safety. It is by nature a concrete value, realized in the congruence of people's needs and the characteristics of a lodging. Since people change endlessly, as does the ability of a dwelling to satisfy basic needs (changes in size through division, in quality through rehabilitation or dilapidation, in accessibility to jobs; because of the different needs of new settlers, of new job locations, and of transportation development), agreement between both terms, as well as the use value represented, keeps swinging back and forth, as time passes, in a typically dialectical way. Use value is largely independent of the quantity of working time invested in the house, that is, of its cost, and finally of exchange value, that is, its average market price. The poorest household has to choose a dwelling for its (low) price, rather than for its convenience. For the poor, conformity between housing and occupants is likely to be particularly bad. There is another feature of this value which is important: use value at a particular time depends largely on prevalent tastes. These will change over time. Poor housing will not consist so much of poorly built houses, but rather of old fashioned constructions which have today turned into unsuitable dwellings.

Poverty may be defined largely as living in housing conceived and built for other people and other needs. Being totally concrete (in contrast to exchange value, which is totally abstract from the object's properties), use value relies entirely on the agreement, *hic et nunc*, of a particular home to a particular occupant.

5.2.1 Correspondence between habitation and inhabitants

For each of the four censuses, we need to measure the relationship between two groups of variables: variables defining the inhabitant (ethnicity, age, family status, degree of crowding, social level) and variables characteristic of the dwelling (type of occupancy and of tenure, vacancy rate, type of housing, capital value, rent). This is best done through a *canonical correlation analysis* that indicates which of the characteristics of the inhabitants and the housing fit together best, as well as the strength of this fit. In Los Angeles, analysis of the four censuses exhibits two kinds of relationship: one between housing and social level, which will be discussed in section 5.3.2 (the economic viewpoint), and another between housing and the type of family (the demographic viewpoint).

In 1940, the strongest relationship (table 5.3) tied together the small families of young professionals starting out in life with the small detached houses they owned in well-off neighborhoods. The two fitted together strongly (81% of variance in common). These families lacked elbow room (correlation with 'number of persons per room': $r = 0.745$).

Population changes during and after the war altered this typical pattern. Young professionals were more likely to accept rather diversified housing, which blurred the clarity of the correspondence. In 1950, a new relationship appeared concerning old people (who had been the least affected by changes caused by war). Old widow(er)s were living by themselves in rented apartments far too large for them. The value of their home was quite high ($r^2 = 0.56$), but rent was not determined ($r^2 = 0.08$): it was high as often as it was low. All this is typical of the retired, who have moved to the city center where they live on very expensive land and where the rent depends on the quality of the building. This is the last step in the 'family life cycle', corresponding in space to concentric waves of diffusion as the age (and the income) of the family head increases until the centrifugal movement toward the periphery is reversed: many old people, when their children have left home and their income has diminished, return to the center.

A new correspondence was identified for 1960; one part consisted of large, generally black, families and a few old people, living in crowded conditions (number of persons per room: $r = 0.74$). The corresponding housing component was the largely owner-occupied detached housing with a low capital value, situated in poor neighborhoods. There was competition for housing in these districts: the vacancy rate was quite low ($r = -0.439$) and the rent relatively higher than capital value. In other words, the best adaptation at this time was to be found in the ghettos, not only the black ghettos but also the poor white communities.

The relationship between housing and people was much the same in 1970, but for a single housing characteristic: almost all poor families now lived in detached houses ($r^2 = 0.91$) owned by the occupants ($r^2 = 0.73$ instead of 0.26 ten years earlier). Over time, there had been an increase in the number of poor households with large families living in miserable houses.

Table 5.3. Types of correspondence between dwellings and dwellers: the demographic viewpoint. (R is the correlation between the two sets of variables, that is, the fit between certain dwellings and certain dwellers.)

Variable	1940		Variable	1950	
	r	r^2		r	r^2
Persons/room	0.745	0.56	Young	−0.925	0.86
Young	0.368	0.14	Old	0.751	0.56
Old	−0.495	0.25	Singles	0.796	0.63
			Persons/room	−0.767	0.59
Owner-occupied	0.810	0.66	Owner-occupied	−0.620	0.38
Renter-occupied	−0.812	0.66	Renter-occupied	0.632	0.40
Houses	0.645	0.42	Houses	−0.840	0.71
Apartments	−0.764	0.58	Apartments	0.775	0.60
Rent	0.641	0.41	Value	0.750	0.56
			Rent	0.274	0.08
$R =$	0.901	0.81	$R =$	0.816	0.67

	1960			1970	
	r	r^2		r	r^2
Whites	−0.518	0.27	Persons/room	0.815	0.66
Blacks	0.547	0.30	Young	0.751	0.56
Young	0.861	0.74	Old	−0.666	0.44
Singles	−0.769	0.59	Singles	−0.645	0.42
Old	−0.717	0.51	Whites	−0.406	0.16
Persons/room	0.740	0.55	Blacks	0.454	0.21
NSY[a]	−0.547	0.30			
Houses	0.859	0.74	Owner-occupied	0.852	0.73
Apartments	−0.854	0.73	Renter-occupied	−0.852	0.73
Value	−0.833	0.69	Houses	0.952	0.91
Rent	−0.345	0.12	Apartments	−0.909	0.83
Owner-occupied	0.508	0.26			
Renter-occupied	−0.489	0.24			
Vacant	−0.439	0.19			
$R =$	0.802	0.64	$R =$	0.853	0.73

[a] NSY ≡ number of school years

They tended increasingly to own them and thereby to be tied down by the length of their mortgages.

Correspondence between housing and people is stronger when a social group is restricted in its choices and moves. In 1940, in a city populated by a recent wave of migrants, the proportion of young couples recently arrived was higher than in other American cities. With a bearish economy, strong unemployment, and a still very low proportion of Blacks, these young people burdened with children had limited choices, and were more tied to a particular type of housing. The war dramatically changed these conditions. In a booming economy, only the elderly, whose fixed incomes had been trimmed down by inflation, were left behind and lost their economic ability to choose their housing. Later, as the peace economy settled down, the real losers appeared: poor, usually black, households with large families, whose choice was already limited, now had it narrowed down further when they set out to buy their homes.

5.2.2 Housing and accessibility

The evolution of accessibility over time, although it is of major importance, has been little studied. Only the 1970 census indicates the average length of the journey to work, which prevents any time comparison. Several studies have been made on the efficiency of successive transportation systems, but not on the differences in accessibility among city blocks. We must rely on a short but interesting study by the UCLA School of Architecture and Planning (Perloff et al, 1973).

Usually, accessibility is measured as a function of existing flows, which is largely tautological. Network planning depends on the flows, and the flows on the network. Such a measure may be used in short-term planning, but not in a deeper and longer study. Perloff's research team used a much better index, $A(t, i)$, expressing the relative number of job opportunities in a radius of t minutes travel time around block i [5], after stratification according to personal income and job type.

The results are impressive (table 5.4)—there are practically no jobs at a fifteen-minutes travel distance from home. Most journey-to-work trips take between half an hour and one hour; for trips longer than this the number of jobs available increases more slowly. Using a means of transport is compulsory in Los Angeles, or in other words, to own a car is a necessity. Actually, a family needs several cars in good condition: the survey shows that many poor families owning cars are neither able to maintain them or to pay regularly for the fuel or the insurance.

[5] Let $A(t, i)$ be the accessibility index associated with tract i for a trip lasting t minutes; j is the income bracket; k is the occupational category, and $E(t, i)_{jk}$ is the number of jobs open to categories j and k at t minutes from tract i. Then we have

$$A(t, i) = \sum_j \sum_k P_{ijk} E(t, i)_{jk} ,$$

with P_{ijk} being the corresponding portion of active persons in tract i.

Los Angeles is the city with the highest number of cars per capita in the world. Cars increase mobility only above a certain income threshold, which explains the huge advantage of wealthy households whose accessibility index jumps to 4.75. Very poor families also enjoy quite good accessibility because they have sacrificed an agreeable location for the need to live close to their work. The most penalized group is the lower middle class living at the periphery—its accessibility is minimal. Characteristically, most freeways link rich neighborhoods to offices downtown.

Except for rich households, most families must face the classical trade-off between housing and neighborhood quality or accessibility. This is a favored topic in urban studies. In Los Angeles, however, alternatives are not so narrow: an increasing number of young bachelors have gone back to the center, choosing simultaneously a convenient location and good housing. Poorer families, however, are often forced to move away from the center into remote neighborhoods because of their many children and their need for safety.

Low accessibility has important consequences: besides inconvenience, causing travel weariness, and supplementary costs, the whole process of finding a job is jeopardized. Indices in table 5.4 show that a low-salaried worker has a choice two or three times smaller than a wealthy professional, which also implies less competition among employers for labor, in turn implying relatively lower salaries, greater employment instability, and more difficulty in finding a job. Poverty is largely related to spatial processes.

Although we lack precise data, it seems that the various population movements observed between 1940 and 1970 did not increase housing use-value, but conversely moved residences away from workplaces. The drift of the middle class to the periphery, the concentric diffusion ('life cycle' moves) of households away from the center, the spread of black districts while so many black service workers kept their jobs in Downtown office buildings, the relocation near the airport of so many industries during the Second World War: all of these factors contributed to a general decrease in accessibility. Conversely, the traditionally rich districts, on the mountain

Table 5.4. Accessibility as a function of trip duration, income, and professional category for Los Angeles County, 1967 (source: Perloff et al, 1973, pages 185–190).

Trip duration in minutes	15	30	45	60	90
Median index	0.25	1.84	2.38	3.13	3.50

For a distance covered in a 45-minute trip			
Income ($)	0–6999	7000–9999	10000–14999	15000 +
Index	2.2	1.2	2.1	4.75
Professional category	Professionals Managers	Clerks, Salesworkers	Service workers	Craftsmen, Operatives, Laborers
Index	4.3	2.5	1.5	1.0

slopes or along the beach, did not experience such changes. Their accessibility increased in a twofold manner: a growing number of offices have left Downtown for more modern locations along the commercial axes (Wilshire Blvd, Westwood district, Santa Monica Blvd, Hollywood Blvd, etc), thereby shortening the professional's journey to work. On the other hand, development of a vast freeway network converging Downtown has also brought together offices and residences.

Thanks to the work of Perloff's team, we can study the accessibility to work for three different neighborhoods in minute detail: rich families in Beverly Crest, the black ghetto in Watts, and Boyle Heights, an area of poor Whites (table 5.5). Accessibility is a direct function of social status. Freeway lay-outs and car availability play as important a role as simple location. Beverly Crest, with twice as many cars per household as in Watts, and three times more than in Boyle Heights, is also well connected with the center through two freeways. Its inhabitants have three times more choice of jobs than those of the other two neighborhoods, in spite of their eccentric location. This result is still more impressive since the absolute number of job opportunities is much lower in the case of professionals.

Distribution of accessibility to job by income groups clearly exhibits the middle-class unfavorable situation ($8000 to $10000 bracket). In each case surveyed, maximum accessibility corresponds to the income bracket most typical of the neighborhood: low incomes in Watts, average in Boyle Heights, high in Beverly Crest. This is a most important observation. It suggests a very close correspondence between socioeconomic structure and accessibility to work. Accessibility appears here as a complex term,

Table 5.5. Accessibility of three neighborhoods. (Source: Perloff et al, 1973, page 194.)

	Beverly Crest	Watts	Boyle Heights
Accessibility index	5.97	1.71	2.11
Cars per household	1.71	0.91	0.64
Accessibility index by income ($)			
0–4999	2.74	2.22	1.86
5000–6999	–	2.12	3.06
7000–7999	1.65	1.15	1.28
8000–8999	–	0.67	0.77
9000–9999	1.72	0.74	1.18
10000–12499	4.19	0.88	2.14
12500–14999	–	–	0.87
15000+	7.97	0.33	0.35
Accessibility index by category			
Professionals, Managers	6.45	2.32	3.58
Clerks, Salesworkers	1.85	3.26	4.12
Service workers	–	2.21	2.76

integrating location on the map, efficiency of the transportation system, and equipment availability to use this system. If a wealthy household were to live in Watts, it would suffer from very bad accessibility to the jobs it would be looking for; conversely, a poor family located by some miracle in Beverly Crest would be handicapped, as far as access to work is concerned, in comparison with a Watts family. This leads to a definition of accessibility much more subtle than sheer location on a map. There exists a close relationship between the social status of a neighborhood and its accessibility to work. This relationship works both ways: even without any social or racial prejudices, and in the absence of any price constraints, it is in the best interests of a household to choose a location among similar households in order to maximize its access to work. Accessibility determines a neighborhood's social status.

Conversely, inhabitants act as pressure groups on job locations, and still more, on transportation investment decisions. Here, we may suspect a complex and fundamental mechanism fitting housing conditions to family needs, and which has not yet been completely elucidated. It helps us to understand the Watts' decay, as this once important rail and street-car crossroads suffered in the 1950s from the development of freeways located elsewhere.

One of the classic themes of United States urban geography insists on the progressive decay of the center and on the resulting growth of the suburban ring. This model leads to an organic conception of the city, which can be compared with a tree whose heart rots and dies, while sap irrigates and develops the healthy bark. Such a general process cannot be denied, but it is a complex and sometimes contradictory one. An over-simplified version of this model betrays a whole ideological content which would have us believe that poor central districts are inhabited by parasites living at the expense of the wealthy periphery. Housing decay is actually a much more complex phenomenon.

Its superficial forms are well known: dirty and peeling paint, graffiti, broken windows, out-of-order elevators, staircases without light and full of garbage, violence and crime. Everything shows a lack of maintenance, of supervision and, sometimes, a complete abandonment. A deeper and much more interesting form, however, appears behind these symptoms of decay. There is a growing lack of housing suitable to the needs and resources of its inhabitants. Blighted housing is characterized by the fact that it has not been designed for its present occupants: offices transformed into apartments without enough bathrooms, huge apartments subdivided by temporary partitions, marble halls leading to slums, old cast-iron elevators which do not work anymore, and broken chandeliers. Poor families' housing has in general been built in earlier times for wealthier occupants. The lack of maintenance with which poor families are often reproached largely stems from the fact that they are burdened with many useless fixtures, while the most necessary facilities are missing.

As far as financing housing is concerned, the lack of adaptation is worse. Poor people live on the most expensive land in town. True, they are closer to their jobs, which are usually located Downtown. But they pay double the price for this doubtful privilege. On the one hand, they are concentrated in small areas; apart from 1960, these decaying districts present the highest rate of vacancies and the largest number of children per family. On the other hand, landlords do not spend money maintaining these buildings anymore.

Finally, there is a poor fit between accessibility to jobs and population needs. Table 5.4 shows that only very poor households have a reasonable index, but they are categories which particularly suffer from unemployment. Lower-middle-class groups live further away from their working places.

Like other forms of discrepancies, these represent a transition—a shift from an old equilibrium to a new one, from the old bourgeoisie who built the buildings which are today dilapidated, to the future inhabitants of these neighborhoods: well-off singles who will live in modern apartment towers, or companies occupying modern office buildings. True, the transition takes time, often a few decades, and it is expressed in the predicament of poor households. They have to occupy dwellings which have not been designed for them, in badly located districts as far as jobs are concerned, amidst a transformation of land use leading inexorably to their elimination. Finally, what characterizes Downtown decay is not the appearance of new housing forms but the growing inadequacy of old housing to meet the needs and means of new inhabitants.

This decay is due mainly to the rapidity of change to which households cannot adapt fast enough, viz:

Changes in land-use patterns taking the form of concentric waves diffusing from the center to the fringe; or of secondary nuclei as in the Ullman–Harris model (Harris and Ullman, 1945).

Changes in the human composition of residential districts: households move, with the change in their income, from one radial sector to another (Hoyt's model); and, with the passage of time, from one concentric ring to another (Burgess's concentric model). There is also a slow drift of ethnic groups, particularly of Blacks.

Changes in accessibility altering a district's use value and, through a relationship which has been shown to be very strong, the social and professional characteristics of its inhabitants. The freeway system, built between 1947 and 1967; the project for a new Rapid Transit System not yet implemented but discussed so many times it has contributed to the modification of neighborhoods directly involved; and finally, transformations at the extremity of the main transportation axes, with new jobs created, and old activities disappearing.

All these changes indirectly influence the composition of residential areas.

With prosperity in the 1950s and 1960s, the process of urban decay took much more complex forms.

Contemporary centripetal movements altered the simplicity of the classical pattern. Downtown tended to be rehabilitated by young professionals who came back to live in the center. More recently, the several 'Linear Downtowns' distributed throughout the city along important boulevards have experienced similar transformations—business along those axes tending to be replaced by modern residential buildings. Wilshire Blvd follows the example set by the Bunker Hill complex, Downtown.

The very development of freeways has tended to reverse relationships: their new role is not only to render peripheral residences closer to the center but conversely, to facilitate the access of young professionals living Downtown to the jobs created in the urban fringe.

Los Angeles constitutes an urban system too vast, too complex, and changing too rapidly for the classical scheme of an old decaying center surrounded by prosperous suburban rings to be still meaningful. In order to understand the process of urban decay one must drop the concept of a unique center, distinguish between the Central Business District and decaying Downtown, add to the usual centrifugal movements very important population returns to the center, and finally, separate the notions of black neighborhoods and decaying ghettos. Although most miserable neighborhoods are in fact black ghettos (for example, several blocks Downtown, Watts, and neighborhoods surrounding the University of Southern California), an increasingly important black bourgeoisie has spread out from the old ghettos and today occupies large areas of the city (Culver City, Palms, Compton, etc).

5.3 Transformations of the exchange value

Even expressed in constant 1940 dollars, to take account of inflation, the average market value of a dwelling in Los Angeles has increased with time. As the number of dwellings has also risen, a definite boom in real estate values is apparent. How could family incomes cover the increasing housing costs? Which mechanisms helped to finance housing? These are the main questions posed by the evolution of exchange value.

5.3.1 Evolution of land capital and real estate income

Table 5.6 shows the increase over time of average rent and capital value. Figures are arithmetic averages computed on medians derived from the censuses: one should not analyze them too closely. Their order of magnitude, however, is important.

Capital value has doubled over thirty years, partly because the quality and size of the average dwelling has increased, but mainly because of changes in accessibility: "Location has played a much more important role than deterioration and aging in determining the increase in real estate values" (Gillies and Berger, 1965, page 5). As the SMSA experienced an enormous growth, the city itself, which formed the main part of the agglomeration in 1940, today represents only its central part. This land has become very expensive. The role of urban freeways is clear. Until the 1960s, land prices became more homogeneous; from 1970 on, the trend was inverted—the vacancy rate increased again, and prices differed more widely throughout the city.

Rent increased too, but at a slower pace. The average annual yield of real estate capital was very high in 1940; it fell abruptly in 1950, and decreased slowly thereafter. Of course, this ratio has been computed from two evaluations, both quite imprecise. It is meaningful, however, and follows the general rate of profit quite closely (average stock yields on Wall Street hovered around 5.5% during the whole period, with an increase in market price which more or less made up for inflation). Only after 1974 and for a few years, with the fall in the buying power of the dollar, has the equilibrium broken down. The slow but regular decrease in land-investments yield seems to indicate that in Los Angeles the real estate market has tended to become overpriced. This could explain why after 1970 investors turned their back on land construction in the city center. This long-term trend has probably reinforced the exceptional drop in 1974. It still remains that the real value of housing stock has multiplied almost four times over thirty years.

Fortunately for the inhabitants, average household income has increased somewhat faster, thus diminishing the housing burden (table 5.7). Meanwhile, the growth of the income coefficient of variation shows social

Table 5.6. Evolution of land rent in Los Angeles 1940-1970 (expressed in 1940 dollars).

	Rent		Capital value		Annual yield (%)	Number of dwellings	Global real estate value (millions of $)
	mean $\bar{x}$	coefficient of variation c.v. = $\sigma/\bar{x}$	mean	c.v.			
1970	35.74	0.315	8343	0.374	5.14	1 029 697	8591
1960	32.82	0.249	7326	0.316	5.38	959 348	7028
1950	25.27	0.277	5595	0.379	5.42	749 409	4193
1940	31.15	0.380	3866	0.463	9.67	575 331	2224

Table 5.7. Evolution of housing relative value in Los Angeles, 1940-1970 (expressed in 1940 dollars).

	Median income		Ratio housing value/income
	mean	c.v.	
1970	3233	0.474	2.58
1960	2258	0.393	3.24
1950	1689	0.266	3.31

disparities have increased. While it has become easier for well-off families to pay for their houses, the lot of the poor has certainly worsened. The evolution of rent in the whole SMSA confirms this (table 5.8: figures are taken from Mittelbach, 1963, page 23). Figures are in current dollars and thus include inflation, which is inconvenient. It would be difficult to correct them into constant dollars, but the transformation is not necessary. It would only produce a monotonic transformation of the rate of increase, the most important data in the table. The fact remains that rent has increased in inverse proportion to income between 1950 and 1960. This may be partly explained by the removal of rent control (established during the war) between these two dates. In any case, inequalities in the relative cost of housing have intensified since 1950.

Table 5.8. Evolution of rent for income groups (Los Angeles SMSA) (sources: US Bureau of the Census, 1950; 1960; Mittelbach, 1963, page 23).

Income ($) in 1949 and 1959	Rented homes (%)		Median monthly rent ($)		Rate of increase 1950/1960 (%)
	1950	1960	1950	1960	
Less than 2000	32.1	20.8	37	64	73.0%
2000–2999	19.4	9.6	42	71	69.0
3000–3999	19.8	11.0	46	75	63.0
4000–4999	11.7	12.1	49	79	61.2
5000–5999	7.3	11.8	53	84	58.5
6000–6999	3.9	9.4	58	88	51.7
7000–9999	3.7	15.6	65	91	40.0
10000+	2.1	9.6	87	111	27.6

5.3.2 Housing cost versus family income

Canonical correlation analysis has already given us our first result in subsection 5.2.1. This produced a second factor showing the relationship between income and housing in detail (table 5.9). Two types of strong relationship between inhabitants and dwellings appear:
(1) In 1940 and also in 1970 white and wealthy households without children correspond (84.5% and 91.9%, respectively, of the variance in common) to dwellings with simultaneously high rent and high capital value. In 1970 the type of housing (apartment or house) and tenure (owner-occupied or tenant) play no role at all; only rent and price are important. On the other hand, in 1940 quite highly educated households without children clearly preferred an apartment to a house. These are wealthy, retired people who have moved Downtown to good apartment buildings. This is the strongest correspondence observable for 1940.
(2) Levels of correspondence have changed a lot by 1950 and 1960. Rich and well-educated families with children are strongly linked to neighborhoods with high rents where most dwellings are owner-occupied, detached, or semidetached houses, with a few high-priced apartments. Surprisingly

enough, housing value plays a secondary role in this association and is much weaker than rent (respectively: 35% versus 70% in 1950, and 23% versus 72% in 1960). This is typical of blocks where house size varies widely, that is of poorly planned districts with a hasty and disordered development, as opposed to the pre-1940 orderly subdivisions of huge ranches by large developers (for example, to produce Beverly Hills), and to the relative stagnation in land development during the late 1960s.

Figure 4.13 shows the evolution of land rent during the last decade. The contrast between center and periphery is very clear. Downtown housing prices and its inhabitants' social status grew together as a significant number of single individuals returned to the heart of the old city.

Table 5.9. Types of correspondence between inhabitant and dwelling: the economic viewpoint.

Variable	1940		Variable	1950	
	r	r^2		r	r^2
Young	0.914	0.84	Income	0.936	0.88
Old	−0.601	0.36	NSY[a]	0.684	0.47
Persons/room	0.578	0.33			
NSY[a]	−0.809	0.65			
Houses	0.684	0.47	Owner-occupied	0.718	0.52
Apartments	−0.609	0.37	Renter-occupied	−0.710	0.50
Value	−0.754	0.57	Rent	0.838	0.70
Rent	−0.738	0.54	Value	0.593	0.35
R =	0.845	0.71	R =	0.882	0.78

	1960			1970	
	r	r^2		r	r^2
Income	−0.915	0.84	Income	0.828	0.69
NSY[a]	−0.635	0.40	NSY[a]	0.781	0.61
Persons/room	−0.404	0.16	Young	−0.591	0.35
			Whites	0.503	0.25
			Blacks	−0.464	0.22
			Old	0.342	0.12
Owner-occupied	−0.765	0.59	Value	0.858	0.74
Renter-occupied	0.735	0.54	Rent	0.940	0.88
Value	−0.478	0.23			
Vacant	0.556	0.31			
Rent	−0.849	0.72			
R =	0.883	0.78	R =	0.919	0.84

[a] NSY ≡ number of school years.

The relationship between land-rent increases and income increases was quite weak; it became stronger only during the last decade. This is probably due to the workings of the economy. In a bullish economy, poor households must make sacrifices to obtain housing because competition is strong, especially as mortgage rates are quite low and confidence in the future is good. In such conditions, inflation is often an incentive to invest in real estate. Later on, when stagflation appears, mortgages become more difficult to find and more expensive. Agreement between housing quality and family means is subject to complex mechanisms strongly influenced by the shape of the national economy. Housing financing plays a basic role in such compatibility or lack of it.

5.3.3 Financing housing in Los Angeles

It is possible to draw a rapid sketch of the principal means of financing housing (Gillies and Berger, 1965). Between two-thirds and three-quarters of the dwellings in Los Angeles were mortgaged as of 1960 (table 5.10). This proportion was much higher than in the country as a whole and even higher than in San Francisco or New York. Owners of unmortgaged houses were much older than the average homeowner (60 versus 42 years old) and had a lower income; they comprised mainly retired people who had completely paid for their homes. The cost of housing, including the interest paid on a mortgage, was slightly higher in Los Angeles than in the

Table 5.10. Mortgage market in Los Angeles in 1960 (source: Gillies and Berger, 1965, pages 4 and 5).

	Los Angeles		San Francisco		New York		USA	
	M[a]	UM[a]	M	UM	M	UM	M	UM
Dwelling								
Value ($)	16700	15900	16300	15500	18100	17300	13800	9600
Buying cost as % of value								
1957/1960	92	90	93	–	92	–	96	95
1950/1956	79	75	82	82	81	84	86	83
1949/–	63	44	65	44	58	47	62	49
Property tax per $1000 ($)	15	14	15	15	22	22	14	13
% of total	74.5	25.5	67.7	32.3	69.8	30.2	57.9	42.1
Owner								
Monthly cost ($)	114	39	100	38	133	67	104	35
Annual cost as % of income	18	9	18	8	21	11	19	10
Income ($)	7600	5900	7600	6200	7900	6800	6700	4300
Age	42	60	42	61	42	56	41	58

[a] M ≡ mortgaged homes; UM ≡ unmortgaged homes.

rest of the country, although lower than the cost in New York, which was exceptionally high by any standard. Since average income in Los Angeles was higher than the national average, housing costs represented a burden relatively equal to or less than that found in other big US cities, viz 18% of income. The average age of homeowners was slightly higher than the national average.

The mean value of mortgaged homes in Los Angeles was higher than elsewhere in the USA, except for New York. The total amount of debt was huge, even by American standards, increasing from 2.4 billion dollars in 1950 to 6 billion in 1960, in current dollars. In constant prices, this is a vast increase from 2 billion to 4.9 billion dollars.

Such a large amount of capital could not be found on the Californian market alone: there was a regular and growing flow of capital from the East to Southern California, maintained by a yield slightly higher than that in the Eastern metropolises. The relative cost to the borrower was no higher, however, since the Los Angeles homeowner received, in general, a better income. This capital flow was vital for the city. Gillies and Berger estimate that in 1960, of the $23 billion in home loans made in the State of California, 40% came from other states (loc cit, pages 55–56). From this viewpoint Los Angeles appears not as a local product but as a national endeavor, concentrating interests and hopes from the whole nation.

The general evolution of housing finance in the United States is characterized by the growing control of the mortgage market by big institutions. These controlled 51% of the loans (in volume) in 1940, and 80% in 1960. The loan market has become more fluid, but also more volatile. It is now closely integrated into the global money market, with rates that rapidly reflect changes in the general rate of interest.

5.4 The nature and evolution of sign value

Sign value has, in essence, a semantic function: its purpose is to express and to illustrate differences; to transform locations into social signs; and to constitute, through the spatial combination of such signs, an urban language. The names of the pleasant districts built on the hills between Santa Monica and Hollywood are signs of opulence and well-being, and the area's high land-values partly reflect such signs of success. This part of the Los Angeles urban region has retained its privileged image for at least thirty years—as a survey made by geographers at UCLA in the 1970s indicated (Clark and Cadwallader, 1973). Asked which district they would like to live in *given their present income*, 1000 Angelenos designated (1) the hill slopes to the northwest of the city, and (2) the ocean-side districts of Redondo, Manhattan, and Hermosa Beach. There is, of course, a use value included in their choices—the presence of nice views, not too much pollution, and so on—but there is also the prestige of the names constituting the sign values of these residential districts.

We only have to think of Pasadena: it appeared high on the list of most desired locations, even though its townscape is visually mediocre, and its pollution rate extremely high. Perloff, intrigued by such a high evaluation, noted that "Pasadena's choice seems to be related to its preeminence as a residential zone forty years ago" (Perloff et al, 1973, page 206), indicating that its sign value is still extremely high.

The importance of the sign appears in the very names of the most desirable locations. In the hill areas we have all sorts of Crests, Hills, Glens, and Canyons signifying relief (in the double sense of the word), domination over the environment and aloofness from other city dwellers, as well as seclusion, quietness, and peace. Similarly, along the shore we find such terms as Beach, Marina, and Ocean expressing a brisk and healthy contact with the sea, surf, sand, and sun, the vastness of the Pacific, and the sense of openness to the exotic countries beyond it.

Modern linguists, particularly Barthes, have shown that language is not only spoken. Many parallel languages—such as fashion (Barthes, 1967), body movements and objects (Baudrillard, 1968)—can tell us as much, and often more, than the usual oral discourses. Inasmuch as urban elements (buildings, locations, landmarks, etc) are linguistic signs, they constitute a *vocabulary*, organized by a *syntax* made up of spatial relations into a language. Lynch (1960) initiated the analysis of such a language and its imperfections in Los Angeles, and his surveys, confirmed by Banham's (1971) analysis, indicate the coexistence of two different levels of language separated by a void.

5.4.1 Two separated languages

At the neighborhood scale we have a local language: the buildings, the pedestrian paths, the street situations, and their happenings are known in considerable detail to those who live nearby. Neighborhoods exist where such concepts as orientation, contiguity, and proximity are correctly perceived, understood, and transmitted. This sort of local language is a static one, based on the architecture and the relative locations of buildings, the street pattern and the general design of the neighborhood. It is also a spoken language as it enters into conversations between neighborhoods, and a tangible language appealing to the visual, hearing, and olfactory senses as they are combined in everyday experience. In Los Angeles such neighborhoods seem to be less extensive than in European cities, probably because pedestrian movement, the best way of discovering them, is so much more limited. Lynch, in a further series of studies in Los Angeles (Lynch, 1971), has shown how the sense of familiar neighborhood enlarges with an increase in the social level of the person surveyed. In Los Angeles, as elsewhere, poverty means a shrinking of the perceived and known space.

On the other hand, we also have a regional language; a language suitable for describing things at the metropolitan scale built on the wide

freeway network of the city.   This is both a *kinetic* language (made up
primarily of impressions of speed, going up and down, turning, stopping
abruptly, and so on), as well as an *abstract* language, because the car
driver must be totally obedient to traffic signs, giving up any confidence
he may have in his own sense of direction and distance.   When you drive
in Los Angeles, it is practically impossible to perceive and master the
orientation of the concrete ramps as they leave the main freeways and are
intertwined in complicated three-dimensional figures.   A person driving
along Hollywood Freeway to the east trying to reach the Civic Center will
see the famous tower topped with a tetrahedron appearing close on his
right-hand side.   He may find it very hard to believe signs ordering him to
cross to the extreme left-hand lane, but if he does not obey blindly he will
rush past the exit and find himself several miles further on before he can
turn back to his destination.   Obedience to paradoxical indications cannot
be thought about at 65 miles an hour—on a crowded five-lane freeway
there is no time for thought.   As a result, the spatial language is *written*
on huge green signboards in common English—not even in symbols as in
Europe—so that the abstract language denies and overcomes the testimony
of the senses.

These two languages, these two systems of relations between signs
located in space, are well known to Angelenos, who 'speak' them more
fluently than drivers in other big cities: "I learned to drive in order to
read Los Angeles in the text" (Banham, 1971).   But the problems stem
from the lack of any link between the two languages, and it is certainly
here that the feeling of disorientation originates, a feeling of anxiety that
bothers visitors and makes them hate the City of Dreams.   Los Angeles
cannot really be considered as an undifferentiated and formless urban
mass, yet these are precisely the common adjectives and clichés which
many people use to describe the city.   There is a missing link, a missing
language, between the small neighborhoods and the large freeway network.
Both are quite familiar to most Angelenos, and even to visitors after a
few days, but their relationship remains unclear for many people.   As
Lynch (1960, pages 40–41) notes:
> "When asked to describe or symbolize the city as a whole, the subjects
> used certain standard words: 'spread-out', 'spacious', 'formless', 'with-
> out centers'.   Los Angeles seemed to be hard to envision or conceptualize
> as a whole.   An endless spread which may carry pleasant connotations
> of space around the buildings, or overtones of weariness and dis-
> orientation, was the common image.   Said one subject: 'It is as if you
> were going somewhere for a long time, and when you got there, you
> discovered there was nothing there, after all'."

A subtle remark by Banham (1971, page 213) confirms the point, when
he noted "... coming off the freeway is coming in from outdoors".   He
observed that when some cars left the freeway for the residential streets
the women passengers would automatically check their makeup in the

mirror on the back of the sunshades, implying that leaving the freeway actually symbolized the entrance into a friend's house. It almost seemed that there was no intermediary space between the freeway and the door of a residence.

One means people adopt to read the urban structure is to replace the missing spatial language by a temporal one. The differences in the ages between districts become signs helping people to orient themselves in the urban space (Lynch, 1960, page 41):

"The apparatus of regional orientation included ... a central gradient of age over the whole metropolis, evidenced in the condition, style and type of structures appropriate to each era in the successive rings of growth."

Banham also commented upon the importance Angelenos place on the signs of the past. These have partly a symbolic value for people, but they also help to identify landmarks (such as the famous Olvera Street), and to organize the urban structure through a useful chronological classification. The very speed of change in Los Angeles disorients inhabitants and visitors—"Each time I come, I don't recognize things anymore, everything has changed"—but at the same time the changes are used by them to introduce some order into the immense city. It is almost as though Time were projected onto the spatial plane, as if architectural signs, expressing age through their ordered distribution through space, take on a particular meaning. There is no question that a temporal language, although still imperfect, appears in order to organize and describe the urban landscape.

5.4.2 Signs and signification

One feels a need for a dictionary of urban signs, and for a corresponding grammar to describe their syntactical relations. Research in this field has only just begun, and it is impossible to go beyond a rough statement of the question at this point. Nevertheless, the multitude of urban signs in Los Angeles, so diverse and yet so aggressive, may be classified under three main types of signification: Nature, Culture, and Power. These themes can be related in pairs, but we can also summarize the combinations in a more convenient way (table 5.11), at the same time making it clear that 'Domination', for example, which signifies Power, is also related to 'Control over Nature', and so on. The categories are not necessarily exclusive.

Inside each principal Signification, the Signifieds are opposed dialectically: Nature is signified by various signs of openness to the external world, which receives it, in a sense, passively. But Nature is also signified by signs of control (over light, temperature, space, etc) which are distinctly active. In the same vein Culture is simultaneously signified by a brutal and often flashy affirmation of modernism, but also by a passionate, moving, and sometimes ridiculous search for legitimacy by today creating links that signify the past.

The same dialectic operates for Power. Pure aloofness and isolation would undermine Power, so one must retire from the crowd, and yet at the same time locate oneself in relation to the crowd in order to express domination over it. Nothing signifies Power better than those Los Angeles houses roosting on a hilltop—a summit location which can be reached only after a long drive over a virtually deserted road, winding for miles inside a canyon. Driving up Beverly Glen or Laurel Canyon, one feels far away from any city, as though one were in the middle of a wild and forsaken mountain area. Eventually one reaches a huge villa standing on the crest, a dwelling that deliberately turns its back on the wilderness, built entirely in order to offer a fantastic panorama over the city. The owner has spent enormous sums of money to separate himself and his home from the city only in order to relate to it again from a superior or dominating position. Even on the ocean shore certain houses tend to dominate the beach and the sea through cantilevered rooms, with wide windows jutting out like observatories. These sorts of sites, which speak so clearly of Power, are scarce, and are reserved accordingly for only the wealthiest. However, it

Table 5.11. The urban language of Los Angeles.

Sign	Signifiant	Signified	Signification
Open views			
Hilltops ... penthouses			
Bow-windows ... glass walls	Space		
Patios ... verandas, balconies			
Drift toward the beach			
Basins, fountains ... individual swimming pools	Water	*Openness*	
Parks ... parkways ...			
Freeways with plastic shrubs	Green space		
Gardens ... lawns ... plants inside the home			**Nature**
Electrical light			
Air conditioning	Artificial power	*Control*	
Access control			
Wood ... stucco ... concrete ... plastics ... light ... steel	Artificial materials	*Modernism*	
Pseudostyles:			**Culture history**
Antique, Colonial, Alpine, Spanish revival ...	Past	*Legitimacy*	
Decoration: neocolonial, pseudomedieval			
Barriers			
Hedgerows, wide lawns, parks ...	Isolation	*Separation*	**Power**
Housing			
On hilltops			
On the top of buildings	Elevation	*Domination*	
On the shore, above the ocean			

is always possible to multiply them artificially by placing them on the tops of high buildings, and in this way the penthouses of Los Angeles are the dominating eagles' nests of the not-quite-so-rich families.

Similar nuances, containing within them the same dialectical seesaws, appear in the language of Isolation. The point here is to show how different one is from one's neighbors. The extremely rich use sheer space: they build their homes in grounds so large and so sheltered from others that one can hardly catch a glimpse of the houses themselves. Since respect and deference are ensured beforehand by the neighborhood's fame, the owner can do without the admiring contemplation of the passerby: in Bel Air, the most expensive part of Beverly Hills, the sidewalks are missing so that one cannot stroll by, but only drive through; stopping is forbidden.

To 'speak' in this way, however, is far too expensive for most people. When a parcel of land is smaller, the relationship swings dialectically: the point is no longer to separate by concealing, but to separate by showing off—as if the owners were afraid the passerby would not be impressed enough by their houses. They feel obliged to attract a person's attention, while at the same time keeping him at arm's length. This is the function of the grass lawn in front of every true American house—at least when it is occupied by a middle-class family. The lawn is carefully groomed, so denoting its important role and the way it is intended to impress the passerby. But it also has the function of forbidding him to come too close—"Keep off the grass!". In most cases, a narrow concrete path or driveway limits one boundary of the private property, and so shows the visitor where he should stand.

But how does one create a distinction from the mass when one has only limited means and is part of the mass oneself? There is no question anymore of delicate refinements, quiet understatements, or huge manorial grounds; there is not even the opportunity to plant a limited but haughty piece of lawn. Instead one must express separation more crudely, and put all the more emphasis on the property that is itself so small. In danger of being lost in the crowd, a person using such social 'talk' cannot afford to murmur subtly; he must scream.

Low fences (so low one could easily stride over them) appear around gardens the size of a handkerchief: symbolic barriers carrying out their unique role of saying "This is not yours, *I* own it!". Fences in the poorer districts bear the same relation to the wide lawns and parks as slang is related to correct and elegant language. They represent a popular way of 'talking', a more direct way, with more immediate images and allusions, with richer metaphors and allegories—in fact, a more rhetorical way of speaking. Fences are often painted or decorated in the most various and imaginative sorts of ways. Narrow gardens are 'embellished' with ceramic statues; the small plots are dotted with earthenware cats, artificial ducks or storks, and even Snow White's dwarves. Such slang can be quite subtle:

the dwarves try to be nice to the passerby and smile at him, even as they guard the property and keep him away. There is also a confused attempt to recover a sense of legitimacy on which to base a newly acquired property, and this effort to root oneself in the past is typical of such a modern city. Everybody knows that in medieval Europe dwarves ran through the land!

The search for legitimacy, the need for cultural landmarks endowed with historical meaning, is particularly noticeable in Los Angeles. Even if we make allowances for some of the fantasies characteristic of North American society, it is still true that there are few cities in the United States where people try so hard to signify the past.

The need and expression of the past are not unrelated to income: at least for those who have recently acquired some money. If poor houses try to relate to the Conquista with their pseudo-Spanish-colonial style, some of the bigger and richer ones go straight back to the Middle Ages, featuring towers with battlements, portcullis chains, flickering torches (burning gas), and armor in the entranceway that can be glimpsed through the pseudo-Gothic porch. Some houses even go back to Antiquity, with frontages based on Greek temples, and columns decorated in a style which could be said to be 'composite'—in the complete and literal sense of the term.

At the same time, resorting to the past in this way is negated by the pride of modernism. In contrast to most big cities on the East Coast, Los Angeles seems to be particularly proud of using the most modern construction materials with great freedom and imagination. The city evolved very quickly from wood to stucco to concrete and steel; it then moved on to plastic, and today to artificial light in order to heighten and accentuate its modern architectural forms: a visual characteristic which constitutes an outstanding feature of the city. Los Angeles is lit by floodlights, searchlights, fluorescent gas tubes with variegated colors (neon, xenon, argon) and gas torches, as well as light in constant movement— flickering flashes, changing luminous signboards, and rotating restaurants lit like old-fashioned lighthouses. These decorative materials, extremely fluid and plastic, have led to fantastic expressions in architecture, where language is changing into myth, and sign into symbol.

It would be all too easy to make fun of a language that is sometimes so excessive that it falls into unintentional *kitsch*, but such smirking and fingerpointing would be unfair. In the ghettos, flashy decoration is a way of expressing human personalities limited and crushed by too many taboos; elsewhere the exuberant language expresses a satisfaction which may appear illusory, but nevertheless forms a basic component of the American way of life. The decorative language denotes a mixture of audacity and candidness which some Europeans tend to brand as uneducated simplicity, but it actually contrasts very favorably with the pretentious vulgarity and the complete lack of personality so typical of European suburbs.

Given the lack of previous analysis along these lines, it is difficult to predict how this sort of language will evolve in the future. We can, however, look for clues in that part of the language expressing certain aspects of Nature, because this is the area where changes have been very marked over the past thirty years. For example, the ability to generate a sense of openness in external space, while at the same time creating an expression of domination, has been increasingly restricted to heights that have been created artificially—essentially at the tops of apartment towers. This may well be one of the reasons why they have developed so rapidly throughout the city, since today the mountain slopes have been totally occupied and are greatly overpriced.

There has also been another trend in the language as Nature has been attacked from all sides and has tended to vanish. The incidence of greenery has evolved from the parks and tree-lined avenues where people once rode horses, to the first Pasadena Parkway in 1938 lined with groves of trees and shrubberies, to the freeways of the 1960s still divided by natural bushes. Since these shrubs died from pollution, an extraordinary project tried to replace them in 1970 with plastic ones, 'bushes' that were 'ever green', smoke-resistant, washable, and unaffected by smog. Words in the urban vocabulary were thus transformed in an interesting effort to express the same signification, viz Nature. Individual parcels of land have followed a similar linguistic evolution: lawns try to say today what tree-planted gardens of old expressed; and for those living in apartments, and not wealthy enough to grow plants on a terrace, there always remain indoor plants (the supply of which has now grown into a large industry) popular particularly among young people and representing the more recent word form that tries to say 'Nature'.

5.5 Symbolic value and urban structure in Los Angeles

Los Angeles is one of the great cities of the world where urban symbols, and their unconscious expressions in myth, are present to an overwhelming degree. Unfortunately, this does not mean that they are always clear and distinct, nor are they always easy to analyze. Any North American city is characterized by a number of basic symbols, and these can obviously all be found in Los Angeles as well. The Central Business District often expresses its economic power through the phallic symbol of the skyscraper, although this particular value appears less prominent, and even quite subdued, in Los Angeles. In comparison with the overwhelming Wall Street towers of New York, or the elegant Hancock Building and Sears Tower (the highest in the world) of Chicago, the center of Los Angeles displays an unimpressive, second-class, almost shabby appearance. Except for a beautiful new complex made of cylindrical glass towers, its skyscrapers are too few, too banal, and too widely spread across the city to make a worthwhile and potent impression.

What is no less surprising is that the classical myths of the West Coast are also poorly represented—the Myth of the Far West and the Myth of the Pacific. Several restaurants try to look as if they were part of the decor in a cowboy movie, but the best saloons of the Old West, and the truest evocations of the Forty-Niners are to be found in San Francisco. In those earlier days Los Angeles was still a small town and not really part of the classical West. Similarly, it contains quite a large population today of oriental origin, but its Chinatown and Little Tokyo are not particularly visible in the huge urban area, and they are no match for the Chinatown of San Francisco.

5.5.1 The Myth of the Star
Nevertheless, if the standard symbols and myths of American cities are not especially prominent in Los Angeles, the city has generated several new ones which typify it exactly. One of the most prominent is the *Star Myth*, a symbol of success that was born in Hollywood and rooted in Beverly Hills. It is related to the *Gold Symbol*: not gold as a source of power and fear, nor the slightly mysterious and occult symbol, as in Wall Street, both concrete and abstract at the same time; but rather gold which shines and sparkles, which wants to exhibit itself, and derives its success from its very exhibition. Baudrillard quite rightly underlines the ambivalence of symbolic values: since they depend on Freudian subconscious mechanisms, they do not respect the logical principle of noncontradiction, but attract and repel simultaneously. Freud has shown that gold is unconsciously perceived as the equivalent of faeces, the infantile gift of the child to his mother.

In Los Angeles, show business is symbolically related to gold in its natural flake or nugget form, and these words are present in the signs of many bars and restaurants—just as they are in Las Vegas. This glittering aspect of glamor is dialectically completed by its opposite, the aura of 'corruption' which Hollywood tries so hard to deserve, as gold and faeces are mixed in Freudian images. A whole mythology of vice and perversion, of hedonism and decadent luxury, of success leading to disaster, of alcohol and drugs ruining a promising career, is kept flourishing in cheap and widely-read newspapers, and even in the B films made in Hollywood itself. The city creates and thrives on stories of its own (supposed) debasement. Such myths are much too complex to take them apart completely and detail all their inner mechanisms here. In fact they are frequently made up from more elementary myths: Cinderella ascending to glory; Gyges spoiled by the gods, trying to win them over by offering them his ring (that is, making a spectacular gift to the Salvation Army), to find his offer disquietingly refused (God is not for sale at such a low price); the myth of the Capitol so close to the Tarpeian Cliffs; the myth of the Vamp, the venomous woman, so attractive and so destructive, a modern siren calling from a bar stool (again the intertwined connotation of gold and faeces); the myth of Balzac's 'Peau de Chagrin', with the image of life's candle burning at both ends, of lives running to self-destruction like the tapes introducing the story in 'Mission Impossible'. All the ingredients are here to excite the dreams of the masses: they get the intoxicating impression that success is around the corner, just within the reach of their outstretched hands; but at the same time they are reminded that the social hierarchy is stable after all, and that in a really 'happy ending' the unheard-of-success that upsets social rules is finally and inevitably broken to pieces. One must keep to one's position and one's dreams.

All these myths are epitomized in a remarkable way in *Hollywood-Babylon* (Anger, 1975), a long list of Hollywoodian glories, excesses, and disasters: 'Fatty' Arbuckle, among the leading comics of his time, accused of murder and ruined; Buster Keaton, a genius dying in misery, broken by his son's leukemia; Erroll Flynn, the gifted swashbuckler under a conviction of statutory rape which almost ruined his career; and then all the lives, several terminated by suicide, that were broken in a few months when sound movies replaced the silent screen. Perhaps the most poignant symbol is the actress, unemployed after playing in thirteen films, who drove up the hill one night to the gigantic illuminated letters reading HOLLYWOODLAND, undressed, and jumped naked to her death in a cactus bush from the last D—the thirteenth letter. Here is success, failure, destruction, movement, light, superstition, sex, linguistic sign, hope, and hopelessness—the symbol is complete.

Nathaniel West (1939) has described in his novel *The Day of the Locust* the violence, the passion, and the bitterness of Hollywood life. In fact, limits between symbols and reality vanish. If Hollywood portrays the world through books, films, and shows, it also turns dialectically upon itself and so becomes its own object. It is the story of the photographer photographed, as reality becomes so totally symbolic that symbol becomes reality. From Nathaniel West to Andy Warhol, how many novels and films do we have about novel writing and film making, about writers, producers, and actors? The narcissism of actors and actresses contaminates the whole system: it is both a mark of its success, as well as one cause of its failure. And, quite typically, the cinema virtually left Hollywood in the 1960s to rediscover the world.

5.5.2 The Myth of the Fantastic

The hopeless mixture between reality and fiction generates the *Myth of the Fantastic*, exemplified in the architecture of the whole city, but particularly prominent in the show-business districts themselves. Grauman's Chinese Theater, the "ultimate shrine of all the fantasy that was Hollywood" (Banham, 1971, page 113), is loaded with redundant symbols; prints of people's feet and hands are actually stamped in the cement in front of this famous movie theater like nonwritten and indelible signatures. On the sidewalks along Hollywood Boulevard, bronze stars

embedded in the cement feature the names of famous personalities from
the radio, movie, and television industries, and people walk on them as if
they were entering a cathedral filled with the tombs of vanished royalty.
Fantastic buildings realize a succession of dreams in plaster and metal:
Simon Rodia's fantastic towers; the house, built in 1925 for Henry Oliver
looking like the eerie scenery inspired from Hansel and Gretel; and,
perhaps more than anything else, Disneyland, the first example in the
world of a real city coming straight from fairy tales.

Banham has described the fantastic styles used in restaurants. Metonymy
is the rule here, and the part speaks for the whole: a plastic totem pole
and three illuminated arrows announce the 'Tahitian Village'; a huge pine-
apple, five meters high and flashing green and yellow says 'Hawaiian Food'.
The symbols form such a luxuriant jungle that even epiphytes grow in its
shadow, parasitic symbols grafted onto others. The old oil derrick, kept
in Santa Monica as a symbol of oil wealth, is now dressed with painted
wood representing a medieval embattled tower, which is dressed
symbolically in turn as an Austrian beer parlor!

The whole city looks like an immense stage, where cardboard pieces of
scenery are dispersed in the most fantastic ways. An old photograph
shows Universal Studios during the 1930s while they were filming *Ali
Baba and the Forty Thieves*. The open air studios are so vast, and their
pseudoexotic sceneries of a totally false Middle East blend so well into
the surrounding townscape, that it is difficult to know where fiction stops
and reality starts. In Los Angeles one never knows for sure.

Baroque forms, *kitsch*, romanticism, and fantasy expressing audaciously
symbolic values are the last thing that the average European traveler
expects to find. These are not the things that for him or her characterize
the United States as it is usually depicted—with coldly efficient, computer
controlled robots with a touch of skeptical English humor. On the
contrary, few visitors expect the overornate style from eastern Europe,
laced with German *gemütlichkeit*, and set in scenes built straight from
Grimm's fairy tales. The true originality of Los Angeles, among all other
American cities, lies not so much in the important role of symbolic value
(after all, this is significant in all cities), but rather in the freedom of its
expression. It is, in fact, the symbol of its libertarian anarchism.

5.5.3 The Myth of Libertarian Anarchism

The *Myth of Libertarian Anarchism* clearly contrasts Los Angeles with the
large metropolises of the East Coast. At the far western end of the
continent, people tried to realize a Utopia by turning their backs on the
urban failures of the East and Midwest—a Utopia that is expressed by a
total freedom for everyone to express themselves in their own symbols and
to live by them. This myth also explains the vogue of the automobile: it
is, of course, a means of transportation in a dispersed city, but it also forms
a distinct means of expression. Nowhere in the United States, and perhaps

nowhere in the world, can one observe a larger variety of forms and colors in the bodies of the cars. Many have been repainted, redecorated, cut, welded, and reshaped into the strangest and most personal forms. Los Angeles is the birthplace of the 'dune buggies', small open cars with plastic bodies sparkling like electric guitars, made to drive on dunes and beaches. They are the humble Volkswagen—the People's Car—dressed up in finery to show off. The same aggressive freedom appears in the incredible motor bikes, with the front wheel pushed far ahead of the engine, and the driver lying lazily back as if in bed; and in the uniforms of the Hell's Angels mixing hippie paraphernalia with the helmet and Iron Cross of the Wehrmacht. This is also the home of the bright green Rolls-Royce upholstered with pink fur. In all these forms of myth, the point is not so much to show off one's money, but to bang one's fist on the table, and to state noisily and freely one's idiosyncrasy. Anarchism passes over into another symbol—movement.

5.5.4 The Myth of Movement

Based on the importance of change in such a volatile city, the *Myth of Movement* is not simply rooted in the everyday experience of rapid urban transformations—in Los Angeles movement itself becomes a myth. The inhabitants tend to exaggerate its importance, because it is not only a fact, but also the very symbol of a Utopia being realized every day. Of course, it is true that many illusions and hopes have crumbled, particularly since the 1970s when the local economy suffered a severe setback, the population stopped growing, and change itself slowed down as the city went into a period of painful self-questioning. Nevertheless, the myth of movement is still there, and quite as important as the sense of movement through time is the sense of movement over space. It is here that the main role of the automobile appears—as a symbol of individual freedom. What Banham calls "autotopia" is obviously a myth. Driving a car at high speed on a freeway (and notice the connotation of the prefix 'free') should symbolize liberty, but it actually submits the driver to a severe discipline and a total obedience to traffic indications he does not under-stand. Myth, as always, is deceitful, and ideology lurks behind it.

5.6 Conclusion

In Los Angeles, as elsewhere, all these different values combine to constitute the satisfaction that people can experience from their homes and their neighborhoods. In a market dominated by competition, they may all be integrated in the concept of land price or rent; but competition is never perfect, and it is often greatly distorted by publicity. Racial and social prejudices, for example, build almost opaque barriers, so that correlations between price and value are likely to be weak. Even more important is the fact that the most interesting values (use, sign, and symbolic values) are not comparable; each depends on a different

qualitative judgment. They are likely to be evaluated quite differently
from one social group to another, from one age group to another, as well
as between different cultures and different educational levels. It will
probably remain impossible for quite some time, to measure them
precisely.

Driving through Los Angeles, one can easily see all values combined,
although in a rather confused way. Hence the first impression of a
disjointed city, a city with a lack of structure, is an impression that is
actually misleading. Yet everything seems to contribute to building the
wrong impression: the dispersion of the business centers; the immensity
of the agglomeration; the variety of perceived land values which cannot
be expressed in a common unit; and the superimposition of two spatial
languages (local and regional) without intermediate links connecting them
—the surface streets and the freeways. A mathematician once said that
Los Angeles was a discrete topological space, made up of equidistant
points. Any two points chosen at random are almost a constant distance
apart in driving time, since it is time-consuming to get on and off the
freeways, although driving on them is extremely fast (Ulam, 1962, page 174).
This tongue-in-cheek mathematical description, that all points in the city
seem almost the same distance from each other, expresses admirably the
apparently amorphous nature of the city's urban structure, and its
excellent overall accessibility by automobile.

Yet, far from lacking in order, this immense urban structure of Los
Angeles is an authentic language, revealing the true nature of the American
city through its signs and its contradictions (Horkheimer and Adorno,
1972, pages 120–121):

"Even now, the older houses just outside the concrete city center look
like slums, and the new bungalows on the outskirts are at one with the
flimsy structures of world fairs in their praise of technical progress and
their built-in demand to be discarded after a short while like empty
food cans. Yet the city housing projects designed to perpetuate the
individual as a supposedly independent unit in a small hygenic dwelling
make him all the more subservient to his adversary—the absolute power
of capitalism. Because the inhabitants, as producers and as consumers,
are drawn into the center in search of work and pleasure, all the living
units crystallize into well-organized complexes."

Modes of change

The purpose of this chapter is to study change in its successive *steps*, making spatial segregation among socioprofessional groups more clearly perceptible; to analyze the various *types* of change through the global treatment of a data matrix with the help of three-way factor analysis; and finally to exhibit change in the properties of the urban space of Los Angeles.

6.1 Change in human relations

The evolution of human relations is inscribed in space, particularly in the case of social segregation. Some social groups tend to live together in the same blocks, while they deliberately shun other groups. Segregation changes over time, largely because people move frequently (almost every two years in Los Angeles) and because of repeated alterations in their social position. Relationships in social space thus form a dynamic equilibrium. Space viscosity (resistance to moving and relocating mechanisms) is low except in the case of minority groups. It is thus legitimate to assume that spatial relationships observed at a given time correctly express social links among professional groups.

6.1.1 Residential mobility

Recent and earlier data on household mobility through urban space are wanting, but the approximate volume of movement can be estimated from the successive censuses. From 1950 onward mobility has been recorded superficially. There were no data at all, however, in 1940. Time lags are not comparable: in 1950, people were asked about their residence one year before (in 1949), whereas in 1960 and 1970 the question concerned their address five years earlier. Data can be compared only between 1960 and 1970. Since mobility is important, some part of movement is lost when it is recorded at a five-year interval covering, on average, two different residences; and mobility at the beginning of each census period is hopelessly lost. In spite of these weaknesses, some conclusions can be drawn (table 6.1). Of the households in 1950, 25% had moved during the twelve preceding months, a surprisingly high proportion in comparison with European cities. Percentages recorded in 1960 and 1970 are very similar, but differences are still significant (mobility has been estimated from samples: 25% of households in 1960, only 15% in 1970). Many households during the latter decade had left the city center (6% approximately), and in smaller numbers the periphery (1%), to live in the city. The proportion of families coming from other states in the Union or from abroad to live in Los Angeles increased.

The relationships between center and periphery seems to have changed during the late 1950s. Previously, traditional flows originated outside

California and were directed toward the city center, and then from this center to the periphery, reproducing faithfully the Burgess model of urban growth (Park et al, 1925). In 1958–1959, however, flows were very different (Mittelbach, 1963, pages 26–27). New migrants preferred to settle down in suburban communities, whereas families living in the city center may have moved, but tended to stay in the city. In the whole SMSA between 1958 and 1960, 60000 households left the center for the periphery, but 66000 others moved in the opposite direction—the centripetal flow was slightly larger. This was a momentous new trend, contradicting traditional ideas on urban growth and confirming observations made in preceding chapters. The phenomenon received much attention in the early 1970s (cf. *Newsweek*, March 15, 1972), but started much earlier, before 1960.

These movements are related closely to economic conditions and to their social consequences. Almost all migrants moved into more expensive housing: only 25% paid a lower rent after moving; 10% bought a house cheaper than the one they had before. There is not enough information on the way the regional economy influences mobility. Between 1958 and 1959, however, as the economy was turning from expansion into recession, 33% of households moved, compared with a proportion of 38% between 1955 and 1958 when the economy was booming—a link is thus likely.

Families who lived outside Los Angeles and settled down in the city center were mainly coming from the big cities (68% of them, although only 63% of the whole US population live in these large cities). Actually, since the end of the 19th century, Los Angeles has attracted more city dwellers than rural families.

For those who move within the city, the choice of a new place of residence follows quite definite rules. Clark has suggested (personal

Table 6.1. Patterns of change of residence in Los Angeles, 1950–1970.

Nature of move	Moves between			Difference 1960–1970	
	1949–1950 (%)	1955–1960[a] (%)	1965–1970[b] (%)	d (%)	s_d
No move	1558209 (75.9)	803328 (40.6)	993541 (41.0)	0.04	0.168
From LA Downtown		553056 (27.9)	537124 (22.2)	−5.70	0.190
From LA outside Downtown	386905 (18.8)	240991 (12.2)	293162 (12.1)	−0.10	0.205
From outside LA, in the USA		317809 (16.1)	441435 (18.2)	2.10	0.199
Abroad	108715 (5.3)	63653 (6.4)	156267	3.20	0.212
Total	2053829	1978837	2421529		

[a] Survey at 25%.   [b] Survey at 15%. s_d standard deviation.

communication) that his studies indicate that families seem to select their successive residences within a narrow sector limited by two straight lines converging on the city center; distances to this center change much more than the general orientation. People would choose according to their knowledge of the city (Lynch, 1971), and this they acquire mainly by driving to their job in the CBD along the freeways. Thus any move of residence would tend to be along the direction of the main transportation axes. Such mechanisms would correspond quite well to the processes described by Hoyt (1939; 1964); families move within a sector towards the periphery in order to find larger and more modern dwellings. On the other hand, the traditional interpretation of the sectorial pattern would not hold as well: the movement of people looking for a better home would certainly not produce consistent social heterogeneity within a sector, with the social groups organized in rings.

6.1.2 Social segregation: the successive steps

Social segregation is defined not only between two groups, but necessarily among all groups: a person cannot live among others without assimilating their prejudices and preferences. In this way, social groups appear as points moving through time in 'social space', where social segregation and residential contacts can be represented as distances and arrows on a map.

The coresidence of two different groups in the same census tract can be measured by a simple coefficient of linear correlation (order zero) between the groups. The lower half of table 6.2 shows these coefficients for the four successive decades. Only the seven main social groups have been used. Correlations divide them into two main sets: Professionals, Managers, and Clerks, on the one hand, and Operatives, Service workers, and Laborers on the other. Correlations which express the degree of coresidence between two categories are not very strong but they clearly show a pattern—they are always positive within each set, and always negative between categories included in different sets. In other words, the two sets avoid each other carefully although the groups within each of them mix quite freely in the same tracts. Craftsmen occupy a peculiar position separated from both sets, which expresses the uncomfortable social position they are in.

The linear correlation coefficient measures the raw relationship between groups, that is, their overall tendency to reside together. It does not represent, however, the bilateral relationship between any two groups. For example, the Professional and Manager categories do live alongside each other; but is it because they feel themselves alike and choose to do so, or is it that they share the same prejudices against all other groups, and in this way are forced to live with each other in order to avoid mixing with common 'undesirables'? In other words, do they live in the same tracts because they mix freely together, or because they both wish to avoid the same other groups? Partial correlation between the two groups, while holding constant the five other groups, answers this question. Spatial relationships between two groups then appear as if the other groups were evenly distributed through the whole city, and their relative influence is thus eliminated.

The order 5 partial correlations are indicated in the upper half of table 6.2. Most differ from −1 because the percentages of the seven social groups do not form a closed set (in general, they do not sum to 100%). Several small groups, like transport equipment operatives, private household workers, and various categories of farm workers, have not been

Table 6.2. Correlations between socioprofessional groups in Los Angeles, 1940-1970. (Entries correspond vertically to 1940, 1950, 1960, and 1970.)

		P	M	CS	C	O	SW	L
				Order 5, partial correlations, after holding constant the five other categories				
	P		−1.000	−1.000	−1.000	−1.000	−1.000	−1.000
			−0.776	−0.776	−0.832	−0.888	−0.710	−0.708
			−0.863	−0.638	−0.832	−0.875	−0.888	−0.753
			−0.508	−0.517	−0.620	−0.638	−0.221	−0.241
	M	0.502		−1.000	−1.000	−1.000	−1.000	−1.000
		0.599		−0.774	−0.888	−0.893	−0.932	−0.811
		0.599		−0.702	−0.826	−0.917	−0.890	−0.825
		0.707		−0.484	−0.759	−0.590	−0.552	−0.550
	CS	0.525	0.402		−1.000	−1.000	−1.000	−1.000
		0.398	0.273		−0.632	−0.849	−0.762	−0.709
		0.525	0.565		−0.651	−0.823	−0.761	−0.735
		0.571	0.555		−0.288	−0.558	−0.388	−0.345
	C	−0.543	−0.501	−0.340		−1.000	−1.000	−1.000
		0.421	0.576	0.466		−0.859	−0.814	−0.870
		−0.369	−0.390	−0.288		−0.771	−0.884	−0.808
		−0.503	−0.468	−0.349		−0.600	−0.133	−0.659
	O	−0.729	−0.657	−0.626	0.662		−1.000	−1.000
		−0.561	−0.416	−0.293	−0.242		−0.831	−0.822
		−0.773	−0.748	−0.812	0.383		−0.869	−0.877
		−0.793	−0.689	−0.791	0.481		−0.074	−0.480
	SW	−0.211	−0.439	−0.348	−0.273	0.019		−1.000
		−0.735	−0.696	−0.672	−0.725	0.412		−0.821
		−0.521	−0.538	−0.532	−0.168	0.379		−0.855
		−0.502	−0.560	−0.507	−0.084	0.256		−0.318
	L	−0.458	−0.089	−0.697	−0.020	0.226	0.145	
		−0.447	−0.542	−0.426	−0.508	−0.151	0.388	
		−0.650	−0.567	−0.732	−0.048	0.697	0.597	
		−0.650	−0.572	−0.613	0.154	0.506	0.522	

Order zero, simple correlations (left margin label applies to lower-left half of the matrix)

P	Professionals		O	Operatives
M	Managers		SW	Service workers
CS	Clerks and Salesworkers		L	Laborers
C	Craftsmen			

analyzed, but the relative importance (%) of each of the seven categories has been computed in relation to the total active population in each census tract. These groups that were left aside were very small in 1940, which explains that order 5 correlations for this census year are practically equal to -1. Their size, however, has slowly increased with time.

The partial correlations are all negative: all groups tend to avoid all other groups. Coresidence is less a proof of similarity in taste and feelings, than the expression of a still stronger distaste towards other groups. This intergroup aloofness, which was very pronounced in 1940, remained quite important during the following years, but generally decreased in 1970. At that point relationships change: Professionals come closer to Service workers and Laborers, while Managers remain separated from them. Service workers and Operatives mix together quite often, as do Laborers. This complex evolution can be mapped, thanks to the definition of social distance between groups as based on residential segregation.

A correlation coefficient is not a distance in the precise mathematical meaning of the term (the triangular inequality does not hold, for instance, and it can take negative values). Other measures of social distances have been used (Duncan et al, 1961), but it is more convenient here to transform the coefficient r in the following way: let d_{ab} be the social distance separating two groups a and b computed as

$$d_{ab} = \cos^{-1} r_{ab} .$$

The social distance is thus measured along the perimeter of the trigonometric circle. Then, from the distance table computed in this way, social 'space', where the groups are represented in the way they intermix or segregate, can be recovered through Multi-Dimensional Scaling (MDS): a set of coordinates is estimated for each point (each social group) such that distances observed between these points correspond monotonically to the distances computed above (Torgerson, 1958; Shepard, 1962). Any number of points, n, will fit perfectly in an $(n-1)$-dimensional space, but the geometric configuration obtained from MDS can be interpreted easily only if it has few dimensions. So, the observed cluster of points must be embedded into spaces of increasingly fewer dimensions. Monotonic correspondence between the observed set of distances and the distances computed within those spaces usually becomes less and less satisfactory. This lack of fit is measured by the *stress*, which should be as small as possible.

All social groups, in this case, can be located on a plane with a low stress (table 6.3), except in 1940 where a three-dimensional space would be more satisfactory.

It is illuminating to compare the four clusters of points corresponding to the four censuses, that is to study the relative movements of the social groups over the thirty years. For that purpose, the three configurations obtained in 1940, 1950, and 1960 have been rotated and projected onto the 1970 cluster chosen as the target. This *rotation to congruence* has been described elsewhere (Marchand, 1974). The four configurations are then comparable and may be mapped together (figure 6.1). Arrows linking the various positions of each social group over thirty years show their evolving relationships as far as residential segregation is concerned. At each of the four census years, the seven groups form a cluster the extent of which has been indicated in order to show its general form.

In 1940 and 1960, the main axis is vertical and the two clusters coincide very closely: the degree of segregation is virtually the same (figure 6.1). Slight differences involve Operatives and Laborers, whose residences tend to mix more often, and the same holds for Professionals and Managers. Craftsmen and Service workers live very much on their own, away from other groups and separated from one another as well.

Circumstances changed by 1950: the cluster keeps the same general form but has shrunk in a remarkable way. War and the housing crisis had merged the different professional groups so strongly that segregation has diminished out of necessity. People took up residence wherever they could rather than where they wished. The pattern of segregation reappears in 1960, practically as it was twenty years before.

Table 6.3. Recovering social space through multidimensional scaling (from zero-order correlations).

Year	Stress (%) for minimal dimension	
	2	3
1970	0.4	0
1960	1.0	0
1950	1.0	0
1940	14.7	3.3

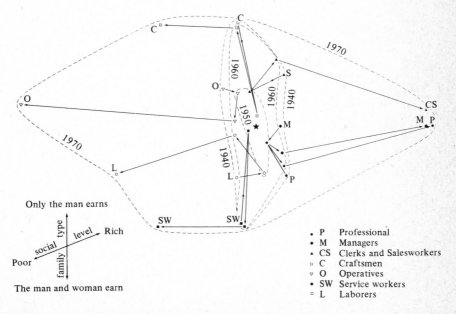

Figure 6.1. Los Angeles: expansion and contraction of social space (1940–1970).

Segregation took on a completely different form in 1970: rich families had definitely moved away from the poor. Separation between high-income and low-income categories became paramount. Not since the 1930s had segregation based on income been so powerful and so effective. This is all the more striking since, in the meanwhile, the black population had spread throughout the city and their diffusion is likely to have increased professional segregation by separating rich Blacks from poor Blacks. No less remarkable is the fact that the relative movements of social groups over time do not intersect, except when the war economy forced all groups to live more closely together. Spatial segregation is very stable; its intensity has changed, but not its form.

Since all configurations (except maybe those of 1940) are inscribed in a plane, they can be explained with two components or axes which, when combined, represent the segregation process. After correlating and analyzing characteristic variables for each professional group, two discriminant axes can be identified:

(1) Family type and structure, conditioned by the woman's role in the family: among the Craftsmen (at one extremity of the cluster) women as a rule do not work; whereas among Service workers (at the other extremity), female headed families with the women working form most of the group.

(2) Social level, with the classic distinction between the rich and the poor. This horizontal axis is slightly oblique in relation to the first one (Service workers and Laborers have the lowest incomes of all groups), which should come as no surprise: family structure (the woman's role in the family) and socioeconomic status are correlated.

Interestingly enough, both axes reproduce the main factorial dimensions exhibited by the many factorial analyses undertaken by Brian Berry and his students on American cities: socioeconomic status and family cycle (cf. several of the Research Papers published by the Department of Geography, University of Chicago). The method used here, however, is completely different and relies only on a few variables measuring the socioprofessional structure of the population.

A complete break occurred in spatial relationships between the 1970 period and the preceding ones. Family structure and the woman's role had been the main factors in separating professional groups for more than two decades. In 1970, level of income supplanted them and played by far the most important role. One explanation could be the general prosperity experienced by the United States, and particularly by Southern California, since the mid-1950s. This contributed, as seen above, to increasing rather than to decreasing social segregation. Figure 6.1 would be strong evidence against the social policy of the Democratic governments since John F Kennedy: it shows they did not, at least in Los Angeles, alleviate social segregation and could not even stem its increase. Another likely reason also plays a role: migration toward the periphery by upper-middle-class families who lived close to the center probably reinforced social homogeneity in the plain. The contrast, between the lower-middle-class neighborhoods in the plain and the rich western districts (from Santa Monica to Hollywood) which did not change, has necessarily increased.

The interpretation of the two axes defining the plane upon which social space is mapped is corroborated by the very form of the cluster of points in 1950: its vertical axis has rotated slightly to the left (a rotation which disappears again in 1960). Opposition between high and low incomes vanishes almost completely, which is typical of a wartime situation; while disparities between family structure remain as the only (weak) discriminating factor. It was also typical of the war period that many more women worked as laborers. In 1950, their position L still appears at the lower extremity of the cluster and only comes back to its intermediary position in 1960, as it was previously in 1940.

In 1940, the seven groups fit into a three-dimensional space, which indicates a more complex degree of social segregation: relationships tend to break down into pairs of opposites. These relationships become less complex as time passes, and since Professionals, Managers, and Clerks (groups P, M, and CS) become closer, relationships tend to simplify into a clearcut opposition between well-to-do white-collar districts and poorer blue-collar neighborhoods.

There is no point in trying to reconstruct the geometry of social space for each pair of groups (partial correlations of order 5: table 6.2, upper triangular matrix). In such cases, the relationships are pairwise and space is always one-dimensional. As distances are all equal in 1940 and maximal (table 6.4), it is particularly convenient to choose this value as the unit to express relatively all social distances in the following years. They are then measured between zero and one, and are all comparable.

Professionals consistently stay equally distanced from Managers and Clerks. This does not show up so well in the simple correlation coefficients because Managers tend to mix more freely with Clerks. The main segregation here is rather between Professionals and the two other groups.

Table 6.4. Social distances between pairs of categories (after holding constant the five others).

	1940	1950	1960	1970
Professionals with				
Clerks	1.000	0.784	0.720	0.673
Service workers	1.000	0.751	0.848	0.571
Managers	1.000	0.783	0.831	0.670
Service workers with				
Craftsmen	1.000	0.803	0.845	0.542
Operatives	1.000	0.812	0.835	0.524

More remarkable still are the relations between Service workers on the one hand, and Operatives and Craftsmen on the other. Service workers tend to shun districts where Craftsmen live (the simple correlation coefficients are negative) and to reside with Operatives. Pairwise relationships, however, are different. When the distorting influences of other groups are removed, Service workers are equally likely to live with both groups, but Craftsmen can move into wealthy neighborhoods more easily than can Operatives, which indirectly influences their relationship with Service workers.

6.2 Types of change through a global analysis

The preceding analyses of change are based on the same principle: to compare two sets of relationships or two spatial distributions at different moments, and to deduce change from the differences between those two points in time. These are not authentic diachronic analyses, but actually a juxtaposition of different synchronic analyses, similar to inferring change by comparing instant pictures. Such a comparative method has much to recommend it: it is quite simple, convenient, and widely used, so much so that it remains at the very core of all studies of change in the field of urbanism.

There are, however, two important drawbacks. The method depicts change quite faithfully only if time is divided into enough fixed points, that is, if one can use a number of observations regularly distributed through time. This is the basic requirement of Time Series Analysis, which needs at least a hundred observation points. With censuses conducted every ten years, this is impossible in urban studies.

It is spurious to compare different factor analyses of different censuses, although it has often been done: the set of eigenvectors forming the new vectorial basis on which observations are projected differs from one analysis to another. Such comparison amounts to comparing measures made on different bases when the relationship between those bases is not known. Hence comparing loadings from different analyses is a spurious exercise.

The main defect is still the need to break continuous time into discrete fragments. One would like to include temporal succession in the analysis, as well as the locations and variables. This leads to the *simultaneous* analysis of three sets of categories which is possible in three-way factor analysis. Introducing time as a supplementary variable has been attempted by Cattell under the name of the P technique (Cattell, 1952), in order to analyze change during psychological tests. For psychologists, Ledyard Tucker has proposed a mathematical method and various algorithms for three-way factor analysis (Tucker, 1963; 1964; 1965; and particularly 1966; see also Levin, 1965). The relationships between three-way factor analysis and multidimensional scaling are important (Tucker, 1972).

In practise this method has not previously been used by geographers or urban planners [except by Cant (1971) who falls back into traditional two-way factor analysis]. Only an outline of the approach is given here; the method is developed, with the computational algorithm, in appendix A.

Traditional factor analysis is used with a matrix in which variables are entered against locations (census tracts). The entries are data taken from a particular census. The four censuses (1940, 1950, 1960, and 1970) produce four matrices in which the entries are observations made on the same variables, at the same locations, but at different times. Put together, these four matrices form the cubic (or rather parallelepipedic) matrix we want to analyze.

The method consists of unfolding the data cube in three different ways:
(1) variables are compared against both time and location—that is, every variable is analyzed as it changes throughout the city over the thirty-year period;
(2) locations are considered against variables and time—each census tract is studied as all its characteristics change over time;
(3) time periods are related to the set of all variables measured over the whole city, emphasizing different types of change.

The final result consists of two different parts. On one hand, three classical principal component analyses organize the data into homogeneous types: *variables* (population and housing) are grouped, on the components or factors of the first analysis, into a few homogeneous 'types of variables' (matrix **P**); *locations* (census tracts), at the end of the second analysis, into 'types of districts' or of neighborhoods (matrix **A**); and the third analysis groups the *time periods* (the four census years) into 'types of periods' (matrix **Q**). By itself, this grouping into homogeneous types is very useful: it shows the links between a mode (say, variables) and the combination of the two other modes (for example, all tracts at all times).

On the other hand, a small cubic matrix is computed. Its entries are *not* correlation coefficients, but *weights* linking the three initial component analyses. This cubic matrix, called **G**, is the most original part of the method.

The computer program that was written calls upon subroutine EISPACK to extract eigenvalues and eigenvectors during the various component analyses necessitated by the method. This package happens to store eigenvectors in the order of increasing eigenvalues. For the sake of simplicity, this order has been kept here, although it is contrary to usual practice. No rotation has been made during this three-way factor analysis.

6.2.1 Population and housing evolution: the main types
Nine variables (all percentages) have been chosen to describe changes in population and housing, but they are not closed (they do not sum to 100%): Whites, Blacks, Young, Old, Owner-occupied dwellings, Renter-occupied dwellings, Vacant dwellings for sale and rent, Single-dwelling

units, Five-and-more dwelling units. Choice has been limited by a
technical constraint. Unfolding the cubic data-matrix leads to successive
standardizations of data by variables, by locations, and by time periods.
All data must be expressed in the same unit: for instance, one of the
unfoldings will compute the mean of all variables measured at four time
periods in each census tract. This is a very troublesome constraint of the
technique, and in this case the difficulty has been overcome by choosing,
from among available data, only those variables expressed as percentages,
that is as ratios, or pure scalars independent of any unit. Clearly, there is
no perfect solution to this conceptual problem of how change be compared
among variables of a different nature.

Types of variables All the factors (that is, the types) extracted during
this three-way factor analysis are labelled PH (for Population and Housing)
with the identification of the type (V for variables, P for periods, D for
districts or census tracts) and the number of the factor.

Combining all tracts at all times groups the nine original variables into
three main types (table 6.5). The main factor (PH-V3) represents the
overall evolution of the city. It accounts for 80% of the total variance;
all loadings are high except for the percentage of Blacks ($r^2 = 0.12$ only).
The loadings are all of the same sign because the variables have not been
standardized and are all positive (percentages). This predominant factor
(the cluster of points is almost one-dimensional, virtually along a straight
line) represents the *overall stability of the urban structure over time*.
Only two phenomena break this general continuity: the development of
apartments, rapidly altering a city made up of single houses; and, more
important still, the widespread and regular diffusion of black families
throughout the city.

Table 6.5. Population and housing: loadings of 'types of variables' (matrix **P**).

Original variable	Type of variable (factor)		
	PH-V1	PH-V2	PH-V3
Whites	0.520	−0.245	−0.994
Blacks	−0.430	0.500	−0.346
Young	0.409	0.028	−0.977
Old	0.375	−0.351	−0.980
Owner-occupied	0.555	0.127	−0.951
Renter-occupied	0.319	−0.304	−0.981
Vacant	0.328	−0.350	−0.975
Houses	0.500	0.131	−0.954
Apartments	0.184	−0.633	−0.851
Eigenvalue	179.21	255.07	1964.27
Percentage of variance	7.3	10.5	80.5

Factor PH-V2 singles out Blacks ($r^2 = 0.25$) and their move away from apartments (negative loading; $r^2 = 0.40$). The weak loading for Houses is due to the high percentage of them in almost all tracts during most periods. The Blacks are mainly adult and young (Old: $r = -0.351$). This change is consistent with a decrease in housing vacancies. In summary, there is a drift of young black families toward single-house homes with a high density of occupation. It is not the creation of a ghetto, but rather the progress by the black middle-class out of the ghetto.

A completely different profile is summarized from factor PH-V1: white families increasingly segregate themselves from the Blacks and move into houses they own. These Whites are disparate: old people or young families with children. They constitute a white bourgeoisie which has settled down in Los Angeles, avoiding the black districts (the proportion of Blacks decreases) to choose low-density tracts.

With a remarkable economy of means, the main characteristics of change in Los Angeles are thus indicated and weighted: the overwhelming stability of population and housing; the important diffusion of Blacks; and the development, away from the Blacks, of single-house neighborhoods for Whites. The two first phenomena account for more than 90% of the total information.

Types of periods The analysis of the nine variables measured for 309 tracts shows two main types of change (table 6.6). The principal contrast separates 1970 from the three other periods, particularly from 1950 and 1960. This dichotomy did not appear clearly in the preceding analysis, when pairs of censuses were compared.

The year 1970 radically distinguished itself from the others only in social space (figure 6.1). Here again, there is a definite break in the overall evolution of the variables representing population and housing factor (factor PH-P2, with 93% of the variance).

Factor PH-P1, though of much less importance, divides this evolution into two halves: 1940 and 1950 on the one hand, 1960 and 1970 on the other. But even on this factor, 1970 stands out from the second group and is poorly related to 1960.

Table 6.6. Population and housing: loadings of 'types of period' (matrix **Q**).

Period	Type of period (factor)	
	PH-P1	PH-P2
1940	0.967	−0.527
1950	0.892	−0.694
1960	−0.443	−0.706
1970	−0.980	0.126
Eigenvalue	138.51	2317.33
Percentage of variance	5.6	93.2

Types of districts By combining nine variables measured over four periods, the **S** matrix groups all census tracts into five different types of district (table 6.7). The general model breaks down each observation into a product (1) of its loadings on the three main axes, and (2) of the coefficient corresponding to those three axes in matrix **G** (figure 6.2). From the way **S** has been computed, interpretation must take into account the entries in the small cubic matrix **G**, and particularly their sign.

Table 6.7. Population and housing—loadings of 'types of districts' (matrix **S**).

Type of variable	Type of period	Type of district				
		PH-D1	PH-D2	PH-D3	PH-D4	PH-D5
PH-V1	PH-P1	−0.007	−0.156	−0.028	0.258	0.966
PH-V1	PH-P2	−0.023	0.178	0.514	0.615	−0.696
PH-V2	PH-P1	0.190	0.265	−0.198	−0.741	−0.600
PH-V2	PH-P2	−0.001	−0.036	0.251	−0.235	−0.972
PH-V3	PH-P1	−0.022	0.156	0.047	−0.236	−0.971
PH-V3	PH-P2	−0.046	−0.048	−0.168	−0.017	0.998
Eigenvalue		10.93	28.87	56.98	88.65	543.02
Percentage of variance		1.5	4.0	7.8	12.2	74.5

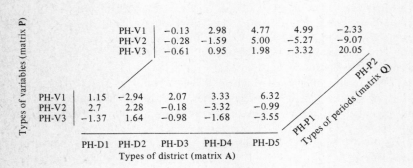

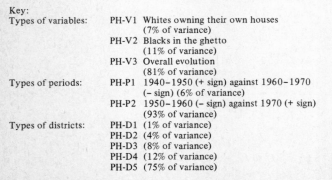

Key:

Types of variables: PH-V1 Whites owning their own houses
                                      (7% of variance)
                        PH-V2 Blacks in the ghetto
                                      (11% of variance)
                        PH-V3 Overall evolution
                                      (81% of variance)

Types of periods: PH-P1 1940–1950 (+ sign) against 1960–1970
                                      (− sign) (6% of variance)
                        PH-P2 1950–1960 (− sign) against 1970 (+ sign)
                                      (93% of variance)

Types of districts: PH-D1 (1% of variance)
                        PH-D2 (4% of variance)
                        PH-D3 (8% of variance)
                        PH-D4 (12% of variance)
                        PH-D5 (75% of variance)

Figure 6.2. Population and housing core-matrix **G**.

Table 6.8. Interpretation of 'type of district'.

Type of variable (factors from table 6.5)	Type of period (factors from table 6.6)	PH-D1	PH-D2	PH-D4	PH-D5
PH-V1 Development of houses inhabited by Whites (+)	PH-P1 (+) 1940–50 (−) 1970		(+) 1940–50 (−) 1970		(+) 1940–50 (−) 1970
	PH-P2 (−) 1950–60 (+) 1970		(−) 1950–60 (+) 1970	(−) 1950–60 (+) 1970	(−) 1950–60 (+) 1970
PH-V2 Drift of Blacks toward one-dwelling districts (+)	PH-P1 (+) 1940–50 (−) 1970	(+) 1940–50 (−) 1970	(+) 1940–50 (−) 1970	(+) 1940–50 (−) 1970	(+) 1940–50 (−) 1970
	PH-P2 (−) 1950–60 (+) 1970				(−) 1950–60 (+) 1970
PH-V3 Overall evolution: stability of urban structure (−)	PH-P1 (+) 1940–50 (−) 1970		(−) 1940–50 (+) 1970		(−) 1940–50 (+) 1970
	PH-P2 (−) 1950–60 (+) 1970				(+) 1950–60 (−) 1970

Type of district and the core-matrix **G**

		PH-D1	PH-D2	PH-D4	PH-D5
PH-V1 Development of houses inhabited by Whites (+)	PH-P1 (+) 1940–50 (−) 1970		−2.9 (2.4%)		6.3 (93%)
	PH-P2 (−) 1950–60 (+) 1970		3.0 (3.2%)	5.0 (37.8%)	−2.3 (48%)
PH-V2 Drift of Blacks toward one-dwelling districts (+)	PH-P1 (+) 1940–50 (−) 1970	2.7 (3.6%)	2.3 (7%)	−3.3 (55%)	−1.0 (36%)
	PH-P2 (−) 1950–60 (+) 1970				−9.0 (94%)
PH-V3 Overall evolution: stability of urban structure (−)	PH-P1 (+) 1940–50 (−) 1970		1.6 (2.4%)		−3.6 (94%)
	PH-P2 (−) 1950–60 (+) 1970				20.0 (99%)

In the bottom half of the table, the entry in the core-matrix **G** is indicated with its sign. The square of the corresponding loading is in parenthesis.

Notes. The signs in brackets identify the directions on the factors (or components); their combination is discussed on page 182.
'Type of district' PH-D3 is strongly correlated with type PH-D5 and has not been presented in this table; it is discussed, however, on page 186.

The general procedure is presented in appendix A. Only a few hints will be given here. The reader who is not interested in technical details might wish to jump to the next paragraph.

All variables, being percentages, are positive. The directions of axes are arbitrary. Loadings on these axes have been mapped, so it is necessary to identify these directions in order to interpret the maps: this is made possible through table 6.8, where signs of the four factors are combined. Consider, for instance, figure 6.3 representing districts of type PH-D4. Its positive (or negative) values correspond to certain types of periods and variables. The sign of a score (the value attached to a tract and mapped) is obtained by taking the algebraic product of four signs (of the variable-type, of the period-type, of the correlation between district-type and variable-type, and finally, of the coefficient g in the core-matrix $\mathbf{G}$). This actually gives the product indicated in the general model:

$$x_{ijk} = \sum_m \sum_p \sum_q a_{im} b_{jp} c_{kq} g_{mpq} \ .$$

Table 6.8 indicates the interpretation for each group of districts and each variable-type, that is to which period-type the positive and negative values correspond. Type PH-D3 districts, which are the negative reflection of type PH-D5 districts ($r = -0.9$), have not been interpreted.

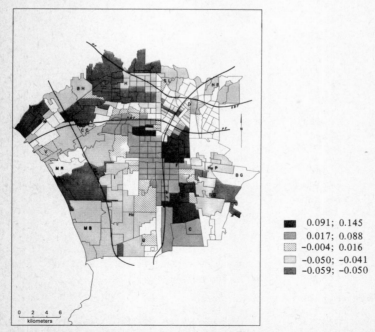

■	0.091; 0.145
▨	0.017; 0.088
▨	−0.004; 0.016
□	−0.050; −0.041
■	−0.059; −0.050

Figure 6.3. Los Angeles: three-way factor analysis of population and housing for districts of type PH-D4 grouping, 1940–1970.

The type PH-D5 grouping of census tracts typifies the general evolution of Los Angeles over the thirty years. It accounts for three-quarters of the information. The city center stands in stark contrast to the concentric rings which extend further outward toward the south and the southeast (figure 6.4). Table 6.8 shows how change has regularly alternated: the axes representing both types of periods switch their direction—1970, for instance, first appears at the positive and then at the negative extremity of the axis. Actually this fluctuation proves the extreme stability of the city structure since no period plays a more important role than the others.

In the short term there is a centrifugal movement of the Blacks (PH-V2) between the 1950–1960 period, and the 1970 one. Another long-term and weaker movement ($r^2 = 0.36$) is centripetal, during the period 1940–1950 and 1970. Movements in the white community are a reflection of movements by the Blacks, but the emphasis is different. The long-term centripetal drift is more important (93%), while movement toward the periphery appears as secondary (48%).

Figure 6.4 summarizes most of the information discussed in this book, and several important points emerge from such an informative map:

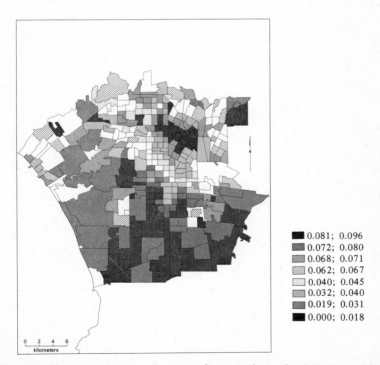

0.081; 0.096
0.072; 0.080
0.068; 0.071
0.062; 0.067
0.040; 0.045
0.032; 0.040
0.019; 0.031
0.000; 0.018

0 2 4 6
kilometers

Figure 6.4. Los Angeles: three-way factor analysis of population and housing for districts of type PH-D5 grouping, 1940–1970.

First The extreme regularity of spatial patterns: the transition from the periphery (with the highest scores) to the city core (with the lowest) is very slow and contains many nuances. If a surface were adjusted to these scores, it would offer continuous and regular slope, with a very smooth appearance. This is clear evidence of the existence of strong mechanisms which have controlled spatial order in Los Angeles over the thirty years, and of the predominance of the concentric pattern. This result has been obtained after an involved mathematical manipulation of the data: two principal component analyses combined through a cubic core-matrix produced a set of 309 scores, that were interpreted after manipulating four different signs.

Second The basic urban pattern, concentrating three-quarters of the information given by nine variables over thirty years, is *concentric*, with very smooth variations when one goes away from the city center. Two phenomena alter it slightly: on the one hand, the appearance of early secondary urban centers, particularly in Hollywood but also along Wilshire Blvd and Santa Monica Blvd, with the development of linear business zones; and on the other, the widening of concentric circles toward the south, in the direction of Long Beach.

The regularity of this general development is altered along the oldest axes of the city: to the west along the piedmont and toward the south and the ocean. The city center has played a far more important role in city growth than is usually acknowledged. It has structured, polarized, and determined its spread, as in more classical and less extended cities. It should not be forgotten that only population and housing variables are taken into account here, and this is not to deny the particular importance, in Los Angeles more than in any other North American city, of secondary centers away from the CBD in providing jobs, attracting shoppers, and breaking or complicating the spatial pattern of the city. A multinuclei model might well fit Los Angeles, where productive functions are concerned. When it comes to people and their homes, however, most of the city's evolution has followed a strongly structured, closely knit concentric pattern.

Third This pattern is dynamic. Its global form is influenced by differences in the speed with which successive rings spread out or in. Toward the south, urbanization, spreading into a homogeneous plain, has progressed particularly fast, so that the successive rings of similar tracts are very wide. Conversely, to the west, the urbanization wave has bumped into the Santa Monica mountains. Districts extending from the sea to Beverly Hills and Hollywood were frozen in position quite early. They have not followed the subsequent evolution of the other parts of the ring they were a part of; in figure 6.3 they appear as the exceptions.

The other types of district (PH-D4, PH-D2, and PH-D1) exemplify geographic peculiarities in the urban evolution; they are also exceptions to the general pattern represented in figure 6.4.

The type PH-D4 pattern sums up the dispersion of Blacks throughout
the city. Two main types of moves appear from the entries in table 6.8:
(1) The drift of Blacks (type PH-V2 variable) from the center to the
periphery in a long-term movement—1940–1950 is contrasted to 1970.
(2) In the short term, that is, in a type PH-P2 evolution from 1950–1960
to 1970, a movement of Whites from the periphery to the center (figure 6.3),
but of less importance than the black drift (38% instead of 55%). Two
causes are combined here: since Blacks and Whites are practically
complementary (they sum almost to 100%), growth in one appears as
decrease in the other. These movements represent relative differences
rather than flows in absolute numbers. On the other hand, Whites return
to the city center, particularly young unmarried adults, as Blacks leave it.

Districts fitting into this type PH-D4 category integrate two spatial
structures: a concentric one, shown above to be paramount, and a radial
pattern. A characteristically long sector goes from the center to the south,
toward Long Beach, along the Harbor Freeway; districts of the opposite
type (with positive scores) are spread out, conversely, along the shore, the
mountains to the northeast, along a line from Hollywood to Silver Lake,
and east from Highland Park to South Gate. In between lies a quite
regular line of tracts with almost zero scores, constituting the front of the
vast black diffusion zone.

Here again spatial patterns are extremely regular; the transition from
one type to another goes through very delicate nuances. Actually,
figure 6.3 depicts the complete diffusion of the black population over
thirty years and, in contrast, the opposite drift of the Whites. The successive
waves of diffusion coinciding with the four censuses are all integrated
together. The map represents their 'envelope' in the mathematical sense
of the term, that is a surface tangent to every one of the four successive
waves. The synthesis of these waves explains why the surfaces represented
on these maps are so smooth and polished.

The type PH-D2 grouping breaks the radial migration of Blacks into two
different phases (figure 6.5):
(1) A long-term (from 1940–1950 to 1970) movement by Blacks (7%)
and some Whites (2.4%) from central-eastern districts (between Downtown,
Florence, and Huntington Park, on both sides of the Pomona Freeway,
and from Watts toward the west, on the other side of the Harbor Freeway,
in the middle of Los Angeles).
(2) A short-term (1950–1960 to 1970) centripetal movement of the
white middle class living in detached houses.

These opposing movements actually correspond to three phenomena:
the relative diminution of Whites in the districts into which Blacks are
moving; the drift of Whites to the old city center, which is the inverse of
black extensions; and the drift of Whites, moving away from black
encroachment, from the immediate ring around the center into a second
one clearly visible on the map. The latter runs from Hollywood to Santa

Monica, then along the shore to Manhattan Beach and Gardenia, thence north to South Gate and Bell Garden.

In short, the type PH-D2 grouping breaks the great black migration mapped by type PH-D4 into its internal components: black families move out from the center to the first ring while white families move away to the second ring, or return in the opposite direction to the black flow, toward the city center.

There is little information left on axis PH-D1 (only 1.5%), once all the preceding phenomena have been accounted for. The corresponding pattern (figure 6.6) is meaningful, however. This contrasts a long-term movement (1940–1950 versus 1970) in districts where the population has changed slowly (Santa Monica, Inglewood, Watts, and Culver City) to those where the change has been sudden and strong as in Marina del Rey, Manhattan Beach, Gardenia, and Highland Park—all recently urbanized.

The type PH-D3 grouping is quite original[6]. It is strongly correlated with type PH-D5 (80.6% of the variance is common), and might be seen as

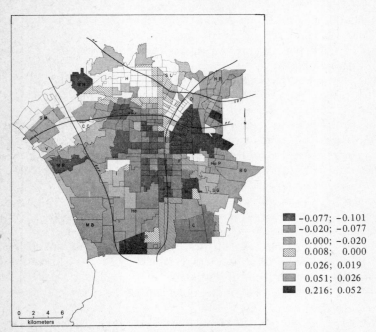

Figure 6.5. Los Angeles: three-way factor analysis of population and housing for districts of type PH-D2 grouping, 1940–1970.

[6] Axes PH-D3 and PH-D5 are not orthogonal. They are not eigenvectors as in principal component analysis. They have been obtained through a complicated calculation, combining two principal component analyses (of variables and of periods) with the core-matrix **G**. The algorithm used here, developed by Ledyard Tucker, is presented in appendix A.

an inverted image of PH-D5, but with some very interesting differences in emphasis. It concentrates on the centripetal moves of the white middle class between 1950–1960 and 1970, and provides new information. We observed in the type PH-D5 grouping a relative increase of Whites in the city center corresponding, naturally, to the centrifugal movement of the Blacks. This is the classical complementarity of quantities when measured by mutually exclusive percentages. It is a long-term change reflecting the uninterrupted spread of Blacks. Type PH-D3 grouping, however, isolates another fact: in contrasting past periods (1940, and particularly 1950–1960) with 1970, it exemplifies the increase in the white population of the city center in the latter period, that is, the very significant return of young professionals to Downtown.

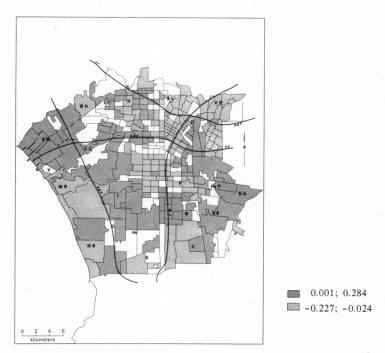

▨	0.001; 0.284
▢	−0.227; −0.024

Figure 6.6. Los Angeles: three-way factor analysis of population and housing for districts of type PH-D1 grouping, 1940–1970.

A case study: the evolution of Santa Monica The different groupings of Santa Monica census tracts obtained on the preceding maps clearly show the analytical power of three-way factor analysis. Let us try to recapitulate these results to produce a local synthesis.

Type PH-D5 grouping of districts contrasts the shore with the center, the old local Downtown to the recently urbanized periphery. At a limited scale, we observe the rough draft of a concentric pattern.

Black migration represented by type PH-D4 districts splits the town in two. The northern, typically white, half remained unaffected by such movements, and borders Pacific Palissades, one of the wealthiest districts on the shore. The southern half presents very low scores—almost zero—and exhibits no clear trend. It is a transitional district between Pacific Palissades, untouched by black migrations, and Venice, where their numbers have increased notably.

Type PH-D2 grouping distinguishes the arrival and departure zones of this black spread. Here again, Santa Monica is split between north and south, but in an opposite fashion. In the north the scores are zero because the blocks, almost exclusively white, do not play any particular role in the great process of ethnic change. Conversely, the southern half has higher scores as Whites from the central districts, moving away from the Blacks, come here in numbers to settle down.

Santa Monica is not subdivided by the type PH-D1 grouping. The contrasts between districts where ethnic changes have been small and those experiencing recent urbanization and racial change does not involve the town. The small neighboring town of Venice, however, is clearly split by the score values on this type PH-D1 axis. It is an old fishing harbor whose ethnic composition has changed very radically over time, with the beach, where hippie communes and different ethnic groups are mixed, and the inner, much more stable, part separated by just a few blocks as the transition between them.

6.2.2 The general evolution of professional categories

The same method as that described in section 6.2.1 and used to analyze population and housing has been used again with different data, namely the seven socioprofessional categories (SP), measured in percentages and in each census tract over thirty years. These categories have been grouped through three-way factor analysis into 'types of socioprofessional categories' (SP-C axes—see table 6.9). The four census periods are grouped, in the same way, into four types (SP-P axes—see table 6.10). Census tracts are

Table 6.9. Socioprofessional status—loading of categories (matrix **P**).

Categories	Factor SP-C5	Factor SP-C6
Professionals	0.605	−0.880
Managers	0.546	−0.908
Clerks	0.397	−0.972
Craftsmen	0.083	−0.976
Operatives	−0.233	−0.907
Service workers	−0.230	−0.872
Laborers	−0.484	−0.727
Eigenvalues	27.8	204.7
Percentage of variance	11	79

grouped into 'types of districts' (SP-D axes). In order to avoid confusion with the first analysis of population and housing data, the groupings (or types) obtained from this second analysis of socioprofessional data are labeled SP. The interpretation of the different types of grouping, with the help of the small core-matrix **G**, is indicated in table 6.11.

Table 6.10. Socioprofessional status—loadings of periods (matrix **Q**).

Periods	Factor			
	SP-P1	SP-P2	SP-P3	SP-P4
1940	−0.084	0.813	−0.575	−0.994
1950	0.016	0.113	0.994	0.487
1960	0.345	0.025	−0.938	−0.575
1970	−0.248	−0.587	−0.771	0.033
Eigenvalues	2.63	7.33	14.38	95.51
Percentage of variance	2.2	6.1	12.0	79.7

Table 6.11. Three-way analysis of socioprofessional categories: interpretation and mapping.

Type of socio-professional category, SP-C	Type of period, SP-P	Type of district, SP-D							
		SP-D3				SP-D5			
		(+)	(−)	g	s	(+)	(−)	g	s
SP-C6 Mostly middle class (79% of variance)	SP-P1 (2%)	1970	1960	−0.3	−0.2	1970	1960	−0.4	−0.96
	SP-P2 (6%)						1940	−1.8	−0.98
	SP-P3 (12%)					1960	1950	−2.4	−0.96
	SP-P4 (80%)					1940		1.3	0.97
SP-C5 White-collar groups WC (+) versus Blue-collar groups BC (−) (11%)	SP-P1 (2%)	BC 1970 WC 1970		0.2	0.2	WC 1960	BC 1970	0.2	0.87
	SP-P2 (6%)					WC 1940	BC 1940	−1.0	−0.70
	SP-P3 (12%)					WC 1950 BC 1960	WC 1960 BC 1950	−1.8	−0.73
	SP-4 (80%)					BC 1940	WC 1940	0.6	0.68
Symbols on figure 6.7:						hatching	dot screen		

White-collar groups: Proprietors, Managers, and Clerks
Blue-collar groups: Operatives, Service workers, and Laborers
g and s are corresponding entries in the **G** and the **S** matrices.

'Types of districts' are axes extracted by the analysis; their directions are arbitrary. In order to map these types and to give them a significant interpretation, it is necessary to identify these directions. This is done through the combination of four different signs (cf section 6.2.1). Consider type of district SP-D5. Census tracts with positive scores (SP-D5 +; represented on figure 6.7 with hatching) are contained mainly in 1940 (SP-P4: 80% of variance, sign −) blue-collar workers (SP-C5, sign −): these two (−) signs, combined with the g (+) and s (+) signs produce a (+) sign on the SP-D5 axis.

The seven categories are grouped into six types. Two of these (SP-C5 and SP-C6) account for 80% of the total variance (table 6.9). The other types will not be considered here. Type SP-C6 groups all the categories together, illustrating the strong stability of their distribution throughout the various tracts. Only Laborers, the least qualified and the poorest of all employed personnel, do not load very strongly on this axis. It is the middle class that forms the core of this group (Clerks and Craftsmen); the poorest (Laborers and Service workers) and the wealthiest (Professionals and Managers) separate slightly from it.

Type SP-C5 clearly contrasts both extremities of the social scale, with a very regular ordering of the categories in accordance with their social status.

These two types of social organization sum up society in Los Angeles: a very large middle class, including most groups, complicated by the secondary opposition between white-collar and blue-collar workers.

The evolution of the socioprofessional structure has taken three different aspects (table 6.10):

(a) An evolution in which 1940 plays the basic role (SP-P4) and which seems to have a cyclical form, the sign changing regularly between one census and another. The results single out the last period (1970), which remains independent (orthogonal) of all these fluctuations. Such cyclical trends constitute most of the change (80% of all variance). The very high loading ($r = -0.994$; $r^2 = 0.988$) for 1940 shows that the basic trait of the three decades has been that of very good stability.

(b) The originality of the social distribution in 1950 appears in factor SP-P3; this corroborates the remarks made while studying spatial segregation (see figure 6.1 and section 6.1.2).

(c) The importance of change over the thirty years appears in the contrast between 1940 and 1970; this last census again occupies an original position, away from the three others.

The three-way factor analysis of professional groups identifies two important types of neighborhood in the city (factors SP-D3 and SP-D5 in table 6.11).

Type SP-D5 presents the overall change in the population, and in the middle class in particular (figure 6.7). In 1940 they located mainly in a ring surrounding the city to the east and south. The change over the thirty years consists of an increased concentration in these districts and in a move away from the center-west (from the neighborhoods around Hollywood and between the Hollywood and the Santa Monica Freeways). The movement is quite complex, consisting of a centrifugal move from the center-west toward the peripheral ring, but simultaneously a drift to the south and the east, leaving the northwest margins to wealthier groups (the mountain slopes and the northern shoreline).

The timing is interesting: the 1940 census accounts for 80% of the phenomenon. Since then, the overall process of change in the spatial distribution of professional groups has remained quite constant. For 6% the movement has been a long-term one, contrasting 1940 and 1970 (SP-P2). The most important discontinuity occurred between 1950 and 1960 (SP-P3), as social groups redistributed themselves after the war had forced them to intermingle.

White-collar and blue-collar groups have separated over time (table 6.11 and figure 6.7), the former toward the west, the latter to the city center and the east. Such segregation has been going on for thirty years, but the movement increased in intensity during the 1960s (intersection of SP-P1 and SP-P5 in table 6.11: $r = 0.87$; $r^2 = 0.76$), which confirms the observations made on figure 6.1: social space (as defined by coresidence) has divided during the 1960–1970 decade.

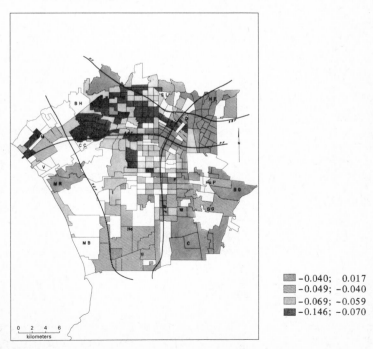

-0.040; 0.017
-0.049; -0.040
-0.069; -0.059
-0.146; -0.070

Figure 6.7. Los Angeles: three-way factor analysis of employment for districts of type SP-D5 grouping, 1940–1970.

6.2.3 Conclusion

The basic findings are both the extreme *spatial regularity* and the remarkable *chronological stability* of the residential structure of Los Angeles. Population and housing distributions form concentric rings separated by very delicate transitions. Distortions of the peripheral rings are due to differences in the speed of development. It was faster to the south, where no important obstacle stood in the way, neither physical (it is only a sedimentary basin) nor social (empty space or poor neighborhoods, with little power to influence urbanization). It was slower to the northeast, where both physical and social reasons combined to freeze the existing structure and to stop change, with the social obstacle (the presence of expensive lots and rich households) by far the most important one. Until 1970, the evolution is dominated by the situation as it existed in 1940.

The general stability of population and housing over the thirty years and the paramount role played by the city center, around which all change has been structured in a concentric pattern, runs against more traditional clichés which would have us believe Los Angeles is an amorphous aggregation of houses without a center, changing in the most erratic and anarchical way. Obviously, this is not true.

Once the overall stability and regularity are taken into account, change can be broken down into a few significant components. The most important is the great drift of Blacks to the west, the southeast, and the south. It is necessary to distinguish different kinds of districts in this vast movement: the arrival and departure zones both of the Blacks and Whites, with their various combinations, and the social neighborhoods, which exhibit in their differences the complex relationships between socioprofessional categories.

6.3 Changes in spatial properties

The spatial fabric of Los Angeles, consisting of the juxtaposed residences and the people who live there, presents particular spatial properties and certain types of spatial organization whose form and evolution are analyzed in this chapter. Let us try and define, then, several important properties of space:
Regularity By the regularity of space, we mean the pattern of its behavior in the immediate vicinity of a point. Consider a variable measured in a tract—the percentage of Whites for instance. If one moves slowly away from this tract to the next, then on to the next, and so on, the percentage of Whites will change, but in what manner? If the measure jumps abruptly and suddenly after a small move from one tract to another, then space is very irregular, even erratic. Conversely, in a very regular space, a variable barely changes after limited movements. Each point in this space can be seen as being surrounded by a ring where the variable under consideration does not change much. This ring could be called a 'neighborhood', because the concept here is quite close to the similar nomenclature that mathematicians use in general topology. Regularity implies that delicate

nuances exist in the spatial evolution of a variable, that there is a smoothness of space.

Coherence   Coherence represents the degree of dependence linking two distinct points. Assume that the average income of a block is very high. The income of the next block is likely to be high as well. But as one moves away, this relationship between the two measures of the same variable at two points increasingly remote from each other tends to vanish. In more precise terms, the correlation of a variable with itself at two distinct points, the *spatial autocorrelation*, usually diminishes with the distance separating the two points. Space coherence, or its structuration, is expressed by this autocorrelation value. In a coherent space, a measure of a variable at a point gives some information, not much perhaps, but something, on that variable at any other point. If spatial coherence is the same in all directions, the space is *isotropic*.

Spatial autocorrelation forms the keystone of human geography. In an incoherent space, where spatial autocorrelation is zero, all spatial structure is absent and the geographer has nothing left to build upon or to explain. Examples will be given for Los Angeles of variables which are distributed in such erratic space, and which depend more on the economist than on the geographer for interpretation. On the other hand, a well-structured space cannot be analyzed in a satisfactory way by classical statistical methods: spatial links perturbate these methods (by the dependence they introduce between measures) and also express important facts which cannot be ignored.

Homogeneity   By the *homogeneity* of an urban structure we mean the relative similarity which may exist between different points. It is a simpler and more intuitive concept representing the uniformity or diversity of space.

These three concepts of space are not independent, but they are sufficiently different to justify the use of methods able to distinguish them and to exhibit them. They are parts of the more general 'Theory of Regionalized Variables' (see appendix B).

Finally, most spatial forms in Los Angeles can be classified into three main types: field space, network space, and framework space. These distinctions will make it possible to include the urban evolution analyzed here in the general frame of the classical growth models.

6.3.1 The evolution of spatial structures in Los Angeles

By spatial structure, we mean here the set of relations linking points in space, such that the whole, the city, is more than the sum of its parts, the districts. Analysis will be limited to the main characteristics as measured in the censuses and to the principal spatial properties as defined above.

The theory of regionalized variables   This is the main instrument of analysis used in this chapter. Let us call a 'regionalized variable' a function $Y(x)$ taking a value at each point x in space. It usually varies from one point to another, which suggests random processes and the resort to probability calculus, but with regularities indicating the presence of underlying structures which need to be uncovered.

The theory was designed to solve a mining problem. From a discrete set of measures on ore concentration, obtained by boring holes (that is, from a finite set of measurements of variable Y at different points x), the problem was how to interpolate the measurements in order to obtain a continuous measure of Y to compute the volume of the ore body. Two schools of thought tried to solve the problem. The American school fitted polynomial surfaces to the data, using the least-squares criterion. The South African (with Krige) and French (with Matheron) schools analyzed the structure of space first, that is the way in which information obtained for point x can be used to predict the value of the variable at point $(x + h)$, h being a small increment in distance. If there is a spatial structure, which is the usual case, then these values are somehow related, and the information acquired at one location is valid in a whole neighborhood around it, whose form and width the method tries to estimate [the controversy between those different approaches is well documented in Davis (1973). For the theory of regionalized variables, see Matheron (1965; 1970) and Serra (1967)]. The theory is currently used in mining; it has also been applied in meteorology (Delhomme and Delfiner, 1973) and, in a simple example, in urban analysis (Ciceri et al, 1977).

Only the *variogram*, that is, the description of the spatial structure (which constitutes the first step of the theory), has been used here. There was no point in *kriging* (that is, in interpolating between the points where data are measured, with the building of a spatial autocorrelation model; see appendix B).

Data must be measured on comparable spatial bases, but census tracts differ in their area and in their population. Mining engineers use densities —the quantity of metal per cubic foot, for example. In an urban study, it is particularly convenient to use percentages or middle values (income median, for instance). The distance between tracts has been measured by giving coordinates to their centers of gravity. Between all pairs of n points separated in space by a distance h, the variogram is computed as:

$$c(h) = \frac{1}{n} \sum_{i=1}^{n} [Y(x_i) - Y(x_i + h)]^2 .$$

Any linear trend is thus eliminated (see appendix B). The successive steps of h (the analysis mesh) have been chosen here as equal to 500 meters. (The computer program used is based on a version sent by Jean Serra, from the Centre de Morphologie Mathématique de Fontainebleau, whose help is gratefully acknowledged. I have largely rewritten it for this particular study.)

Two preliminary problems had to be solved:
(1) The spatial basis of the data: miners use geological borings representing discrete data and covering only a minimal part of the area studied.

Conversely, census data are medians or means computed for the whole area of the tract, and the union of all tracts is equal to the area analyzed. In other words, we are forced to use aggregated data instead of discrete raw measures. Hopefully, the consequences seem limited, but they have not yet been fully investigated.

(2) The irregularity in the form and size of the tracts: this problem may superimpose on the spatial structure of the variables a spurious structure due to the administrative grid itself. This can be easily investigated using a method invented by Waldo Tobler and suggested by Leslie Curry (personal communication). Superimpose on the map of the 316 tracts a regular square grid with a fine mesh. Attach a random variable with equiprobable distribution to each grid intersection. Aggregate, in each census tract, all random values included in it. The tract size will manifest itself through this aggregative process; tract form in the anisotropy of the variogram. The random variable, which is 'white noise', should produce a horizontal variogram (a pure nugget effect; see appendix B) if the administrative grid had no effect whatsoever. Deviation from the nugget effect illustrates the parasitic structuring role of the grid.

In Los Angeles the effect is slight: in the northwest–southeast direction, no spurious structure appears, only a pure nugget effect with some spurious periodicity (cf Ciceri et al, 1977, page 147). Conversely, in the northeast–southwest direction, a limited structure appears with moderate regularity and a 1.5 km to 2 km range. This results from the contrasts between the old, small Downtown tracts, and the largest and more recent tracts along the ocean. This parasitic influence should be remembered when interpreting the variograms.

The main types of spatial structure and their evolution The figures starting from figure 6.8 onward present variograms of the main variables for the four census periods. The origins are different to avoid confusion but the scales are the same for all periods, so that the slopes are comparable. Miners, mainly interested in kriging (cf appendix B), concentrate on the variogram function close to the origin. Serra, as a rule of thumb, suggests considering the variogram for values of the increment h up to a quarter of the main dimension of the field analyzed. As Los Angeles approximately forms a diamond 20 km by 30 km, this rule would limit the interpretation of the function at h equal to 8 km. The rule, however, is concerned with kriging and assumes a symmetrical interpolation on both sides of each point, that is, for a neighborhood with a diameter equal to half the largest dimension. For a simple description of spatial structures, it seems legitimate to accept values of h up to 12 km. In any event, the number of pairs of points increases until one reaches 5 km and thereafter remains constant until 12 km, which is a further justification.

Spatial regularity The distribution through space of 'Vacant dwellings' (figure 6.8) is by far the most irregular. In 1950 the variogram corresponds to a pure nugget effect with a total absence of spatial organization. This was not the case in 1940. Space was not very regular, but it was structured with a 4.5 km range. After dismissing the first value for 1960 and 1970 as aberrant because it is based on too few points (80), the intrinsic function (cf appendix B) shows a weak structure with similar ranges. After the war and the peculiar situation of the housing market (1950), vacant dwellings are located randomly and contiguity relations do not play any role. As different analyses have shown in the preceding

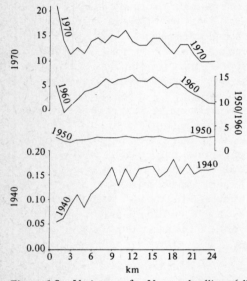

Figure 6.8. Variogram for Vacant dwellings (all directions) in Los Angeles.

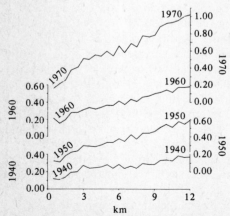

Figure 6.9. Variogram for Capital value (all directions) in Los Angeles.

chapters, this variable is largely autonomous and has very little to do with spatial patterns.

For the 'Capital value' of the dwelling (figure 6.9), the curve close to the origin is upwardly concave (the parabolic model) and exhibits a strong regularity at short distances.   Land rent is strongly related from one tract

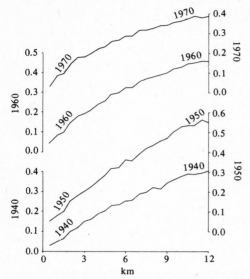

Figure 6.10. Variogram for Owner-occupied dwellings (all directions) in Los Angeles.

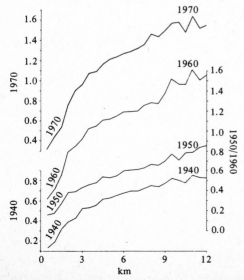

Figure 6.11. Variogram for Young people (all directions) in Los Angeles.

to the next, but the link tends to disappear quickly. The same structure occurs for 'Owner-occupied' dwellings (figure 6.10) (both variables are correlated anyway).

The greatest regularity is observed with the population variables: 'Young' (figure 6.11), Number of persons per room (figure 6.12), and particularly with the ethnic variables, 'Whites' (figure 6.13) and 'Blacks'. Here the function is clearly parabolic. The regularity is impressive and increases over time. Contiguity insures a strong relationship between

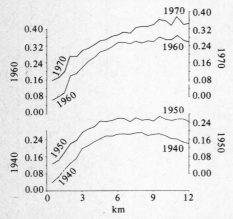

Figure 6.12. Variogram for Number of persons per room (all directions) in Los Angeles.

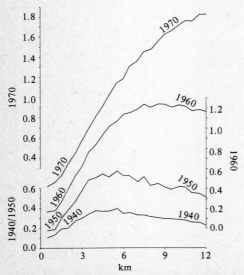

Figure 6.13. Variogram for number of Whites (all directions) in Los Angeles.

neighboring tracts, and its effect is widespread. Income (figure 6.14) is at first linear (that is, only moderately regular), but tends to the parabolic form as time passes by—another proof of increasing spatial segregation.

The evolution of spatial regularity over three decades is remarkable. The variables signifying social status (Whites, Income, Number of persons per room) become increasingly regular. Their behavior suggests the appearance and development of authentic 'neighborhoods', where households are very similar to their closest neighbors, with very subtle transitions which become wide breaks as distance increases. This concept of neighborhood is radically different from the usual one based on factorial ecology.

Since the variogram $c(h)$ is not computed at a particular location, but for all pairs of points (that is, census tracts) in the city separated by the distance h, its results are meaningful over the whole urban space. A neighborhood defined in this way is a portion of a city where transition between adjacent blocks is very small (regular space), but which quickly becomes very large as the distance between blocks increases. It is not an element of the spatial partition of a city which can be mapped, and it owes little to the old traditional concept of the 'region'. It is rather defined as an element of a *structure*, that is, of a set of relations characterized by their form and their intensity. Nor is it a homogeneous piece of land, clearly delimited on the map and located in a particular area of a city; rather it is the strength of a relationship and its change with distance. With this definition, a neighborhood is based on the *modes of relation* between urban dwellers.

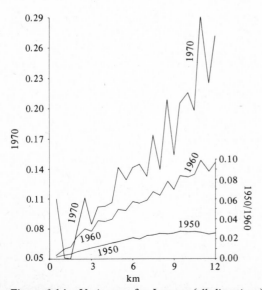

Figure 6.14. Variogram for Income (all directions) in Los Angeles.

On the other hand, types of housing, as represented by percentages of single houses and apartments in a tract, present a much weaker spatial regularity which does not increase over time. Residences remain distributed through urban space in an irregular and broken pattern, with abrupt lateral changes from one type to another, while the population housed in these dwellings has a spatial variation displaying very delicate nuances. This again illustrates the increasing mismatch between housing and residents which characterizes the whole period. The stronger spatial relationships, and the firmer ones, exist between ethnic and social groups rather than between dwellings.

Spatial interdependence The variogram of the percentage of Whites (figure 6.13) is the perfect example: the range of the structure is 4.5 km in 1940 and 1950. It increases to 7.5 km in 1960, and exceeds 12 km in 1970. Close to the origin the curve is linear at first but then reaches a plateau. From there it tends toward the spherical model, and finally becomes logarithmic. Its interpretation is important. In 1940 there was a relationship between the ethnic content of two tracts only if they were close to each other (less than 4.5 km). Beyond this distance, the ethnic composition of any two tracts was unrelated. The spatial coherence of this variable has increased steadily until in 1970 it included the whole city. Whereas urban space in 1940 was made up of quite independent communities of Blacks and Whites with only close range relations, that is, composed of broken and almost independent areas, the city in 1970 forms a very coherent whole where any point is, at least from an ethnic consideration, related to any other. To know a district was black or white, just before World War II, gave information only on its immediate surroundings. Today, it is enough to deduce the ethnic structure of the whole city. The same can be said, but with a slightly weaker structure, for family type (percentages of Old and Young).

Socioeconomic status, mainly measured by average income (figure 6.14), follows a different spatial pattern. Spatial regularity increases over time (the variogram slopes get steeper), and the interdependence between points gets stronger and stronger. In 1970 the variogram is almost a parabola that is upwardly concave and shows a very strong regularity. The curves present no plateaux, however. There is no observable range in these structures. In this case, the complete urban area, although poorly organized at first (in 1950, the variogram shows a slow drift, almost a nugget effect), slowly acquires a structured whole. As far as Income is concerned, the interdependence between city blocks has, today, become strong and regular.

The variables representing housing offer a third type of spatial evolution. They are spatially organized in small structures (the range for all of them is about 3 km) which remain unchanged over thirty years. Stability is very strong in the case of single houses (figure 6.15), and still more so for apartments. Since the number of apartment buildings has grown in absolute and relative numbers their grouping in the urban space must have remained identical. Residential buildings divided into apartments have been consistently organized in ribbons and nuclei whose size and form have not changed since 1940, even if their number has increased largely. *The heterogeneity of space* On the variograms the height of the curve above the horizontal axis measures spatial heterogeneity: it indicates by how much any two points, distance *h* apart, differ on average. Almost all variables analyzed here show an increasing heterogeneity. Most variograms reach plateaux or increasingly extreme values between 1940 and 1970. The only exceptions are Houses and Owner-occupied dwellings, both variables being strongly correlated in any case; and vacant dwellings, which practically behave like a spatially random variable.

Such increasing heterogeneity implies a more intimate blend of differing census tracts. For instance, the diffusion of Blacks throughout, the city transforms a space clearly divided into two ethnic blocks into an urban mosaic where Black and White contacts are much more frequent. Most of the variables are concerned with this evolution, and it may form the basis for the impression of increasing disorganization in Los Angeles and the belief in a developing anarchy, which is so widely held among the city's residents. Reality is the complete opposite of such an impression. As has been shown above, the spatial coherence of the population has increased and the city, formerly consisting of quasi-independent areas, has slowly evolved into a tightly knit spatial structure.

Spatial anisotropy: the spatial structure of land rent The preceding variograms represent the spatial structure in all directions around any point.

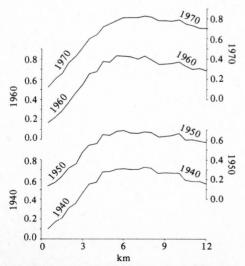

Figure 6.15. Variogram for single-dwelling units (all directions) in Los Angeles.

They may be disaggregated, however, for different orientations, in order
to discover the spatial anisotropy of the variable. This is notable only
in the case of land rent (figure 6.16). The curves close to the origin
do not noticeably differ. Beyond 3 to 4 km, however, the variograms for
the two orthogonal directions (NE–SW and NW–SE) increasingly diverge
as distances (that is, the parameter h) grow. Furthermore, the divergence
becomes wider with time—it is weak in 1940, but very strong by 1970.
In the NW–SE direction, the spatial structure presents an almost constant
range of 3 to 4 km. For any two tracts separated in this direction by a
wider gap, housing values are practically independent. Conversely, in the
NE–SW direction, land values remain correlated even at large distances.
These correlations, although weak in 1940, become increasingly regular by
1970, when they take a parabolic form, signifying a very strong regularity
in the spatial distribution of land rent.

   In the case of this variable, space is definitely anisotropic. The urban
'backcloth' is *fibrous*, with narrow fibers or threads extending from the
northeast to the southwest. Choose a tract at random: its mean land
value gives little information about the same value in tracts located to the
northwest or to the southeast; this is the width of the thread. It gives a
lot of information, however, about land rents toward the northeast or the
southwest. Land rent, among all the variables studied here, offers the
clearest example of a fibrous structure. But the same spatial organization,
albeit weaker, is observed for other variables—Blacks, Young, Number of
school years completed, and particularly median rent. Housing, more
than any other urban phenomenon, is definitely organized in this way.

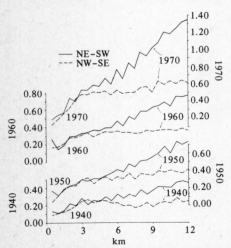

Figure 6.16. Variogram for dwelling value in Los Angeles, showing the anisotropy of
spatial structure.

This anisotropy remains to be explained. Land rent does depend on the geographical site and the local amenities it offers. Land on the Santa Monica mountains, with their south facing slopes, is the most expensive in the city; and this orientation (SE–NW) might be a significant factor. It is not enough, however, to explain the spatial structure covering the whole city of Los Angeles.

Land rent depends heavily on accessibility, that is on the layout of the transportation network. Today, however, the main freeways are not oriented in the directions of the threads exhibited by the land-rent structure. They run from north to south (the Harbor Freeway), from east to west (the Santa Monica Freeway), and even perpendicular to the threads, from northwest to southeast (the Hollywood and San Diego Freeways).

The key to the problem is given by the map of a much older network, that of electric streetcars, which formed the main axis along which Los Angeles grew. This network connected Downtown to Hollywood, and these two towns to the old towns (Santa Monica and Venice) or to the recent beach resorts on the shore (Manhattan Beach, Redondo Beach, Ocean Park, ...). The paramount role played by the streetcar in the city's development has been indicated above (see section 4.2). Long before the automobile boom, it was instrumental in organizing the pattern of city growth. Basically the network ran from the foot of the mountains, where urban centers were initially located, to the shore. Along the lines, accessibility differed little, and land rent tended to be homogeneous in the NE–SW oriented ribbons. Today, these ribbons form the threads picked out by spatial analysis.

It remains to be explained how a spatial pattern, dating back to the 1920s, could persist until 1940 and be constantly reinforced over the last three decades. Two different processes probably account for this structure. The spatial segregation of social groups has increased in Los Angeles (as described above) since 1940. In 1970 it was stronger than ever, and based mainly on income differences. Since home values and household income are very closely related, the contrast between expensive and cheap land has increased, particularly in the last decade. Social segregation accounts for the growing contrast between home values. But what about the stability of the spatial structure, still determined by the transportation network of the 1920s, and yet decipherable under the modern freeways? The point is that land rent forms a system, its evolution obeys built-in equilibrium mechanisms that maintain the spatial organization and even reinforce it. The more expensive lots, because they were wider and closer to the transportation line (that is, more accessible to the center and the shore), attracted wealthier households and necessitated larger investments (bigger houses, for instance). In the following decades landowners tried to maintain their property values through zoning laws, effective (if not always legal) screening of newcomers, and common local policies

strengthened by close neighborhood ties. This complex and involved
network of human relations, both at the adult level (neighborliness) and
at the juvenile level (community schools), tended simultaneously to
perpetuate a certain attitude to life, a definite homogeneity in the local
population, and the preservation of the value of the property to be
handed down to the next generation, all of which constitute the essence
of the neighborhood concept. The preservation of land rent, as exhibited
here, shows the efficiency of this urban unit. Particularly strong
neighborhoods (the well-off and simultaneously well-organized communities)
form autonomous municipalities within the Los Angeles agglomeration.
Wealthy households can manage their own tax money and their own
schools. Typically enough, they developed in roughly NE–SW oriented
ribbons.

Such efforts to preserve property values and conserve the homogeneity
of a district are largely conscious. In a deterministic way, they partly
explain the observed stability of a neighborhood. Given the perpetual
turmoil of moving households, with a fast turnover of dwellings and
individual efforts to climb the social ladder, they are certainly not strong
enough to make up for the surprising stability of urban patterns observed
even in Los Angeles. Everything happens as if neighborhoods, as very
complex networks of relations between people, households, and dwellings,
were able to *organize themselves*. In other words, to use the constant flow
of random disturbances (that is, of external noise represented by new
dwellers, changes in accessibility, building turnover, etc) to maintain or
increase their inner order. This complex question will be discussed in
subsection 7.2.3.

All variograms, whatever their particular form, show the strength of
spatial coherence. The measure of most variables (apart from Vacant
dwelling) still gives some information on other tracts located miles away.
Spatial structures are wide (from 3 to 12 km, and more) and are often
reinforced as time passes. Obviously, it is false to present Los Angeles as
an amorphous and disorganized mass of houses. Its urban space exhibits
a superimposition of structures (of embedded patterns), a complex
organization of space which becomes more tightly knit every decade, and
tends today to include the whole city.

It is puzzling to observe structures of different size and different form
for variables that are so closely correlated. Look at the 1950 data:
Land rent presents a range of 3 km, whereas income has a 6 km range.
It can be explained as follows: let us measure Income and dwelling
Value in any tract, chosen at random. In some other tract, located 4 or
5 km away, the Value of the dwellings is not related to the Value in the
first tract, while Income is still correlated in both tracts. Over the whole
city, however, there is a strong relationship between these two variables,
although they behave differently through urban space, and this is the
source of the problem. The overall correlation is an average. The actual

cross-correlation between Income and Value varies with the distance separating the tracts where these variables are measured. The usual coefficient of linear correlation does not take into account spatial structure and, representing an average, may hide important variations.

The different evolutions of spatial structures confirm the preceding distinctions made between three main groups of variables:

Patterns of family types have become increasingly coherent over the city. The urban space, which was separated in 1940 into small, almost independent structures, is today completely organized through the progressive extension and coalescence of its elements.

Socioeconomic status (Income, Number of school years completed, ...) has evolved toward the same global organization, but in a different way. The totality of the city, although forever changing, was slowly structured, not by the extension of smaller embedded structures, but through internal differentiation.

Housing (types of dwelling, occupation, and tenure) remains poorly organized in small structures over the thirty-year period, and each variable is quite dissimilar, although practically stable in shape and size.

This takes us back to the problem of conformity of housing and population: their spatial organizations differ, and change over time has only increased the differences. While population characteristics have become increasingly mutually interdependent from one part of the city to another, dwellings are organized spatially only within the neighborhood, at a much smaller scale. This may explain why, as shown above, housing in Los Angeles is increasingly mismatched to the needs of the population.

Finally, the more important conclusion arising from this spatial analysis is the importance of history, even in such a recent and fast-changing city. The spatial structure of land rent as it is observed today dates back to the 1920s and the development of streetcar lines, but its origins are even more remote. The drift of population toward the shoreline was to be expected, but why did it settle at the foot of the mountains, away from the ocean, in the first place? Explanation lies in the purpose and the strategy of Spanish colonization. Los Angeles was not founded as a harbor like San Francisco, nor as a fortress along the coast, but as a missionary and agricultural center dedicated to supplying other missions and military establishments. It was natural to locate it on alluvions, well supplied with water, 25 km from the shore. This site, traditional for an agricultural village in a semiarid environment, determined the whole development of the city until the present day. The strategy of Spanish colonization generated several agricultural settlements from Los Angeles to Hollywood, on the piedmont line parallel to the seashore. As a consequence, during the 1910s and 1920s, streetcar lines developed perpendicularly from this piedmont line to several beach resorts, in a NE–SW direction.

The original choices, back in the eighteenth century, have finally led, through the complex interplay of social and economic factors (the importance of real estate development, a free market system, the increasing role of beach resorts and the growth of the city when electric streetcars were the main transportation technology) to the present spatial organization of housing values. Even in Los Angeles, the weight of the past remains of paramount importance.

6.3.2 The various types of spatial organization

There is a *grain* to space, a texture to the urban fabric, as far as population and housing are concerned. As a consequence, space may take three different forms:

Space as a field: organization through contiguity Some variables change slowly from one census tract to another, as a direct function of spatial contiguity. This organization lends itself easily to the fitting of poly-nomial trend surfaces, because data measured at a point are approximately a function of the coordinates of that point.

The distribution of ethnic variables (percentages of Blacks and Whites) and family structure (Family cycle) are organized in this way, revealing the role of everyday contacts between close neighbors. Such variables are distributed in space in a concentric fashion around the city center, located slightly to the south of Downtown.

Evolution over time takes the form of a progressive drift of the concentric rings in a centrifugal movement. This is particularly clear in the case of the black population which is a typical case of *diffusion through contact* where concentric waves radiate away from the center. As exhibited by three-way factor analysis, this process is the most important by far and summarizes the global evolution of the city.

Space as a network: organization through flows Socioeconomic variables are organized by sectors or by threads (Land rent). Transportation systems, particularly the older ones, play a leading role in their genesis and growth. Space is no longer isotropic but is supported by a network of axes along which similarities, changes, and influences circulate more rapidly.

Space as a frame: the lack of organization In the case of a few variables, space plays the role of an empty frame where events happen which seem to be completely indifferent to their absolute or relative position. Spatial autocorrelation is practically zero. The variogram functions are constant, and variables are almost randomly distributed over the city. This case is well illustrated by the housing Vacancy rate: except maybe in 1940, it is not spatially structured. This is at the limits of geography, or rather beyond the border and into the field of economics.

Given the reputation of Los Angeles for rapid growth, fast building turnover, and strong population mobility, one would not expect that the classical models of urban growth developed in the 1920s for cities with strong foreign immigration to fit very well. Even in a different socio-logical context, such as Berry's factorial ecological studies, the regularity of the concentric and sectorial pattern would be so blurred by the city's complexity as to disappear. The multinuclei model (Harris and Ullman, 1945) was proposed specifically with Los Angeles in mind. This is erroneous, however, and the most striking conclusion of the present spatial analysis is that of the persistence of the classical patterns as far as residence is concerned (of course, the multinuclei model remains the best choice for explaining the distribution of commercial and service activities).

Since the end of World War II and the seminal analysis of Los Angeles by Shevky and Williams (1949), the general characteristics of its urban structure have not radically changed.

The prevailing spatial organization is that of the concentric pattern. Three-way factor analysis has shown that a system of rings radiating from the city center does account for most of the evolution of population and housing over the thirty-year period (three-quarters, actually). This pattern is produced by processes of change based on contiguity: change moves from one block to the next. Beneath the spatial pattern, one can imagine complex mechanisms of human relationships occurring: door-to-door connections, contacts between children at school, community action, racial and social prejudices, displays of architectural taste, physical zoning, and finally, in a more or less conscious way, a careful screening of the inhabitants, the preservation of land rent, and the maintenance of family customs—that is, of values, in every meaning of the word.

In such a space, whose strong cohesion depends on everyday contacts between inhabitants and on similarities between their dwellings, the diffusion of the black population in a wave-like pattern fits naturally. A few black families cross the street to a white block and occupy a house. At first the move is usually opposed strongly by many practices, mostly illegal. Beyond a certain threshold, however, change is accelerated, instead of being retarded, by white behavior, as a certain anxiety (often exaggerated, and sometimes accentuated by real-estate speculation) increases the changeover. In some cases three-quarters of the white house-holds may move out within two or three years (Rapkin and Grigsby, 1960; Taeuber and Taeuber, 1965). The dividing line separating two communities split by strong tensions shifts only under frontal attacks, that is, according to contiguity processes. In Los Angeles, the expansion of the Blacks across the city, probably the most important change during the thirty years, did not really confuse the basic pattern of concentric rings, but was superimposed on them with only minor variations. Black diffusion moved east–west, perpendicular to the north–south axis which joined the black ghettos in 1940 (Downtown and Watts). It produced a transition from the sectorial pattern to the concentric pattern (Lieberson, 1963; McEntire, 1960).

Factorial ecology showed socioeconomic variables were distributed in sectors (Shevky and Williams, 1949). This pattern did not disappear, but instead was reinforced as income inequalities and land-rent disparities increased. This was further complicated by the drift of Blacks through the city and the growing differentiation of land-rent structure (the "threads" discussed above). As far as land rent is concerned, the pattern of stability is partly explained by local physical amenities. Land on the mountain slopes and along the shoreline has traditionally been more expensive, and this has certainly contributed to the freezing of the spatial distribution of land prices. They have been the most costly parts of the city for the last fifty years. Physical amenities are not determinant, however: prices along the shore demonstrate the limits of their influence. Land along the beach is very much in demand, but the socioeconomic sectors radiating from the city center intersect the shoreline and determine the actual prices. The fibrous structure of land rent, with its NW–SE orientation, strengthens the pattern. As a result, prices and socioeconomic status vary considerably along the ocean front: very high in Pacific Palissades, still quite high in Santa Monica, lower in Venice, higher again in Marina del Rey (at least since the building of the marina), low in Playa del Rey and Dockweiler Beach, close to the International Airport, high in Manhattan Beach, and so on. This relative stability in the social use of space cannot be ascribed to physical determinism. The urban structure itself, that is a set of equilibrium mechanisms integrating social and racial segregation, bank policies, the prestige of certain districts, the size of lots, zoning laws, and real estate speculation, plays the leading role. All these mechanisms should be included in the concept of neighborhood.

Los Angeles: order and change in a metropolitan system

The foregoing research on the population and housing of Los Angeles over the thirty years of this study emphasizes several fundamental phenomena, but also leads to some puzzling conclusions.

One of the most interesting points to have arisen is the dialectic between stability and change. What has remained constant and what has fundamentally changed during these three decades of rapid evolution? The answer (presented in section 7.1) is far from obvious and is actually quite involved. It implies the need for a drastic transformation of the classical urban models (section 7.2). Although the following development is based on the observation of Los Angeles, most of it can and should be extended to other North American metropolises.

7.1 Los Angeles: a strongly ordered space
7.1.1 The basic findings
Among the many phenomena elucidated in this analysis, three deserve particular attention because of their importance and generality.

Black migrations The movement of Blacks through the city plays a paramount role in the evolution of the area which has been studied here. Obviously this is due to its central location, but there are other reasons. Residential expansion of the Blacks is by contiguity, from one block to the next, and not, like the Whites, by jumps to remote districts. As a result, the spatial effects of the black diffusion are particularly important in restructuring the urban space. Also when black migrants move, they fundamentally transform most of the local characteristics: land values, vacancy rate, type of tenure, degree of crowding, average income, family size, etc. Because the population they form is more typified, and because they are discriminated against, Blacks structure space as they move much more strongly than do Whites. Other minorities might produce the same effects, but they are far less numerous. Through their migration across the city, Blacks appear as the main structuring factor of space.

The evolution of social segregation The occupation of the central city by a black population that is increasing in size has not in the least reduced the strong social segregation which existed in 1940 (cf subsection 6.1.2). Only wartime conditions forced people to mix together, and the fact that the groups separated again in 1960, when the housing market was free, clearly shows this was against their will. The stability of the segregation pattern from 1940 to 1960 is very impressive. During these two decades people were segregated according to two factors: the size of the family (their *needs*), and their socioeconomic level (their *means*). This equilibrium was destroyed after 1960. In spite of the welfare policies devised by the Democrats, differences in means became determinant. This may partly reflect ethnic segregation, since Blacks have, on average, a much lower status. Well-off bachelors returning to the city center also tended to exacerbate social segregation, but whatever the reason, it is certain that during the last decade, the housing needs of most households were not so easily met.

Agreement between dwellings and dwellers' needs The importance of dwelling suitability is confirmed by the way in which families are restricted to a certain type of housing. Although households with money are able to choose any type of housing they like, individuals and families with insufficient means are increasingly restricted to certain kinds of dwelling. This rigidity in the choice of a home takes different forms as time goes by. In Los Angeles in 1940 this rigidity affected the first step in the family life cycle as a result of the arrival there of young middle-class people starting out in life. The small families of young professionals were to be found in owner-occupied detached houses in well-to-do neighborhoods (subsection 5.2.1). In contrast, the last step in the family life cycle was the most constraining in 1950. Elderly widowers without children (the last group to be able to profit from the war-time boom) were strongly associated with rented apartments in decaying neighborhoods. From 1960 onwards, families burdened with many children, crowded into small, single, low-value houses, constituted the group with the most restricted choice in housing. Typically, they tended to be owner-occupiers, and even more so in 1970, but this is hardly a sign of social progress. On the contrary, a heavy mortgage tends to tie them down still more. Here again, the design and the implementation of social policies in favor cf the poor do not seem to have had any important positive effects on their housing situation, and indeed have even failed to stop the worsening of their situation.

These are sad conclusions, but hardly surprising. The distribution of Federal money, even in huge quantities, cannot replace the structural reforms it is precisely designed to avoid. But this research leads to more surprising conclusions.

7.1.2 Some intriguing conclusions

Contrary to what most people seem to believe, Los Angeles appears as a strongly organized city, both in its evolution over time and in its structure through space.

The strength of the spatial structures The space comprising Los Angeles, at least as far as the population and housing distributions are concerned, has a texture or 'grain', that is, different arrangements similar to fibers, layers, or nodes, which is produced by variations among the main variables, relating to household dwellings, but which is itself an agent in distorting and altering these variables and their locations. Except for the very rare cases where space is not organized at all (for instance, the distribution of Vacancies in the city), spatial autocorrelation is usually apparent, and expresses phenomena which are paramount in urban life.

The Los Angeles city center played a very important role during the three decades considered here. All of the city's evolution pivots on, radiates from, and converges on this center. In complete contrast to all that has been said about it, Downtown was throughout the whole period, the cardinal point on which all other points in the urban space depended. That is not to imply that this center played an important function during this period. Actually, most of the usual functions of a city center had left it in 1940. The true meaning is that a city center may lose its activity, its population, and its visitors, undergo such a deep decay that it looks like a blighted area in a poor suburb of a provincial town, yet still retain all of its remote influence on the geometry of the city.

Actually it seems that the more depressed the center is, the more influence it has on a city's evolution. Two conclusions are clear at this point: dialectic is again at work, and forms are completely divorced from functions. In fact, it is only when and because important central functions leave the center to relocate on radiating boulevards (in Los Angeles: Wilshire, Sunset, Hollywood, ...), that the radiating geometry based on the center develops. In other words, metropolitan space becomes organized in a regular way (for example, in sectors and rings) around the center.

As basic activities move from Downtown out toward the periphery, depressing the center until it is nothing more than a vacated ghetto with poor run-down shops, they simultaneously ensure the power and the perenniality of the axes radiating from Downtown, that is, they ensure the remote influence of the decaying center. This fascinating dialectic explains why so many attempts in Europe to re-create an artificial center in cities bombed during the war (Warsaw, for instance) failed. The competition for activities which had been relocated immediately after the war in avenues away from the ruined downtown proved too strong[8]. The very triumph of a city center in organizing the overall urban geometrical pattern may be possible only if and when this center is blighted to the point of losing a large portion of its functions. Here again, geometry and functions, forms and content, are dialectically opposed.

As a result, the most important movements of the population of Los Angeles are to and from the center. The flight of the white middle class to the periphery has been well documented for most North American cities; it also plays an important role in Los Angeles. Other more interesting movements, however, are superimposed on this classical scheme. Blacks also move toward the periphery in an effort to segregate themselves from poorer black households, but racial discrimination forbids them to jump over large white areas, so they move painfully from one block to the next, forming during the thirty years a few long tentacles extending rapidly outward on the map of the city.

[8] This idea was suggested by Jean Zeitoun, director of the CIMA, Paris.

More important still, white bachelors with means are coming back to the city center in a surprising centripetal movement. First noticed in the late 1960s, such returns seems to have started early in Los Angeles, probably during the 1950s. The phenomenon is complex and recalls, but in the opposite direction, the trends analyzed by the sociologists of the Chicago School during the 1920s. The breakdown of the family, with bachelors refusing, at least temporarily, to get married; a more extrovert way of life, with a heavier reliance on shows, bars, sport, and car-rides, and much less on home life and the TV; and a more natural sexuality, with an indulgent acceptance of promiscuity, and the beginning of the recognition of equal sexual and social rights for women. These people are white collar or well-to-do professionals.

The consequences cannot be exaggerated. It may be the beginning of a new culture, not a counter-culture opposed to modern industrial society, but on the contrary, a way-of-life freely using the prosperity, the division of labor, and the liberty granted by this society, and based on the individualism and the careerism it increasingly fosters. It will be fascinating to see what the recent economic crisis, the resulting pessimism and puritanism, the anxieties about getting and keeping a job, the return in force of the Christian faith, sexual repression, and obsolete clichés will do to this basic trend. It may break it or rather reinforce it, since it is full of inner contradictions, emphasizing profit and modern business as well as morality.

In any event the impact on urban forms is paramount. The return of white-collar groups to the city center is a way to erase the basic contra-diction in US urban land rent. The most expensive land paid the lowest rent, as far as housing was concerned. For Alonso (1964a; 1964b) the rich are not likely to come back to the center, urban renewal or not, because they are not basically interested in *new* structures, as the Chicago School believed, but in *large* ones. Even up-to-date and luxurious new buildings in the center cannot offer a family the large amount of space Alonso believes they are looking for. He sees the success or failure of urban renewal in attracting rich households back to the Downtown as the acid test which decides between Burgess and himself. In Los Angeles, well-to-do people are returning Downtown, but that does not settle the controversy, which was couched in either–or terms—which is an over-simplified dichotomy. If families really are breaking down, the point Alonso is making loses most of its meaning, as does his test.

The importance of past history Europeans are so steeped in history and are so accustomed to a 2000-year-old tradition that they take the importance of historical factors for granted. This is not the case with North American social scientists. Many US geographers still find it necessary to try to prove the importance of history in molding modern cities. Actually, history plays a fundamental role in determining the spatial structures and the urban forms of a modern metropolis—even in the United States, even in California, and even in Los Angeles. The spatial structure of land rent for at least thirty years was molded by the old electric streetcar network (cf subsections 4.2.1 and 4.2.2). The complete layout of this network is due to the fact that Los Angeles was founded at the foot of the mountains, away from the sea but on well-irrigated land as befits a settlement planned as an agricultural center. In short, the transportation network in the 1920s and 1930s, and the land rent structure in 1970 still exhibit the remote effects of decisions taken two centuries earlier by a captain-general representing the Spanish crown in Mexico.

This is, of course, an impressive example, but it is not the only one. The very fact that a city grows implies that its center, whatever its location and its original functions, existed before the other parts of the settlement and cannot but help influence its development: in this case, change is necessarily irreversible. Downtown, for the very simple reason that it came first necessarily plays a leading role in urban sprawl.

A kind of 'collective unconscious' History manifests itself through a kind of city memory, or rather an urban hysteresis. It is important, however, to note that it is not only, and not even mainly, a question of passive *objects* like old names, old streets, or long-past reputations, but also of active *subjects*. The remnants of the past (be it threads of correlated land rent, the remoteness of the city center from the sea, or large cattle ranches preserved inside the city limits for a long period) have an influence on people, on urban life, on economic functions, and on the city structure. In the dialectical sense of the term, they are *subjects* with a power of their own to arrange, orient, or hinder modern development of the city today.

In that sense, past influences are quite similar to a collective unconscious which would weigh heavily, although in a latent way, on modern urban evolution. Let us avoid the polemics between Freudian and Jungian analysts about this concept; we are using the expression in a different context, rather as an image. Instead let us try to define it more precisely.

What would be the content of such a collective urban unconscious? It consists of ancient forces which have been superseded today by new ones and have hence become latent, but have not been destroyed. The logical mechanism which produced them is close to the mechanism ('repression') demonstrated by psychoanalysts in the human unconscious, which justifies the analogy. The role of the city center is one of these 'repressed', or rather latent forces. Its functions have declined and often disappeared as time passed by, but its role in determining the overall pattern of the city, far from abating, has on the contrary increased and taken on a new importance.

Another example is to be found in the mechanisms by which land rent is preserved. Although, over a fifty-year period most proprietors will have died or sold their estates and moved away, and although many houses and apartment buildings have been torn down and replaced by different structures, land rent is still largely organized along the accessibility patterns determined in the 1920s. Individuals, when they sell, try to maintain or increase the value of their property; neighbors join together, usually in an informal way, to protect property values and, at the city level, building codes and zoning laws have the same purpose and a similar effect. For these reasons, land values determined in the past still tend to influence modern action: witness the frequent conflicts over freeway location.

Urban language, as defined above in chapter 5, offers still another example. Neighborhoods organized by the street network, and the whole city serviced by the freeway network, represent conflicting forces largely inherited from the past which have little meaning in the city today, but retain enough power to modify contemporary decisions. Take for instance Beverly Hills, a large cattle ranch which was divided into huge parcels of land after World War I, and developed into a very rich community. The decision was largely arbitrary, or rather determined by the conditions of the housing market at the time. The land, although well located, might as easily have been developed, as in the case of Silver Lake, into a strong but not very rich middle-class community. The limits of Beverly Hills follow those of the cattle ranch, which avoided the upper slopes, that were too steep for the cattle, and the plain, which was too rich and moist, and was covered with sugar cane plantations. These agricultural limitations no longer have any meaning but they still orientate important urban investments, such as the route of the stillborn freeway which was planned to bisect Beverly Hills.

The powerful uproar of well-to-do landowners succeeded in moving the projected freeway to the limits of the community, and finally in dropping the project all together. The contradictions between the needs of homogeneous neighborhoods with their own street systems, and those of a large city with so many distinct neighborhoods linked by elevated freeways are very clear. Influences from the past are still there, latent, meaningless, but powerful, and able to affect the decisions of modern planners.

What are the *mechanisms* by which this 'unconscious' manifests itself? If it does consist of latent forces which have lost most of their meaning but retained some effective power, how do they cope with change? We have identified a *chasm* between the neighborhood's system of streets and the city's freeway network which causes so many complaints about the disorganization of this 'fragmented metropolis'. On the other hand, this hiatus between local life and general activity allows both to change at their own rate. Disjunction between neighborhood and city, as far as spatial organization, perception of space, movement, and type of activity are concerned, is necessary inasmuch as it allows the coexistence, albeit difficult and disturbing, between old latent forces still at work in the neighborhood, and new different modern forces at the city level. It should not be surprising that Los Angeles, probably the fastest changing metropolis in the USA, offers the strongest separation between the two levels. The geographical hiatus between both networks plays a role similar to the sudden and illogical intervention of a freudian lapsus in an otherwise fluent and coherent discourse. It interrupts the efficient and logical facade of present activity to let hidden repressed trends appear.

Contiguity is another mode of change which allows the realization of past forces in today's world. Changes in land rent, the migration of Blacks, and the transition between different types of families, all usually take place through a slow expansion into adjacent blocks, rather than by long jumps. Contiguity as a change mechanism simultaneously integrates (a) stability, as it only works on the fringes and maintains the core intact, and (b) otherness, as it alters peripheral blocks, that is the fringe of the whole, which means finally the definition of the whole itself.

Radial axes also play a basic role. They channel the spatial diffusion of trends away from the center more rapidly, but they also confine them in space. Through them the role of the old center is maintained at a distance; or to put it another way, they ensure the remote influence of the old center as it loses its local functions and acquires a higher level, more global role. Finally, these axes determine a spatial structure in which ribbons of activities, new types of buildings, and social changes diffuse perpendicularly to these radial lines.

The incidence of important gaps between different levels of urban life, diffusion by contiguity, and the circulation of influences projected away from the old center by radial axes, all are mechanisms which allow the persistence of, and manifest the importance of, ancient forces still at work in the urban structure, although new ones have superseded them and 'repressed' them to a latent condition. This account justifies the term 'collective unconscious' used before to represent this condition and its mechanisms, although the analogy should obviously not be extended too far. It is nothing more than a convenient way to express the intricate relationship between old waning structures which are still very much alive, and new ones which are in the process of becoming predominant. In this way, the analysis is again confronted with the difficult problem of change, built simultaneously of stability and alteration.

7.1.3 Stability and change in Los Angeles

Let us now try to distinguish more precisely what, in the thirty years, has remained quite stable in Los Angeles, and what has changed the most.

What has remained stable? The global spatial structure of Los Angeles, as a system of concentric rings, sectors, and axes radiating from the center and channeling the main activities, has remained surprisingly stable over these three decades. This may be the most substantiated and the most remarkable conclusion of this study.

Land rent, particularly in a relative sense (for instance, as used in an ordering of the various districts of Los Angeles) has changed very little, so little that it still exhibits the layout of the long defunct electric streetcar system. Of course, there are powerful mechanisms at work to preserve it: official ones, like zoning laws and building codes, and unofficial ones, that are probably more efficient, like the internal control of the neighborhood, the protection of its reputation (its sign-value), and the two-way relationship between rent and transportation (each variable influences the other, creating an interlocked system where change is strongly restricted).

The spatial location and global form of the neighborhoods have changed very little. Changes by contiguity may encroach on a neighboring district but this does not radically alter its core.

The duality of the transportation network, that is, the typical separation between homogeneous fragments of space (neighborhoods) connected by surface streets and linked by a superimposed network of freeways, or in the past by electric streetcars, allows a remarkable fluidity, an elasticity in a system where elements may change while the whole remains coherent. Urban language, as defined above, integrates change but is basically stable.

Finally, symbols as a source of value have also changed very little in Los Angeles. Hollywood is a good example. Although most studios have had crises, television and rock recording has largely taken the place left by the movie industry; if economics have changed a lot, the symbol has not. Modern, speculative, fast growing industries have also experienced drastic transformations: local oil production has lost much of its importance, but electronic and aerospace firms have grown in its stead and maintained Los Angeles as a symbol of up-to-date, venture technologies.

What has changed? The population living in the various parts of the city has changed mainly because of the racial movement of Blacks across the city, forming two important tentacles, but also because of social segregation, which has certainly increased. In 1940, families of different income level could sometimes be found in the same districts if they had the same housing needs. This was much less true in 1970; spatial segregation was then principally based on differences in income.

The convenience and the efficiency of housing has changed too. The congruence of dwellers and dwellings has kept altering, mainly because of the different rhythms in the evolution of these two variables. Families have constantly moved at a very high rate, while housing, although characterized by a much higher turnover than in European cities, changed at a much slower pace.

Transportation has changed dramatically; in its nature (a collective system of electric streetcars replaced by individual transportation in automobiles) as well as in its role (small streets have become nothing more than sidewalk parking and lines separating blocks, while most of the important through-traffic is channeled along the urban freeways).

Finally, the image of Los Angeles has been radically altered. Viewed before World War II as a sort of ideal counter-city, the American dream come true, the final success after the failure of those imperfect blueprints represented by the East Coast cities; Los Angeles is often cited today as the nightmare city where pollution, crowding, dispersion, dehumanization, and ugliness clearly show what modern cities should try to avoid.

The change–stability dialectic   Clearly, the network of relationships has been more stable while the fragments of urban space have experienced the most change. Logical structures appear more stable than the physical elements of urban space.

Relationships form three main types of network. Geometrical relations (distances, orientations, axes, and nodes) form a quite permanent grid on which population, activities, and money flow and mold the city life.

The complex web of social relations plays several basic roles. It contributes to the preservation of one's heritage, which consists not only of inheritance (real estate, stocks, etc) but also of family traditions and social level. It protects and maintains the *identity* of the subject over time.

On the other hand, it protects the *distinctions* that individuals and households try to maintain between one another. The urban language of sign-value is the main expression of this effort (Bourdieu, 1979), tending to preserve the *otherness*, the quality of being different. A particularly important example where these roles combine is offered by the Blacks, who occupy urban space and move through the city in such a way that they can retain their identity and develop their differences with other ethnic groups.

Symbols throughout Los Angeles create a kind of fantastic network which strongly contributes to ensuring the originality of the city and the maintenance of its unity.

These various networks of relationships are the most stable aspect of Los Angeles. This does not mean that they do not evolve somehow. Their very nature is dialectical, but their evolution is slow and ordered. Their meaning and their content slowly change, while their form remains the same over time. They reproduce nothing more than the old dialectic of the Self and the Other, the One and the Multiple, a classic contrast which reappears here with a geographical slant.

The network of fantastic symbols spread over the metropolis is composed of internal oppositons: attraction versus revulsion, admiration versus disdain, social relevance versus marginal revolutionary trends. Its very contra-dictions fuel it with a tremendous power over the minds of Los Angeles' inhabitants, as well as over those of people throughout the world.

There are no fewer inner contradictions in the geometric pattern of spatial relationships: contradictions between *points, lines,* and *fragments of planes* form the elements of this geometry and reproduce the dialectical development of space exhibited by Hegel in his transcendental mechanics (Hegel, 1970, volume 1, page 224): contradictions between the *center* and the *periphery* which engendered most of the city's evolution for thirty years if not more; contradictions between *centrifugal* and *centripetal* movements, each one of those directions being contingent on the other; and contradictions between the *metric properties* of urban space (the role of distance in these movements, whether we compute it in time, miles, or any other unit) and, on the other hand, the nonmetric properties (in the topological sense of the term) of an urban space where many movements are made through *contiguity* and contact.

Finally, the network of ethnic relations is probably the most loaded with inner tensions and contradictions: contradictions between Whites and Blacks, of course, but also between the roles played by the categories of difference and similarity. Blacks, in their drift across the city, tend to occupy housing left by the Whites in sites which acquire a different role. Since the Blacks have their own zones of employment, shopping, and social contacts, the relative location of this housing changes radically, as does its meaning. A black family newly located in Culver City does not visit other parts of Los Angeles as did the white family who previously lived in the same house. On the other hand, Whites, as they come back to live in Downtown, occupy central sites abandoned by Blacks, sites with easy accessibility to all points, to office buildings, and to downtown bars. However, they require very different dwellings, and luxurious apartments in modern and expansive towers replace the old run-down houses left by the Blacks. Both ethnic groups look for the most accessible location, but for opposing reasons: the Blacks because of their large, traditional families and their very limited means, which force them to save on transportation costs; the Whites, because of their adequate resources, change their morality and turn away from the traditional family to the swinging life-style.

This is not the place to analyze in detail these multiple contradictions which form the very framework around which life in Los Angeles is built. The point here is only to suggest the complexity of the logical structure underlying the evolution of such a large metropolis, with contradictions within the main concepts (like dwellings, urban sites, family means) and also between these concepts. The most remarkable finding is that what appears as the most stable element in the transformations in Los Angeles over time is the impalpable and immaterial, namely the networks representing social contacts, flows of persons or of ideas, and relative distances. Conversely, what has been most affected by change, what appears as particularly unstable and fluctuating, is material: things like fragments of space (districts, zones), social groups, and buildings, all of which have kept changing at a rapid pace. Here again there is a dialectical relation, the deepest of all, between the mutability of physical objects and the steadfastness of logical relationships.

7.2 Los Angeles and the urban models

There is enough material now for us to come back to the classical urban models and theories summarized in chapter 2, and to try to fit them to Los Angeles.

7.2.1 The collapse of the classical models

All the basic mechanisms proposed by the various theories to explain urban evolution simply do not exist, or at least do not play any important role, in Los Angeles during the three decades under review.

Foreign immigration, the mainspring which moved the whole city, according to the Chicago School, had practically stopped by 1931. In any case, it never played an important role in Los Angeles, a city populated not by poor foreign immigrants but by native Americans, many of them well-to-do citizens from the big cities back East.

No easy explanation is to be found, either, in national demographic growth. The birthrate was relatively low during the late 1930s and the war years. True, an impressive babyboom happened after the war and went on for some time, but the birthrate declined again during the late 1960s and early 1970s. No demographic dynamism, anyway, is strong enough to replace the huge and regular flow of immigrants who came to settle down in the dilapidated centers of the eastern cities, and who later moved to the periphery. And it would still be necessary to prove that any population pressure from Downtown would correspond to very poor families: a hopeless task.

Hoyt assumed that the rich led the way in the centrifugal migration which created sectors of different land rents. This has definitely not been the case in Los Angeles, where the rich count among the more stable groups in the city. Attracted during the 1920s to the mountain slopes and some parts of the shore, they have remained there for fifty years without much change.

The opposite assumption would not be any more useful: the poor have not led the way in the most important migrations across the city. True, a very important extension of the black population has stretched a few long tentacles across Los Angeles, but meanwhile many Whites were coming back to the city center. And the black families who moved the farthest were not among the poorest but, on the contrary, formed a black middle class.

Even the interesting discussion by Alonso of his 'structural' theory opposed to Burgess's 'historical' one has no meaning in Los Angeles (Alonso, 1964a). Whites coming back to the center and participating in the Los Angeles' Urban Renewal policy are very different from their parents who moved to the periphery. Their morality, their refusal to have a family, at least for the moment, their relative prosperity from the beginning of their career, in short, their extroversion, is so different from the behavior of their own parents that, even in similar socioprofessional groups and with analogous income brackets, no comparison is really possible. Alonso's hypothesis cannot be tested in this way. This is another version of the classical problem when studying change: the elements under study change so much that a comparison between the starting point and the final stage becomes illegitimate.

If the evolution of Los Angeles does not in any way substantiate the assumptions on which classical models are based, it does exhibit an important factor usually forgotten and omitted in all such models: historical remnants of past structures still play an important role, although they generally remain latent. This is not only important in the construction of a new urban model, but also in answering a preoccupation often found in the North American geographical literature. US cities are so new in comparison with European or extreme oriental metropolises that their structure and their evolution seem to be completely free of the heavy heritage determining the forms, the content, the customs, and the urban way of life of these old settlements. This is certainly an illusion, owed to the apparent newness and to the fast turnover in North American cities. Even in Los Angeles the past is always active, hidden in latent forces which determine, to a surprisingly large extent, the spatial and logical structure of today's population and housing.

The processes advocated by the classical urban theories and models do not work in Los Angeles. Practically none of the forces which have been described as molding the city have had any important impact on its evolution since 1940, and there is little evidence they had more weight in earlier times. Geographers still describe the urban forms (rings, sectors, nuclei) demonstrated time and again by factorial ecology, but with increasingly fewer references to the classical theories underlying these forms which attempt to explain them. Drastic changes in demographic trends (foreign immigration coming to a stop, important declines in the birthrate, and recent inverted flows of population away from the larger cities) have been largely overlooked, although they play a paramount role in reality as well as in urban theories. Urban geography has largely become a description of forms without content.

The puzzling fact is that spatial forms, on the contrary, are extraordinarily vivid and stable. All analyses performed in this study, and particularly the three-way factor analysis, prove the surprising clarity of rings and sectors as they structure the urban space. At the end of this study, urban forms appear as much more important and durable, pervasive, and pregnant with significance than is usually assumed. They constitute the truly stable elements in an otherwise everchanging urban world. This may be the most important conclusion of this book: it implies a drastic separation of forms and processes, and makes it necessary to attempt to construct a new model of urban change, keeping the classical forms, but discarding the old processes used to explain a city's evolution.

7.2.2 Towards a new model of urban change

Empirical evidence offers two basic findings on which to build a new model. First, human behavior in urban space changes with changes in geographic scale. Although they are aggregations of the same individuals, the areal units of districts, neighborhoods, and households appear to behave quite differently. Beyond a certain threshold, an increase in the size of a group determines a qualitative change in the way it organizes space. Second, urban spatial forms are very stable. They represent one of the most stable elements in a city whereas the physical elements (buildings, households, individuals) keep changing. Actually, spatial forms appear as largely independent from their content. This is the reason why spatial patterns described in classical theories are still so obvious although their substance has virtually disappeared.

Independence between form and content should not appear as a paradox. Mathematics is built on contentless forms: a triangle is defined without any reference to the matter from which it is built. This is what is meant here by the concept of 'pure, empty form'. To say that forms and processes are largely independent only means that in a city growing regularly from a central point, the characteristics of the population and of the buildings will tend to organize themselves according to some geometrical spatial logic. This logic has little to do with the phenomena which it is organizing (for example, social segregation, ethnic separation, ...).

The engine of change In this new model, urban change is fueled by contradictions in the behavior of people at different scales of aggregation within the metropolis. Change, in other words, is determined by a kind of geographical dialectics.

The North American ethos is such that each individual constantly strives to move up the social ladder. Urbanites are aggressively pursuing ways of changing their position, their profession, their income, their home, even their way of life. The city can be likened to a boiling cauldron of excited particles running to and fro, similar to a social Brownian movement.

On the other hand, at the neighborhood level this social pattern is clearly reversed, becoming the complete opposite. The goal is to preserve the integrity and the interests of the group by avoiding any form of change. A wide range of attitudes, institutions, and activities help to limit change and preserve homogeneity, including zoning laws, building codes, concealed racism, social prejudices, snobbishness, gossip, door-to-door relations, charity meetings, and school segregation.

A synthesis occurs between these two conflicting processes at the spatial scale of the whole city. The central problem is one of managing coexistence within a heterogeneous set of homogeneous neighborhoods. In a sense, this is the whole idea behind liberal city planning.

The whole system is dialectical. It consists of the same elements at each level (namely, citizens trying to get the best for their families and themselves) following the same goals, and it leads them to adopt, at different geographical levels, actions which are dialectically opposed. This analysis does not apply so well to those at the extremes of the social ladder—the very poor and the ultra rich—who are both confined in remote ghettos with quite fixed locations.

The very efforts made by individuals to transcend their social groups are the main reason for the formation and persistence of homogeneous neighborhoods which attempt to preserve their acquired status, and to transmit patrimonies, land values, and ways of life, unchanged, to the next generation. Conversely, the very juxtaposition of different neighborhoods makes it necessary, at the higher level of the city, to play off the communities against one another (for example, conflicts over the location of urban freeways), to keep them distinct (building codes, physical planning), and to soothe their oppositions and gloss over their conflicts (bussing, the extension of taxes to the whole metropolis).

The incessant tensions corresponding to these dialectical relations are not always checked by countervailing forces. Sometimes, one of these trends wins the day—a neighborhood becomes powerful enough to constitute itself as an independent municipality, completely controlling the amount and the use of its resources (Beverly Hills is a typical example). Conversely, the disaggregating effect of the efforts by families to better their condition by moving to a more comfortable district may succeed—witness the wide expansion of the black population across the city.

These dialectical mechanisms entail no particular spatial patterns. Indeed, a most volatile variable, the housing vacancy rate, which perhaps best captures the perpetual competition between households on the one hand, and renters and landlords on the other, is distributed randomly in space, without any clear spatial structure.

The relations described here have been suggested before by other authors, but without the emphasis on their dialectical form. For Wirth, the main problem in the city was the growing disparity between the increasing independence of individuals and households from one another, and simultaneously the necessary capacity for them to act as a unit at the level of the neighborhood (Wirth, 1938). With more perspicacity, Smith criticizes the Chicago School for failing to see that the decline of the family and the loosening of ties reinforces instead of weakens, the neighborhood (Smith, 1980). The breakdown of the city into distinct homogeneous communities is perennially at the center of the sociologist's concerns: "The city tends to resemble a mosaic of social worlds in which the transition from one to the other is abrupt" (Wirth, 1938, page 15).

Finally, a new contradiction begins to appear in the three-tier dialectical system analyzed above, generating a fourth tier at the lowest level:

whereas previously individuals tended to act within the family structure in their efforts to climb up the social ladder, the case of the 'swinging singles' shows an increasing separation between the individual and the family interests. As a pure product of the inner logic of the social system, the young white-collar worker grows up and graduates thanks to the help and protection afforded him by his family. But, as he enters a new career, he tends to consider the family structure as a burden, if not a handicap, to his success. Transcending one's social level also tends to mean breaking family ties and avoiding acquiring new ones. This quite new development reinforces the dialectical system expounded above, and accelerates the turnover in housing and migration.

Forms and spatial order   Upon this sort of Brownian movement of individuals and families (trying simultaneously to better their social position while grouping with others to protect their privileges) order is superimposed over the city's space through the development, by an inner logic, of spatial forms. Mechanisms generating and imposing these forms in cities are largely, if not totally, independent from the social dialectical relations indicated above.

The spatial forms of the growth process are based on a simple fact: the relative antiquity of the center. The center promotes remarkably clear forms as long as urban growth is quite rapid and persistent. The very fact that a city is founded at a point grants a unique privilege to this point, whatever its properties. It necessarily orientates the main traffic lines, and begins structuring the surrounding space. The location of this particular point, for whatever reasons, induces the development of converging lines. In turn, these lines (or axes) modify the properties of the space along them. For example, if the surrounding environment is not too irregular, these axes represent an isotropic projection in various directions of the center's influence. The dialectic of 'center–periphery' and the centrifugal–centripetal system of flows and influences are both clearly at work. But by the same token, these traffic lines make space between them anisotropic, since they represent privileged avenues of circulation not only of people and commodities, but also of activities and influences. As a result the space in the triangles enclosed between three main traffic lines is necessarily organized as a function of the direct distance to those lines.

The logical development described here is very close to the dialectics of space as outlined in Hegel's "Transcendental Mechanics" (1970, section 1, paragraph 253, A: Space and Time). The idealization of urban growth discussed above is assumed to take place on an isotropic plane. But although various forms of differentiation of the space would alter the details of the development, they would not alter its inner logic. The whole point of the argument is that to found a city is to distinguish a point which subsequently (and necessarily) induces the development of radial lines, differentiated triangles, and, by sheer logical consequence, the generation of center–periphery relations, of centrifugal and centripetal flows, and finally rings and sectors. The development of such classical urban patterns results from a pure spatial logic and is almost completely independent of the political, military, economic, or social factors which determined the original location of the city and subsequently governed its growth. Los Angeles is a clear example of this. It was founded at the foot of the mountains away from the coast as an agricultural center. In the 19th and 20th centuries, it grew outward from this center for reasons which had nothing at all to do with its role as an agricultural settlement.

This is not to say that economic factors, social tensions, and political events, etc, have had no influence on the city's growth; although they do play a paramount role, this role does not seem to be strongly related to the organization of space. What they do is to supply the energy for change—in other words, the incessant turmoil of individuals going through their life cycles, changing jobs and careers, families changing residence, developers building new homes, and making investments which alter accessibility surfaces, etc.

The inner logic of the spatial system which imposes order on the city is actually more complicated. There is first a *geometrical* system of forms which has been analyzed above. But a *topological* mechanism also exists based on contiguity movements. This kind of spatial process maintains *nodes* and creates *fronts* moving across the city, and these forms have been widely documented in this study.

A third kind of mechanism can also be identified. It is more ambiguous: the role of *physical amenities*. It cannot be neglected in determining land rent or the location of social groups (for example, mountain slopes or the seashore). It is, however, different; not a part of an inner logic but rather an extraneous element blocking the self-induced evolution of the spatial system of forms. The role of physical amenities is not to promote change but, on the contrary, to freeze it: to stop the evolution of land rent, fixed at a high level for decades, and to immobilize certain social groups, typically the wealthiest and the poorest. Their ambiguous nature, as generators of forms as well as factors related to social dialectics, explains their limited effects. The rich do not necessarily locate on mountain slopes and on beaches; on the other hand, long stretches of the shore are occupied by lower-middle-class and even poor social groups.

Except for the dubious role of physical amenities, such systems of spatial forms are by and large independent of economic and social factors. These forms seem to have a logic of their own. But then, should not all big cities exhibit a similar spatial organization throughout the United States, or even the rest of the industrial world? They probably do, in a superior way, but with infinite variations owing to the energy, the speed, and the rhythm of the growth process. This point is central and needs further elaboration.

When urban growth and sprawl take place rapidly and continuously, as they have in many US cities, spatial patterns are harmoniously developed and quite clear. It is little wonder that almost all the factorial ecology studies of North American cities have tended to rediscover them (peculiar findings can almost always be traced to peculiarities in the physical environment or in the history of the city). On the other hand, when urban development has extended over centuries, as in Europe, with long periods of quasi-stagnation, even of contraction, followed, as in the 19th century, by a violent demographic explosion, a complicated combination of embedded forms results.

Synthesis: irreversible change The evolution of the urban structure of Los Angeles, and probably of most other US metropolises, can be represented by a compound model uniting two almost independent processes of very different kinds (Marchand, 1984). On the one hand, there is a hierarchy of social tensions such that the nature of human endeavor changes into its opposite as the geographical scale changes. Efforts to cross social barriers are checked by efforts to reinforce those barriers and preserve neighborhood homogeneity. These are themselves checked by city-wide policies designed to accommodate distinct, juxta-posed groups and defuse tensions. Although these trends are loaded with human energy, and constantly stimulate urban change, they are probably quite neutral as far as spatial patterns are concerned.

On the other hand, there is a complex system of spatial forms, of a geometrical or topological nature, which develops in accord with its own internal logic. Two conditions seem necessary for the appearance of such a system of forms: (1) growth must originate from a point, and (2) some kind of distance–decay function must be at work. With these weak and general assumptions spatial patterns of urban growth can be generated quite straightforwardly without any precise reference to the economic and social forces at work. Except for their inner rules of development these forms are empty, void of any energy. They do not feed urban change, but organize it and shape it in space.

The combination of these two independent processes is largely random; it is difficult to say that any one particular step in the development of a neighborhood or in the prosperity of a household corresponds to a particular step or a particular form in the extension of the spatial pattern. On the contrary, both systems are linked in each city in a particular way. As a result, *urban change is definitely irreversible*: there is an 'urban memory', a kind of hysteresis represented by the inscription in space of most economic and social variables through the layout of avenues, buildings, neighborhoods, parks, land rent, commercial and industrial activities—through them the past determines the present.

The intersection of two independent deterministic chains of events produces random events following each other in an irreversible sequence.

Irreversibility is ensured because at each moment, a variety of branchings are possible, that is, the intersection of the two logics may take many forms and is largely or mainly random. Once the event is determined, however, local conditions are fixed; there is no turning back. As Monod (1970, chapter 7) recalls, time is reversible only in a unique sequence of logically determined events. It acquires a direction and is no longer reversible when events result from the random combination of two independent sequences. Events are still logically determined (by the inner logic working within each sequence) but the randomness they embody makes time irreversible.

An analogy might illustrate the model proposed here: imagine a very active turmoil of particles animated by a sort of Brownian movement, but caught in a net of old, relic forms inherited from the past. These forms would remain empty, and the net would be completely transparent without the particles to make it perceivable. On the other hand, the cloud of particles, without the ordering net would be nothing but a formless, ever-changing blur whose individuality and characteristics would be difficult to define. As particles get caught and start forming a pattern, they determine the nodes and the lines which they form on the web—that is the way other particles will subsequently be trapped. Flies moving randomly and getting trapped in a cobweb would be a similar analogy.

Such a model of true (that is, irreversible) change would explain simultaneously the regularity of spatial forms and the variety of growth processes which have been observed in Los Angeles for the last thirty years. But a new difficulty appears: if forms are no longer the direct effect of a particular growth process, how is it possible to account for the evident stability of these urban forms? Some mechanism of *self-organization* must be present.

7.2.3 Self-organizing urban systems

Biologists have encountered the same problems in modern life sciences. They use solutions borrowed from cybernetics, treating living organisms as complex machines (Atlan, 1972; 1979; Dupuy, 1982; von Foerster, 1960). Their findings may be carefully transposed into the urban context by considering a metropolis as a self-organizing system. The prime difficulty lies in the definition of the order of a system; the others in explaining how order can possibly increase 'by itself' either by a redundancy transfer (von Foerster), or by the use of random perturbations (Atlan).

How to define the order of a system   The concepts are not yet perfectly clear or distinct. The 'system' considered here is a large set of many (N) elements which may be combined in a great number of ways. Consider for instance the various households and dwellings of a neighborhood in their various relations (congruence of dwellers and dwellings, social relationships between households, potential family ties, architectural relation-ships between buildings, ...). Atlan suggests that a system might self-organize when it is "extremely highly complex" (von Neumann, 1966), that is, with a great number of elements which may be connected. He gives the example of the human brain, with 10^9 neurones. Let us take 5000 households classified in ten different types in a neighborhood, and equal numbers for the dwellings. There are 2.5×10^9 possible combinations between them, so the order of magnitude is the same.

With such a system, let us try to define the basic concepts, with the help of Shannon's Information Theory (Shannon and Weaver, 1949). Let $p(i)$ be the probability that a particular element (or relationship between elements) exists in the system.

(1) The *complexity* is measured by Shannon's entropy H,

$$H = \sum p(i) \ln \frac{1}{p(i)} .$$

(2) The *variety*, H_{max}, is defined as

$$H_{max} = \ln N ;$$

it is a function of the total number of configurations that are possible within the system, assuming that all of them are equally likely.
If $H = H_{max}$, everything is possible; the system is completely disordered.
(3) The *order* is measured by the relative loss of complexity through the interdependence of elements, or in other words, through the constraints impeding some configurations; order is given as

$$R = 1 - \frac{H}{H_{max}} .$$

It is thus equivalent to the concept of *redundancy*.
(4) The *reliability* of a system is its capacity to keep working in spite of the distortion or destruction of some of its components. This quite complicated notion involves some of the concepts defined above. For instance: the redundancy of the elements, the redundancy of the functions performed within the system, the high complexity of the elements, the possibility for the functions to change their location, etc ... (cf Winograd and Cowan, 1963). Such properties are typical of an 'extremely highly complex' system.

Order through redundancy transfer If order is defined in the usual way as redundancy, what are the conditions ensuring its increase in a system? We want

$$\frac{dR}{dt} > 0 , \qquad \text{recalling} \quad R = 1 - \frac{H}{H_{max}} .$$

This becomes

$$\frac{dR}{dt} = \frac{1}{H_{max}^2} \left(H \frac{dH_{max}}{dt} - H_{max} \frac{dH}{dt} \right). \tag{1}$$

Thus assuming that H and H_{max} both increase, order can increase if and only if

$$H\frac{dH_{max}}{dt} > H_{max}\frac{dH}{dt} \ . \tag{2}$$

The variety of the system, H_{max}, can change only through an external influence increasing the potential number of combinations. On the other hand, H represents the inner structure. Equation (1) exhibits the relationship between internal and external influences.

Assuming the variety increases, that is, $dH_{max}/dt > 0$, and recalling the definitions of H and H_{max}, we have

$$1 \geqslant \frac{H}{H_{max}} > \frac{dH}{dt}\bigg/\frac{dH_{max}}{dt} = \frac{\text{change in complexity}}{\text{change in variety}} \ .$$

For a system to increase its order, its complexity (a function of the number of combinations actually achieved) can grow only if its variety (a function of the total number of combinations possible) grows still faster.

Consider Chicago during the 1920s. The constant flow of European immigrants regularly increases H_{max}, that is, the variety of the urban system. The system's complexity, H, (the intricate relations between varied neighborhoods) may increase, and at the same time, the redundancy increases, that is, the constraints organizing, locating, and segregating the neighborhoods. Order in the Burgess model depends upon the immigrant influx.

Los Angeles may suggest another example of a self-organizing urban structure. Let us propose a quite simplified scenario of its evolution since World War II. The city in 1940 is quite homogeneous—the variety H_{max} is small. Many of the possible combinations among households within neighborhoods, or of neighborhoods within the city, have been achieved; H is large and dH/dt is quite small. During the 1940s, the inflow of soldiers and workers, and the in-migration of midwesterners and Blacks greatly increases the variety (dH_{max}/dt is large). The level of redundancy becomes much greater; spatial order in neighborhoods and in the city increases by itself.

During the late 1960s and early 1970s, migration to Los Angeles slowed down; variety no longer grew. Many combinations had not been achieved (because of social or racial prejudice, for instance); H was quite small. Revolutionary ideas from the counter-culture tended, in the late 1960s, to generate new combinations (dH/dt was positive and quite large). Then, redundancy can only decrease: the city was probably in a process of self-disorganization.

A basic function of such a model is to relate external influences transforming a city or a neighborhood (through H_{max}) to internal changes appearing in the H term. Let us assume that, within a city with a constant population, moves by households increase H_{max} in some neighborhoods. Variety will decrease in other neighborhoods. Redundancy is transferred from one district to another: the beautiful ordering of North American suburbs (spatial ordering, social homogeneity, and harmonious human relationships) might be seen as order developed at the expense of decaying central districts where disorder, namely lack of constraints, would increase.

The redundancy transfer might also happen between hierarchical levels or geographical scales: in a city where every neighborhood becomes more homogeneous, order within neighborhoods is clearly growing. On the other hand, the city becomes increasingly heterogeneous, and the city order decreases. Social or racial tensions, for instance, lessen within the neighborhood but are stronger at the city level: they have been transferred from a low geographical level to a higher one.

A transfer of redundancy may thus explain how a city can increase its inner order by itself. It does not explain, however, how order may be preserved through time, in spite of external perturbations.

Self-organization through the absorption of noise Atlan changes the definition of order by making a distinction between *static* (or structural) order, measured by redundancy, and *dynamic* (or functional) order, that is, the ability of the system to cope with random disturbances (noise) and to keep functioning in spite of them. One of the reasons for altering the definition is this: let us consider a system (the macrostate) formed by subsystems (the microstates). If all microstates are different, H is maximal and R is zero—there is no order. On the other hand, if they are all exactly similar, R is maximal and equal to unity. But the system in this case is nothing but the replica, in many copies, of one subsystem, a state which hardly satisfies any intuitive notion of order. Order, then, should correspond to a state located between these extreme situations, and the concept should also include something about the ability of the system to cope with change.

For Atlan, order is no longer measured by redundancy but by the rate of change in complexity dH/dt. A system is able to self-organize when it increases its complexity in spite of (and thanks to) random perturbations. Change in a city may be considered as a message sent by the city at time t (called X) to the same city at time $(t+1)$ (now called Y). According to a theorem attributed to Shannon, noise is able only to obliterate part of the message (decrease the information transported), but never increase it. Order in a city can only perpetuate itself or decrease. There is, however, a subtle way in which H may increase, assuming that other connections, relations, or elements are *realized* in Y which were not present in X. The old order can only decrease, but a new order may be added to it 'spontaneously', that is, by the effect of noise alone.

The problem is this: if order, defined in terms of complexity, does increase, there must be a way for dH/dt to be positive:

$$\frac{dH}{dt} = H_{\max}\left(-\frac{dR}{dt}\right) + (1-R)\frac{dH_{\max}}{dt} \qquad (3)$$

$$= A + B, \quad \text{say.}$$

When noise disrupts a message, $H_{\max}$ can only decrease (Atlan, 1972); B in equation (3) is negative and represents the destruction of information through noise. On the other hand, the same random disturbances tend to violate constraints, that is to decrease redundancy, and A is positive. In these circumstances, the sum $(A + B)$ may then be positive.

Noise plays a dialectical role: it always destroys some information but at the same time it makes it possible, by eliminating some constraints, for new combinations which were impossible before to appear within the system. In this way, noise increases the overall complexity, or the dynamic order as defined by Atlan.

A different approach may also account for self-organization in an urban system. A graph proposed by Bourgeois (Atlan, 1979, page 66) will help to clarify the model. Consider a neighborhood called X at time t, which becomes Y at time $(t + 1)$ (figure 7.1). Only a part of the past complexity is transmitted, namely $I(x, y)$, the joint information common both to X and Y. The quantity of order obliterated by change is $H(x|y)$, the *equivocation* (the entropy of x given y). Noise adds some ambiguity to the old structure, that is $H(y|x)$. At the neighborhood level, order has decreased by the quantity called equivocation.

Assume, however, that the neighborhood has not been destroyed by change. Relationships between households and between dwellings, as well as the various kinds of congruence between dwellers and dwellings,

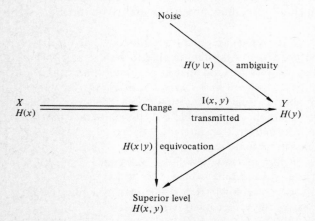

Figure 7.1. Conservation of information at a superior level, after change.

have somehow changed. Some have disappeared, new ones are now functioning, but local life and local unity are still there. New relationships have appeared within the city, and the old ones which have vanished from the neighborhood have left their mark on the urban community. At the city level, equivocation is not completely lost, and ambiguity is added to the order transmitted. On this global scale (city level), total order, after change, is measured by

$$H(x, y) = H(x) + H(x \mid y)$$
$$= \underset{\substack{\text{order} \\ \text{transmitted}}}{I(x, y)} + \underset{\substack{\text{order} \\ \text{added}}}{H(y \mid x)} + \underset{\substack{\text{order} \\ \text{lost}}}{H(x \mid y)}. \tag{4}$$

Equation (4) assumes that all existing functions are still performed somehow in the new neighborhood, which is not always true. Figure 7.1 shows how information lost at a local level may be recovered at a higher one. This is a quite new approach. Shannon did not consider systems organized in a hierarchy, nor the information transfers which might happen through aggregation.

One other important concept is also missing in Shannon's theory: the *meaning* of a message, and it too may lead to an interesting approach in this case. Entropy depends only on the probabilities of different elements of the message, or combinations of elements, whatever their significance. How is the meaning of a message (in this particular case, of change in a neighborhood) to be defined? Atlan (after Poincaré) suggests that it is nothing else than the *effect* the message has on the receiver. With such a definition, $H(x, y)$ the global information transferred through change in a neighborhood to the whole urban organism, would represent the *meaning* of such change, inasmuch as it might induce effects either in the global city order, or in other particular neighborhoods. A large city would then appear as an ordered system ('extremely highly complex'), with an ability to adapt to incessant random perturbations and to receive meaningful messages from its components. It could, in favorable cases (as when the system has enough potential relations or functions to substitute new ones for the old ones which change has discarded), feed on noise to maintain or increase its internal (and particularly spatial) order. It would react meaningfully to changes in its neighborhoods as a *subject*[9] does, without any reference, of course, to life or consciousness. These many similarities to the behavior of living organisms may explain the confusion to be found in so many writers: urban ecologists treating the city as a growing tree, radical geographers seeing conscious and malevolent plots in the most spontaneous urban changes.

---

[9] The word is taken here in the meaning of the Frankfurt School; see Marcuse (1960, page viii), where the term has an important dialectical meaning.

The order in a system is defined by von Foerster and by Atlan in different ways but they are less contradictory than they might appear. Von Foerster sees order in redundancy; Atlan, in the transformation of redundancy into complexity. The first definition is static, the second, dynamic. For Atlan, a system able to self-organize must contain, initially, a certain amount of redundancy, that is, inner constraints which are successively broken as the complexity (the entropy) of the system increases. The speed of this increase, the velocity with which redundancy is consumed, determines the *reliability* of the system; in other words, the time during which the system persists as an ordered structure.

The model proposed here is not complete. Rather, it is intended to show a direction of research which should lead to the preparation of a model of urban growth. Difficulties still exist: definitions of the basic concept are not yet unequivocal, and more conceptual research is necessary. Measurements are difficult if not impossible at this stage: how does one express in figures the redundancy or the entropy of an urban system?

On the other hand, several interesting points may be highlighted:

First the separation of forms and processes as well as the existence of redundancy thresholds beyond which a system suddenly breaks down seem to lead directly to Catastrophe Theory: the link with Thom's work remains to be investigated (Thom, 1974; Wilson, 1982).

Second the dialectical relationship between the individual and the group, one of the basic problems in social science today, is expressed here in terms of Redundancy and Information transfers. This is an important addition to Shannon's theory, and a fascinating method of research.

Third the definition proposed by Atlan makes order a dynamic concept— it is not so much the state of a system, but rather its ability to withstand change; opposition between the concepts of *structural* order (redundancy) and *functional* order (the entropy derivative over time) is most important.

Fourth Redundancy plays a contradictory role in the model. In one way, it does represent order in the system; but in another, it is a reservoir of limitations which are designed to be subverted in order to ensure higher complexity, assuming that the system is so abundant in unused combinations that it will be able to propose new ones to do the job. From this viewpoint, urban constraints, be they prejudices, traditions, or zoning laws, are useful to ensure order inasmuch as they might be broken and violated: such a model is typically Hegelian in its dialectical structure.

Last a system, in this model, is ordered if, and only if, it has a sufficiently large number of latent, unused combinations (that is, a high redundancy). This is a long way from, if not completely opposed to, the concepts of *efficiency* and *equilibrium* pervading most economic models.

7.3 Conclusion: Los Angeles and the urban planning process

Even if urban forms and urban content are independent in their nature and in their origin, they obviously react upon each other. Geographical patterns, once formed and frozen, influence economic and social changes; on the other hand, the movement of people and activities generates new forms and tends to complicate the overall geographical pattern. Change in the city results from the dialectic between these two systems.

If this is actually the structure hidden behind the turmoil of apparent facts, what role is left to planning? Obviously, to facilitate the operation of these complicated dialectical mechanisms—at least as far as we consider the problem to be to accommodate the population, that is to say, to adjust housing, education, recreation, transport, etc, to its needs in a situation of competition and of fast turnover. Hence the contradictory nature of planning in Los Angeles; trying to preserve land rent, to house the poor, to protect the integrity of neighborhoods, to ease social progress, to avoid discrimination (for instance, by bussing), to safeguard privileges, and so on.

The role of planning is certainly very different in other industrial societies with strong socialist policies: in Western Europe, planners in Sweden or in France, in Italy or in the United Kingdom have a more ambitious role. The double system of mechanisms described above tends also to be at work, but many of these processes are slowed down, distorted, reinforced and sometimes even stopped by urban planning. Social segregation in different homogeneous neighborhoods is opposed quite often with various degrees of success. Interestingly enough, policies tending more energetically toward such a goal, as in Scandinavian countries, at the same time weaken at the microlevel the interindividual or interfamily struggle for progress in the social field. One cannot alter one step in the social dialectics without altering the whole dialectical system. Actually, socialist planning tends to create a strong relation between the two systems, which are so radically separated in a free-market economy. In New Towns for instance, be it in England, France, or the Netherlands, the system of urban form, that is, the layout of the city, is determined from scratch in order to house a population which is well defined, and to defuse social tensions as much as possible.

This is in complete contrast with the evolution of Los Angeles, which definitely does not appear as the necessary model toward which all big cities in the world should evolve. On the other hand, the fact that Los Angeles is certainly not the unique model of all future metropolises does not imply that it is a failure. Far from being a disorganized suburb of monstrous size, Los Angeles appears as a well-patterned, logically evolving and strongly organized city where everyday life is probably easier, safer, and sweeter than in most metropolises on the East Coast. The dream has not come true, but certainly it has not turned into a nightmare.

Appendix A: three-way factor analysis

Data taken from a particular census are usually organized in a two-way
table with locations in rows and variables in columns. The study of the
historical evolution of a city leads naturally to the analysis of several
censuses taken at different periods and put together in a three-way table,
that is a cube, with time constituting the third dimension to locations and
variables. It is well known, but sometimes forgotten, that factor analyses
run separately on different censuses may not be compared—their vector
bases (the eigenvectors defined from each data set) are different. Data
taken from different censuses must be grouped into such a cube and
analyzed together.
   A method for such three-way factor analysis has been proposed by
Ledyard Tucker: the method itself is presented in Tucker (1963; 1964);
its first applications in Tucker (1965); and with different algorithms in
Tucker (1966). A more detailed presentation does not add much to
Tucker's papers (Levin, 1965). The relationship between three-way factor
analysis and multidimensional scaling is investigated in Tucker (1972).
A recent publication presents an excellent review of the method
(Kroonenberg, 1983). This methodological approach has been virtually
ignored by geographers (see Cant, 1971).

A1 The mathematical model
The method consists of unfolding the cubic data matrix (called $\mathbf{X}$) into
three parts which are subjected to a factor analysis, and then relating
these three analyses through a central cubic matrix (or core-matrix),
which forms the most original part of the model.

A1.1 Preparing the data
It will be convenient to use Tucker's notation. Let $\mathbf{Z}$ be an i rows,
j columns matrix, and $\mathbf{Y}$ a j rows, k columns matrix. Then, their product
will be

$$\mathbf{Z} \cdot \mathbf{Y} = {}_i\mathbf{Z}_j\mathbf{Y}_k \; ,$$

where the order in which matrices are multiplied is clearly shown. In
classical matrix calculus, operations are defined for two-way matrices only.
Tucker does not propose new operations, but a way of transforming the
data cube $\mathbf{X}$ by collapsing two of its three entries. This can be done in
three different ways: ${}_{kj}\mathbf{X}_i$, for instance, represents the two-way matrix
where each row corresponds to variable j measured at time k, and each
column to location i.
   Unfolding the data cube presents the problem of how to standardize
the data for each of the three entries. Let I be the set of census tracts
(locations), J the set of variables, and K the set of periods (census years).
Standardizing ${}_{ik}\mathbf{X}_j$ along j is straightforward, but the same exercise (which
involves computing the mean, the standard deviation, and the z score)
along i for ${}_{jk}\mathbf{X}_i$ is, in general, impossible. It would involve adding together

data in different units of measurement such as average income in dollars and median school years completed. Tucker suggests a few solutions but none of them are really satisfactory. There is, however, one easy way out of this predicament, namely by converting all the data into percentages (scalars without units). In this analysis nine variables have been used. They describe the population and housing of Los Angeles as percentages of the total value in each census tract.

Each of the three matrices resulting from the unfolding of the original cube matrix is analyzed into its principal components (a new vectorial basis is calculated from the eigenvectors weighted by the square root of the corresponding eigenvalues).

A1.2 The model

The analysis consists of two steps:

First the three original data matrices are each subjected to a principal components analysis. Locations, i, are grouped into 'types of neighborhood', m; variables, j, into 'types of variables', p; and periods, k, into 'types of periods', q.

Second These groupings of neighborhoods, variables, and periods (which Tucker calls "derivational modes" or "idealized modes") are then related by a small cube matrix **G**, the 'core-matrix' (figure 6.2).

In the Los Angeles analysis the 309 census tracts have been grouped, by means of a principal components analysis, into five different types of neighborhood. Hence the cardinals of the different sets are:

$$\text{card } i = 309; \quad \text{card } m = 5 .$$

In the same way, the nine original variables (card $j = 9$) have been grouped into three general types (card $p = 3$), and the four periods form two types of evolution (card $k = 4$; card $q = 2$).

The core-matrix **G** relates the three different groups of principal components, that is, the three groups of 'types'. An observation x_{ijk} is broken up into a linear combination of idealized types of places, variables, and periods, and a global coefficient g relating these types. The model is:

$$x_{ijk} = \sum_m \sum_p \sum_q a_{im} b_{jp} c_{kq} g_{mpq} . \tag{A1}$$

The value of the method lies both in the power of the unfolding procedures, which ensure that the data are treated simultaneously and completely, and in the core-matrix **G**, which synthesizes the three analyses. For instance, the analysis of $_i\mathbf{X}_{kj}$ produces types of changing neighborhoods, since each census tract is characterized by nine variables measured at four different times. In the same way, the analysis of $_j\mathbf{X}_{ki}$ produces different types of variables, which are basically dynamic since each variable is measured over all census tracts and for all census periods.

A1.3 Kronecker's product

The model may be represented easily by the use of the *dirext matrix product* defined by Kronecker (Bellman, 1970, page 235 et seq; Stenger, 1968).
Let us consider two matrices $_i\mathbf{A}_m$ and $_j\mathbf{B}_p$. Their Kronecker product $\mathbf{H}$ is

$$_{ij}\mathbf{H}_{mp} = {}_i\mathbf{A}_m \,\&\, _j\mathbf{B}_p$$

(where & represents the Kronecker operation).

Actually, $\mathbf{H}$ is a supermatrix, where each entry is the matrix $\mathbf{B}$ multiplied by a scalar which is precisely the corresponding element of matrix $\mathbf{A}$.

If $\mathbf{A}$ and $\mathbf{B}$ are nonsingular, we have (with $\mathbf{I}$ being the identity matrix)

$$(_m\mathbf{A}_i^{-1} \,\&\, _p\mathbf{B}_j^{-1}) \cdot (_i\mathbf{A}_m \,\&\, _j\mathbf{B}_p) = {}_{mp}\mathbf{I}_{mp} \,.$$

The basic model (1) can now be written

$$_i\mathbf{X}_{jk} = {}_i\mathbf{A}_m\mathbf{G}_{pq}(_p\mathbf{B}_j \,\&\, _q\mathbf{C}_k) \,. \tag{A2}$$

Recall that $\mathbf{A}$, $\mathbf{B}$, and $\mathbf{C}$ are matrices representing locations, variables, and periods, after these have been regrouped, by three initial factor analyses, in synthetic types. The role of the core-matrix $\mathbf{G}$ is to act as the transformer between the general types and the original observations.

A1.4 The unfolding of the original cube matrix

Let us represent the three different ways of unfolding the original data matrix:

$$\left.\begin{array}{l} _i\mathbf{M}_i = {}_i\mathbf{X}_{jk}\mathbf{X}_i \,, \\[4pt] _j\mathbf{P}_j = {}_j\mathbf{X}_{ik}\mathbf{X}_j \,, \\[4pt] _k\mathbf{Q}_k = {}_k\mathbf{X}_{ij}\mathbf{X}_k \,. \end{array}\right\} \tag{A3}$$

Substituting equation (A2) in equations (A3), we get

$$_i\mathbf{M}_i = {}_i\mathbf{A}_m^*\mathbf{G}_{pq}(_p\mathbf{B}_j \,\&\, _q\mathbf{C}_k)(_j\mathbf{B}_p \,\&\, _k\mathbf{C}_q)_{pq}\mathbf{G}_m^*\mathbf{A}_i \,.$$

It is more convenient to factorize all the internal products (between *) by defining

$$_m\mathbf{M}_m = {}_m\mathbf{G}_{pq}(_p\mathbf{B}_j \,\&\, _q\mathbf{C}_k)(_j\mathbf{B}_p \,\&\, _k\mathbf{C}_q)_{pq}\mathbf{G}_m \,. \tag{A4}$$

Then we have

$$_i\mathbf{M}_i = {}_i\mathbf{A}_m\mathbf{M}_m\mathbf{A}_i \,. \tag{A5}$$

Equation (A5) suggests a particularly interesting idea (cf. Tucker, 1966, page 289). The transformed matrix $_i\mathbf{M}_i$ appears as the product of an equivalent matrix $_m\mathbf{M}_m$, taking the role of a covariance matrix, and $_i\mathbf{A}_m$, representing factors. In other words, matrix $_i\mathbf{M}_i$ seems to be broken up into a principal components analysis, where $_m\mathbf{M}_m$ is the equivalent of the diagonal matrix containing the eigenvalues, and $_i\mathbf{A}_m$ the matrix containing the eigenvectors. Hence, three-way factor analysis may take the usual form of classical component analysis.

A particularly important instance is when matrices **A**, **B**, and **C** are orthonormal (viz. when their square product is the identity matrix). Equation (A4) then simplifies to

$$_mM_m = {_mG_{pq}}\,G_m \,. \tag{A6}$$

In this case, each entry in the diagonal of **M** is the sum of the squares of the entries located in the corresponding plane of the matrix **G**. In this study of Los Angeles, only principal component analyses will be used. As a result, matrix **M** will be simply a diagonal matrix containing the eigenvalues of $_iM_i$. Thus each of these eigenvalues will be the sum of the squares of the entries in core-matrix **G** chosen in the plane corresponding, within **G**, to each value of index m. Unfortunately such a simple relation is not true any longer if one of the decomposition matrices **A**, **B**, or **C** is not orthonormal. Eigenvalues written in $_mM_m$ are not obtained by the simple formula (A6) but by the more general equation (A4), where the sum of the squares of the entries in a plane within matrix **G** is weighted by a double Kronecker product.

A2 The computer algorithm

In order to analyze the change in population and housing in Los Angeles, I have used a parallelepipedic matrix **X** constructed as the cartesian product of
   a set of locations I (card I = 309); seven tracts where data were
   dubious or missing have been omitted;
   a set of variables J (card J = 9); all of which are expressed as percentages;
   a set of periods K (card K = 4); representing the four censuses: 1940,
   1950, 1960, and 1970.
Matrix **X** can easily be unfolded in two ways:
   as a $_jP_j$ matrix (9 by 9) entering variables against each other, and
   as a $_kQ_k$ matrix (4 by 4) entering the periods.
A third unfolding is needed, producing an $_iM_i$ matrix entering census tracts, but this would be a 309 by 309 matrix, far too large to allow the extraction of its eigenvalues and its eigenvectors. Furthermore, it will have a high redundancy and a very low rank; that is, most of its eigenvalues will be close to zero.

Tucker proposes a convenient algorithm to avoid such obstacles (see method II in Tucker, 1966, page 298). Instead of directly calculating **M**, **P**, and **Q** and then computing the core-matrix **G**, he suggests calculating **P** and **Q**, computing **G**, and finally reconstructing **A**. In the Los Angeles case this is the only practical method. However it has a defect, since **A** is no longer the result of a principal component analysis and is not orthonormal.

A completely new program has been written in FORTRAN for the computer; eigenvalues and eigenvectors are extracted with the help of the EISPACK program from Argonne Laboratory.

A2.1 Calculating the P matrix

From equation (A3) it can be seen that

$$_j P_j = {}_j X_{ik} X_j .$$

A principal component analysis of **P** shows that only three eigenvalues are clearly larger than zero (table 6.5). In this analysis, eigenvalues accounting for less than 1% of the total variance have been omitted, and the corresponding eigenvectors have been dropped.

The nine variables have thus been replaced by three eigenvectors ($j = 9$ is replaced by $p = 3$), which simplifies the computations that follow. Finally, the transformation leads to the construction of two matrices:

a diagonal matrix, $_p P_p$, containing the first p eigenvalues; and

an orthonormal matrix, $_j B_p$, whose columns are the eigenvectors of $_p P_p$.

It is then possible to return to the original data and to simplify them by computing

$$_p X_{ik} = {}_p B_j X_{ik} .$$

This smaller **X** matrix, with p instead of j rows, is thus obtained through a change of variable with little loss of information.

A2.2 Calculating Q

Time periods can be arrayed against each other in a similar fashion:

$$_k Q_k = {}_k X_{ij} X_k ,$$

but it is far easier to use the following estimation of **Q**, viz

$$_k Q_k = {}_k X_{ip} X_k ,$$

which is the square of the transpose of **X** as obtained above. A principal component analysis of **Q** again gives the opportunity to omit eigenvalues too close to zero: the k ($= 4$) periods are reduced to q ($= 2$) time groups (table 6.6). $_q Q_q$ is a diagonal matrix, containing the two significant eigenvalues, and $_k C_q$, an orthonormal matrix, whose columns are the corresponding eigenvectors of $_k Q_k$.

The size of the data matrix **X** may be conveniently reduced by replacing the four census periods by the two types which summarize them:

$$_q X_{ip} = {}_q C_k X_{ip} .$$

The data matrix is then unfolded in $_i X_{pq}$.

A2.3 Calculating the S matrix

It is advisable to avoid the calculation of a matrix as large as **A**. It can be seen that

$$_{pq} S_{pq} = {}_{pq} X_i X_{pq} ,$$

where **S** is a small matrix ($pq = 6$) which is easy to analyze (table 6.7).

One eigenvalue is zero, therefore only five remain ($m = 5$). The following matrices can be constructed:

$_mS_m$ a diagonal matrix containing these five eigenvalues, and

$_{pq}V_m$ whose columns are the eigenvectors of S.

A2.4 Estimating the core-matrix G

A principal component analysis of S produces a matrix G conveniently unfolded as:

$$_{pq}G_m = {}_{pq}V_m S_m^{\frac{1}{2}} .$$

In this case Tucker uses a method for approximating the matrix with another one of smaller rank (cf. Eckart and Young, 1936). The same method was used in section 6.1.2.

A2.5 Estimating matrix A

It is now possible to reconstruct matrix A.

$$_iA_m = {}_iX_{pq}V_m S_m^{-\frac{1}{2}} .$$

Matrix A enters 309 tracts with 5 types of neighborhood, which provides the possibility of mapping these neighborhoods (see figures 6.3–6.6).

Matrix A, however, has a defect: it is obtained through successive orthogonal rotations by multiplying the original data matrix X by matrices B, C, and V. In general, matrix X is not orthogonal; its column vectors, that is, the variables in the analysis, are usually correlated. Consequently matrix A, the result of these rotations, is not orthogonal. Table 6.9 indicates the correlations between the five column vectors in A; the fifth type of district is strongly correlated with the third type. Since A is not orthogonal, it is not possible to use formula (A6). The two matrices, B and C, are orthonormal since their columns are eigenvectors—the core-matrix G links them exactly. This is the reason why M is the only matrix in this study which verifies equation (A6), each of its eigenvalues (table 6.10) is actually the sum of the squares of the entries in the corresponding slice in G.

This is not the case for P and Q. Differences between their eigenvalues and the corresponding sum of squares are generally small, except for their bigger eigenvalues. Since the two eigenvectors corresponding to the bigger eigenvalues of P and Q represent the most important, but also the most obvious and banal, phenomena, such a deficiency is not too dangerous. It does not hinder the interpretation of the other eigenvectors where less conspicuous and more intriguing phenomena are represented. More important still, the mapping of the different types of evolution of the districts, which is the main objective of this analysis, is not disturbed in any way by the particular properties of P and Q.

Appendix B: the theory of regionalized variables

Mining engineers have to draw continuous maps of ore content from discrete data obtained from separate drillings. Two different approaches are used. One method consists of fitting a polynomial surface to the data (*trend surface analysis*); this method is quite safe because it makes no initial assumptions. Its shortcomings, however, are well known: the choice of the polynomial degree is arbitrary—an $(n-1)$-degree surface fits perfectly an n-points distribution, but if n is large, the surface is quite intractable. Usually, the researcher tries through various methods to find a low-degree polynomial with quite a good fit. Another drawback is that the method describes the data but gives no indication of the sampling errors, which makes comparisons very difficult.

Another approach, the *theory of regionalized variables* (TRV), is based on spatial autocorrelation. First it identifies the spatial structure, if any, making interpolation much easier. After computing the 'variogram', which describes the spatial structure, the researcher must assume a spatial model that fits the empirical curve of the variogram. This is the delicate part of the method. But the information added in this way (by assuming a model) allows one to produce not only a continuous map of the data, but also a map of the sampling errors.

Both methods are widely used: trend surface analysis is common in North America, and TRV more fashionable in Europe and in South Africa. Only the first step of TRV is used here, that is the description of spatial structures by means of variograms; no delicate assumption will be necessary [for a good comparison of both approaches, see Davis (1973); for TRV, see Matheron (1965; 1970); Serra (1967); for a short introduction Ciceri et al (1977)].

B1 The foundations of TRV

A 'regionalized variable' is a variable Y taking a value $Y(x)$ at each point x of a certain portion of space. Its 'field', V, is the domain where its value is not zero.

B1.1 The 'transitive' approach

Consider a regionalized variable Y and its field, V. Let x and $(x+h)$ be two points in this field separated by a vector h representing the translation or 'transition' from x to $(x+h)$. The transitive covariogram of Y is the function g(h) defined by:

$$g(h) = \int_V Y(x)Y(x+h)\,dx \ .$$

It is a spatial autocorrelation function depending only on the small translation vector h.

B1.2 The 'intrinsic' approach

Let us define a random variable, Y, at each point x of the field. The random function $Y(x)$ takes on a value at each point x, which is not a scalar but a random variable, that is a vector (Matheron, 1970, page 50). Any random sampling which is applied to the function $Y(x)$ will produce a particular scalar value y, across space, at each point x. In fact, y is a particular realization of the random variable Y. Thus, a regionalized variable, y (the set of measurements of an empirical variable across space) may be considered as a realization of some random variable Y at point x. This approach is particularly useful because it makes it possible to apply probability calculus to empirical (that is, observed) regionalized variables: for instance to compute the statistical moments of the function $Y(x)$.

Unfortunately, statistical inference is not possible if there is only one realization of Y. The missing information must be replaced by some hypothesis: for instance, that the random variable is somehow 'stationary' — Y is assumed to be invariant under translation; the choice of the origin is then immaterial. Such a condition, however, is very strong and it is not very often met. Matheron suggests a weaker assumption, namely that Y is "order 2 stationary", meaning that the variance of the variable is finite. Many studies of mining ores, however, have exhibited a priori variances which were infinite. For instance, when the size of the sample taken where the measurement is made (say, the volume of ore extracted to estimate its gold content) decreases, as the field where the regionalized variable is analyzed, increases, the variance may tend to the infinite.

Such difficulty is avoided by making a more convenient assumption. Suppose that the increments of the variable $[Y(x) - Y(x+h)]$ have a finite variance; this is the so-called *intrinsic hypothesis*, a very weak assumption. Then the method consists of studying not the value of Y at two different locations, but the difference between these two values. The intrinsic function, or 'variogram' r(h) is defined by:

$$r(h) = \frac{1}{V}\int_V [Y(x) - Y(x+h)]^2 \, dx \, ,$$

with x moving across the field, V, and h representing the mesh of the spatial filter.

B1.3 The variogram

When dealing with n regionalized observations, one computes the discrete sum:

$$r(h) = \frac{1}{n}\sum_{i=1}^{n} [Y(x_i) - Y(x_i+h)]^2 \, ,$$

that is, the quadratic mean of the differences between all points separated by a distance h. The function r is not attached to any particular point but describes the whole field.

Actually, h is a vector, with a direction and a length. If space is *isotropic* (with the same properties in all directions), h is only a measure of interval; the intrinsic function, in this case, indicates the average relation between any pair of points separated by h. Space anisotropy may be identified by studying the r function along different directions.

Let us plot the values of $r(h)$ for increasing values of h. Such a curve is the basic tool used here to analyze spatial structures. Each part of the curve has an important meaning:

Slope at the origin This describes the regularity of space. A parabolic curve, concave upwards $[r(h) \approx h^2]$, shows an extreme regularity—the variable varies very little for a small translation, but changes a lot for larger transitions. A linear variogram $[r(h) \approx h]$ indicates an average regularity; the function is continuous only by parts. A curve concave downward $[r(h) \approx h^{1/2}]$, say, with an almost vertical slope at the origin, is characteristic of a very irregular space—two measurements of the same variable taken at very close locations may produce very different results; such spatial structure is quite similar to the 'nugget effect' explained below.

Range Usually, points increasingly distant differ more and more [that is, $r(h)$ increases with h] up to a certain distance, h_0. Beyond this threshold, differences between the measurements of a variable do not increase any more and the variogram shows a plateau. The threshold h_0, if it exists, has an important meaning—it measures the spatial extension of a structure. For instance, assume that census tract A is quite rich. The neighboring tract B is likely to be quite rich too. In other words: knowing the average income in A gives certain information about the income in B. As we move away from tract A, however, this joint information usually decreases; 20 km from A, local income may have any value. The range shows the existence, for a given variable, of a spatial structure, and measures its extension.

Embedded structures As h grows, the variogram may reach a plateau, then increase again to a new plateau. In this case, the variable is organized through space in two different (embedded) structures, like two sedimentary lenses of different size nested in each other.

The nugget effect Obviously, $r(h)$ can be computed only for values of h different from zero. If one extrapolates the variogram to the left (toward the origin), it may not meet the vertical axis at the origin; in other words, $r(O)$ may not be zero. A not infrequent example would be an almost horizontal variogram running at a constant height above the horizontal axis. This 'nugget effect' is typical of sediments where gold nuggets are embedded in clay. It reveals the presence of hidden structures existing at too small a scale to be picked up by the analysis: the mesh of the net (the size of increment h) is too large to display such minute structures, which are detected only in a negative manner.

The theory usually progresses in two different stages. The description of the eventual spatial structures for a given variable is based on the variogram. The intrinsic hypothesis is weak and generally met; actually it is even possible, through the transitive approach, to define the variogram and to compute it without caring about the initial assumptions. This first step is very safe. The r function is only a descriptive tool, but a very powerful one. Serra gives the example of iron mines in Eastern France: more than 10000 deep drillings have been made over a century, and various generations of geologists have carefully observed the deposits. Many sedimental structures at a large scale (10 km) or at a small scale (a couple of meters) have been described, but most lenses of an intermediate scale ($\approx$ 500 m) have been overlooked for the lack of an adequate means of analysis (Serra, 1967, page 296).

The second step, *or kriging*, replaces the empirical variogram by an assumed mathematical curve, and proceeds to interpolate the variable and to build a map of sampling errors. This is the most useful, but also the most delicate part of the method. In this urban analysis it would have no meaning.

B2 Building variograms for Los Angeles

The theory of regionalized variables has been used outside the field of mining (for example, Delhomme and Delfiner, 1973), but not previously in urban analysis. Actually, census data are quite different from mining samples and a careful adaptation is needed.

The measurements of a variable taken at different locations must be comparable, but census tracts have different areas and varied populations. Mining engineers use densities (grams of gold per ton, for instance); in this study, either percentages or statistical moments of first order, like means or medians, have been used. The location of the tracts has been defined by giving coordinates to their centers of gravity. In order to compute the intrinsic function, a FORTRAN program sent by J Serra has been used, which has been extensively modified. The mesh, h, is regularly increased in 500 meter increments.

The nature of the tracts, their forms, and their variety creates the main problems: (1) the variables analyzed (say, median family income per tract) are not calculated from a sample taken at a point, but by an average measure over the area of the census tract; and (2) the union of all tracts is equal to the whole city area, whereas mining samples represent only a very small portion of the field which is being analyzed.

There seems to be no easy solution to such problems. One might like to take a sample among 'block groups', smaller spatial units included within the census tracts, but this would omit a large amount of available information, which seems a bad approach. Thus one must assume that within a census tract all points have the same average value, and that by studying only the center of gravity of the tract, this represents the whole spatial unit. Such an assumption is always made when dealing with means or medians.

The irregularity in the shape and the size of the tracts may introduce another bias—it has the effect of superimposing the structure of the administrative grid onto the structure of the variables. The result may not be so bad because the administrative grid is obviously related to the spatial distribution of most values characterizing population and housing. Curry has suggested checking the bias with a method invented by Tobler: construct a regular grid of very small square cells and superimpose it onto the irregular grid of census tracts. Attach a random variable to each square cell, and compute its mean value for each census tract. The effect of the different shapes of the tracts, if any, will appear in the anisotropy of the variogram. The random variable, as a white noise, should produce a flat variogram, that is, a perfect nugget effect. Any important deviation from the horizontal indicates the structuring effect of the administrative grid.

Actually, the experiment shows that no perturbation appears along the northwest–southeast transect: it is a clear nugget effect. On the other hand, along the northeast–southwest transect the administrative grid weakly structures the urban space with a range of about 1.5 to 2 km. This structure has an historical origin in the combination of small tracts around the Downtown with the larger ones in the more recent districts along the ocean. This small effect is taken into account in the interpretation of the variograms (chapter 6.3).

References

ACSC, 1957 *Los Angeles Metropolitan Peak-Hours Driving Study,* Engineering Department, Automobile Club of South California

Alonso W, 1964a, "The historic and the structural theories of urban form: their implications for urban renewal" *Land Economics* **40** 227–231

Alonso W, 1964b *Location and Land Use* (Harvard University Press, Cambridge, MA)

Alonso W, 1971, "Urban growth in California: new towns and other policy alternatives", WP-150, Institute of Urban and Regional Development, University of California at Berkeley, CA

Anger K, 1975 *Hollywood-Babylon* (Bell, New York)

Arnold D, Robert K, and others, 1960 *The California Economy, 1947–50* Stanford Research Institute, Menlo Park, CA

Arthur D Little Inc., 1963, "The control of land development and urbanisation in California" in Governor's Advisory Commission on Housing Problems, Appendix to the *Report on Housing in California,* Sacramento, CA

Atlan H, 1972 *L'Organisation Biologique et la Théorie de l'Information* (Hermann, Paris)

Atlan H, 1979 *Entre le Cristal et la Fumée* (Editions du Seuil, Paris)

Bachelard G, 1957 *La Poétique de l'Espace* (Presses Universitaires de France, Paris)

Banham R, 1971 *Los Angeles: The Architecture of Four Ecologies* (Penguin Books, Harmondsworth, Middx)

Barthes R, 1967 *Système de la Mode* (Editions du Seuil, Paris)

Baudrillard J, 1968 *Le Système des Objets* (Denoël, Paris)

Baudrillard J, 1972 *Pour une Critique de l'Économie Politique du Signe* Collection TEL (Gallimard, Paris)

Bell W, Shevky E, 1948 *Social Area Analysis* (Stanford University Press, Stanford, CA)

Bellman R, 1970 *Introduction to Matrix Analysis* second edition (McGraw-Hill, New York)

Benzécri J P, 1976, "Histoire et préhistoire de l'analyse des données" *Cahiers de l'Analyse des Données, Volume 2* (Dunod, Paris)

Berry B J L, 1971, "Introduction: the logic and limitations of comparative factorial ecology" *Economic Geography* **47**(2) supplement

Berry B J L, Horton F, 1970 *Geographic Perspectives on Urban Systems* (Prentice-Hall, Englewood Cliffs, NJ)

Bogue D J, 1953 *Population Growth in SMA, 1900–1950* Housing Research, Housing and Home Financing Agency, Washington, DC

Bogue D J, 1959 *The Population of the United States* (Free Press, New York)

Bogue D J, Harris D L, 1954 *Comparative Population and Urban Research via Multiple Regression and Covariance Analysis* Studies in Population Distribution 8, Scripps Foundation, Miami University, Oxford, OH

Bourdieu P, 1979 *La Distinction, Critique Sociale du Jugement* (Minuit, Paris)

Bowman L, 1974 *Los Angeles: Epic of a City* (Howell-North, Los Angeles)

Box G, Jenkins G, 1970 *Time Series Analysis: Forecasting and Control* (Holden-Day, San Francisco, CA)

Brodsly D, 1982 *Los Angeles Freeways, An Appreciative Essay* (University of California Press, Berkeley, CA)

Brooks de Graaf L, 1962 *Negro Migration to Los Angeles: 1930–1950* Doctoral Dissertation, University of California, Los Angeles

Burton R, Dyckman J W, 1965, "Defense expenditures in forecasts of California's economic growth" *The Western Economic Journal* **3**(2) 140–151

Cant R G, 1971, "Changes in the location of manufacturing in New Zealand 1957–1968: An application of three-mode factor analysis" *New Zealand Geographer* **27** 38–55

Carlin A, Wohl M, 1968 *An Economic Re-evaluation of the Proposed LA Rapid Transit System* P-3918, The Rand Corporation, Santa Monica, CA

Carr H, 1935 *Los Angeles, City of Dreams* (New York)

Case F E, 1972 *Black Capitalism: A Case Study of Los Angeles* (Praeger, New York)

Castells M, 1972 *La Question Urbaine* (Maspéro, Paris)

Cattell R B, 1952 *Factor Analysis: An Introduction and Manual for the Psychologist and the Social Scientist* (Harper and Row, New York)

Caughey J L, 1976 *Los Angeles, Biography of a City* (University of California Press, Berkeley, CA)

Ciceri m-F, 1974 *L'Analyse Multivariée dans la Géographie de Langue Anglaise* Institut de Géographie, Université de Paris, Paris

Ciceri M-F, Marchand B, Rimbert S, 1977 *Introduction à l'Analyse de l'Espace* (Masson, Paris)

Clark W A, Cadwallader M, 1973, "Residential preferences, an alternate view of intraurban space" *Environment and Planning* **5** 693-703

Clark W A, Nelson H J, 1976 *Los Angeles: The Metropolitan Experience* (Ballinger, Los Angeles)

Clayton J L, 1962, "Defense spending: key to California's growth" *Western Political Quarterly* **XV** (June) 280-293

Coale A J, Stephan F F, 1962, "The case of the Indians and the teenage widows" *Journal of the American Statistical Association* **57** 338-347

Cohen J, Murphy W S, 1966 *Burn, Baby, Burn! The Los Angeles Race Riot, August 1965* (Dutton, New York)

Colby C, 1933, "Centrifugal and centripetal forces in urban geography" *Annals of the Association of American Geographers* **XXIII** 1-21

Coulter E J, Couralmick L, 1959, "Analysis of vital statistics by census tract" *Journal of the American Statistical Association* **54** 730-740

Crouch W, Dinerman B, 1963 *South California Metropolis. A Study in Development of Government for a Metropolitan Area* (University of California Press, Berkeley, CA)

Dash N, 1976 *Yesterday's Los Angeles* (Seemann, Miami, FL)

Davis J, 1973 *Statistics and Data Analysis in Geology* (John Wiley, New York)

Delhomme J-P, Delfiner P, 1973 *Application du Krigreage à l'Optimisation d'une Campagne Pluviometrique en Zone Aride* Centre de Morphologie Mathématique, Ecole Nationale des Mines de Paris, Paris

Duncan O D, Cuzzort R P, Duncan B, 1961 *Statistical Geography: Problems in Analysing Areal Data* (Free Press, New York)

Dupuy J-P, 1982 *Ordres et Désordres* (Minuit, Paris)

Eckart C J, Young G, 1966, "The approximation of one matrix by another of lower rank" *Psychometrika* **27**(1) 211-218

Fogel W, 1967, "Mexican Americans in Southwest labor markets" Report number 10, Los Angeles Mexican-American Study Project

Fogelson R M, 1967 *The Fragmented Metropolis: Los Angeles 1850-1930* (Harvard University Press, Cambridge, MA)

Foley D L, 1953, "Census tracts and urban research" *Journal of the American Statistical Association* **48** 733-742

Foley D L, Drake R L, Lyon D W, Yurenga B A, 1965 *Characteristics of Metropolitan Growth in California* 2 volumes, Institute of Urban and Regional Development, University of California, Berkeley, CA

Forstall R L, 1970, "A new social and economic grouping of cities" in *The Municipal Yearbook 1970* International City Management Association, Washington, DC

Fortune, 1968 *The Exploding Metropolis* (Doubleday, New York)

Georgescu-Roegen N, 1971 *The Entropy Law and the Economic Process* (Harvard University Press, Cambridge, MA)

Gillies J, Berger J, 1965 *Financing Home Ownership: The Borrowers, the Lenders and the Homes* Real Estate Research Program, Report 7, Graduate School of Business Administration, University of California at Los Angeles, CA

Glaab C, Brown T, 1967 *A History of Urban America* (Macmillan, New York)

Goldman S, 1953 *Information Theory* (Dover, New York)

Gottmann J, 1961 *Megalopolis: The Urbanized Seaboard of the United States* (Twentieth Century Fund, New York)

Harris C, 1943, "A functional classification of cities in the USA" *Geographical Review* **33** 86–99

Harris C (Ed.), 1963 *Problems in Measuring Change* (University of Wisconsin Press, Madison, WI)

Harris C, Ullman E, 1945, "The nature of cities" *Annals of the American Academy of Political and Social Science* **242** 7–17

Hegel G W F, 1970 *Philosophy of Nature* (George Allen and Unwin, Hemel Hempstead, Herts)

Hegel G W F, 1975 *Logic* (Oxford University Press, Oxford)

Hildebrand H, Mace A, 1950, "The employment multiplier in an expanding industrial market: LA County 1940–47" *Review of Economics and Statistics* **23**(3) 241–249

Hirsch W (Ed.), 1971 *Los Angeles: Viability and Prospects for Metropolitan Leadership* (Praeger, Los Angeles)

Hirsch W, Hale S, 1970 *Agenda for the Los Angeles Area in 1970* Institute of Government and Public Affairs, University of California at Los Angeles

Holden W H T, 1963 *Los Angeles Freeways and Their Effect on Assessed Valuations* The Rand Corporation, Santa Monica, CA

Hoover E M, Vernon R, 1959 *Anatomy of a Metropolis* (Harvard University Press, Cambridge, MA)

Horkheimer M, Adorno T, 1972 *Dialectics of Enlightenment* (Seabury Press, New York)

Hoyt H, 1933 *One Hundred Years of Land Values in Chicago* (University of Chicago Press, Chicago, IL)

Hoyt H, 1939 *The Structure and Growth of Residential Neighborhoods in American Cities* US Federal Housing Administration, Washington, DC

Hoyt H, 1964, "Recent distortions of the classical models of urban structure" *Land Economics* **40** 199–212

Humlum J, 1969 *Water Development and Water Planning in the South Western United States* (University of Aarhus Press, Aarhus, Denmark)

Kendall M, Stuart A, 1966 *The Advanced Theory of Statistics* 3 volumes (Charles Griffin, High Wycombe, Bucks)

Kidner F, 1946 *California Business Cycles* PhD thesis, Department of Economics, University of California at Los Angeles

Kroonenberg P M, 1983 *Three-way Component Analysis* (DSWO Press, Leiden)

Kuehn G, 1978 *Views of Los Angeles* (Portriga, Los Angeles)

Lancaster H, 1969 *The Chi-squared Distribution* (John Wiley, New York)

Lefebvre H, 1972 *Le Droit à la Ville* (Anthropos, Paris)

Levin J, 1965, "Three-mode factor analysis" *Psychological Bulletin* **64**(6) 442–452

Lewis E L, 1951, "Street railway development in Los Angeles and environs" in *Interurban* special issue 11 *Los Angeles Railway History*, Ed. I Swett

Lieberson S, 1963 *Ethnic Patterns in American Cities* (Free Press, New York)

Lipietz A, 1977 *Le Capital et Son Espace* (Maspéro, Paris)

Lojkine J, 1977 *Le Marxisme, l'Etat et la Question Urbaine* (Presses Universitaires de France, Paris)

Los Angeles County, 1973 *Street Atlas* (Thomas Bros, Los Angeles)

Los Angeles Metropolitan Transit Authority, 1954 *Report on a Monorail Rapid Transit Line for LA*

Los Angeles Metropolitan Transit Authority, 1959 *A Study of Public Transport Needs in the Area* prepared by Coverdale and Colpitts, New York

Los Angeles Metropolitan Transit Authority, 1960 *Rapid Transit Program* prepared by Daniel, Mann, Johnson, and Mendenhall, New York

Louis B, Perry R S, 1963 *A History of the Los Angeles Labor Movement: 1911-1941* (University of California Press, Berkeley, CA)

Lynch K, 1960 *The Image of the City* (MIT Press, Cambridge, MA)

Lynch K, 1971 *The Visual Environment of Los Angeles* LA City Planning Commission, Los Angeles

Mabry J H, 1958, "Census tract variation in urban research" *American Sociological Review* **23** 193-196

McElhiney P T, 1960, "Evaluating freeway performance in Los Angeles" *Traffic Quarterly* (July) 296-313

McEntire D, 1960 *Residence and Race* (University of California Press, Berkeley, CA)

Marchand B, 1972, "Information theory and Geography" *Geographical Analysis* **4**(3) 234-257

Marchand B, 1974, "Pedestrian traffic planning and the perception of the urban environment: a French example" *Environment and Planning A* **6** 491-507

Marchand B, 1975, "On the information content of a regional map: the concept of geographical redundancy" *Economic Geography* **51** 117-127

Marchand B, 1982, "Dialectical analysis of value: the example of Los Angeles" in *A Search for Common Ground* Eds P Gould, G Olsson (Pion, London) pp 232-251

Marchand B, 1984, "Urban growth models revisited: cities as self-organizing systems" *Environment and Planning A* **16** 949-964

Marcuse H, 1960 *Reason and Revolution* first edition, 1941 (Beacon Press, Boston, MA)

Markey M, 1932 *This Country of Yours* Boston

Mason W M, McKinstry, 1969 *The Japanese of Los Angeles* LA County Museum of Natural History, 900 Exposition Blvd, Los Angeles, CA 90007

Matheron G, 1965 *Les Variables Régionalisées et leur Estimation* (Masson, Paris)

Matheron G, 1970 *La Théorie des Variables Régionalisées et ses Applications* Centre de Morphologie Mathématique de Fontainebleau, Ecole Nationale des Mines de Paris, Paris

Meyer J R, Kain J F, Wohl M, 1965 *The Urban Transportation Problem* (Harvard University Press, Cambridge, MA)

Milbank Memorial Fund, 1947 *Postwar Problems of Migration* Conferences (29-30 October 1946)

Mittelbach F, 1963, "The changing housing inventory" RR-4, Real Estate Research Program, Graduate School of Business Administration, University of California at Los Angeles, CA

Mittelbach F G, McAllister D M, Gasparis D D, 1970 *The Role of Removals from the Inventory in Regional Housing Markets* OP-4, Graduate School of Business Administration, University of California at Los Angeles, CA

Monod J, 1970 *Le Hasard et la Nécessité* (Editions du Seuil, Paris)

Moskovitz A, 1957, "Quality control and re-use of water in California" *California Law Review* **45** 586-603

Murphy R E, 1974 *The American City* (McGraw-Hill, New York)

Nadeau R A, 1960 *Los Angeles: From Mission to Modern City* (Longman, New York)

Nakamura A, 1973 *The Politics of Air Pollution Control in Los Angeles and Osaka: A Comparative Urban Study* Dissertation Series, volume 34, number 2, University of Southern California

Neff P, Weifenbach A, 1949 *Business Cycles in Selected Industrial Areas* (University of California Press, Berkeley, CA)

Nelson H J, 1955, "A service classification of American cities" *Economic Geography* **31** 189–201

Nelson H J, Clark W A V. 1976 *Los Angeles: The Metropolitan Experience* (Ballinger, Cambridge, MA)

Niedercorn J H, Hearle E F R, 1963 *Recent Land Use Trends in 48 Large American Cities* RM-3664-FF, Rand Corporation, Santa Monica, CA

Nunis D, 1973 *Los Angeles and Its Environs in the 20th Century. A Bibliography of a Metropolis* (Ward Ritchie, Los Angeles, CA)

Ostrom V, 1953 *Water and Politics: A Study of Water Policies and Administration in the Development of Los Angeles* (Haynes Foundation, Los Angeles)

Park R E, Burgess E W, McKenzie R D (Eds), 1925 *The City* (University of Chicago Press, Chicago, IL)

Perloff H, and others, 1973 *Prototype State of the Region: Report for Los Angeles County* School of Architecture and Urban Planning, University of California at Los Angeles, CA

Preteceille E, 1975 *Equipments Collectifs, Structure Urbaine et Consommation Sociale* (Centre de Sociologie Urbaine, Paris)

QB 15, 1945 (April)
QB 18, 1946 (January)
QB 28, 1948 (July)
QB 32, 1949 (July)
QB 33, 1949 (October)   *Quarterly Bulletin* The Regional Planning
QB 77, 1962 (July)   Commission County of Los Angeles
QB 98, 1967 (October)
QB 108, 1970 (April)
QB 110, 1970 (October)
QB 120, 1973 (April)
QB 122, 1973 (October)

Rae J B, 1971 *The Road and the Car in American Life* (MIT Press, Cambridge, MA)

Rand C, 1967 *Los Angeles. The Ultimate City* (Oxford University Press, New York)

Rapkin C, Grigsby W, 1960 *The Demand for Housing in Racially Mixed Areas* (University of California Press, Berkeley, CA)

Reps J W, 1969 *Town Planning in Frontier America* (Princeton University Press, Princeton, NJ)

Robertson R M, 1964 *History of the American Economy* (Harcourt, Brace and World, New York)

Robinson W W, 1959 *Los Angeles from the Days of the Pueblo* California Historical Society, San Francisco

Robinson W W, 1968 *Los Angeles, a Profile* (University of Oklahoma Press, Norman, OK)

Rossi P H, 1980 *Why Families Move* (Sage, Beverly Hills, CA)

Rubin B, 1977, "A chronology of architecture in Los Angeles" *Annals, American Association of Geographers* **67** 4

Sauvy A, 1967 *Histoire Économique de la France entre les Deux Guerres (1918–1939)* 3 volumes (Fayard, Paris)

SCRC, 1964 *Migration and the South California Economy,* Report 12, South
    California Research Council, Occidental College, Los Angeles
Scott M, 1949 *Metropolitan Los Angeles: One Community* (Haynes Foundation, Los
    Angeles)
Sears D O, McConahay J B, 1969, "Participation in the Los Angeles riot" *Social
    Problems* 5 – 12
Sears D O, McConahay J B, 1970, "Racial socialization, comparison levels, and the
    Watts riots" *Journal of Social Issues* **26** 121 – 140
Security First National Bank, 1965 *South California Report, a Study of Growth and
    Economic Structure: Los Angeles* Research Division
Serra J, 1967, "Un critère nouveau de découverte de structures: le variogramme"
    Sciences de la Terre **12**(4) 275 – 299
Shannon C E, Weaver W, 1949 *The Mathematical Theory of Communication*
    (University of Illinois Press, Urbana, IL)
Shepard N R, 1962, "The analysis of proximities: multidimensional scaling with an
    unknown distance function" *Psychometrika* **27**(2) 125 – 140; **27**(3) 219 – 246
Shevky E, Williams M, 1949 *The Social Areas of Los Angeles* (University of
    California Press, Los Angeles)
Smith M P, 1980 *The City and Social Theory* (Basil Blackwell, Oxford)
Smith W F, 1966 *Aspects of Housing Demand: Absorption, Demolition and
    Differentiation* number 29, Center for Real Estate and Urban Economics,
    University of California, Berkeley, CA
Smith W, and others, 1963 *Transportation and Parking for Tomorrow's Cities,* Los
    Angeles
South California Rapid Transit District, 1967 *A POreliminary Report to the People
    of the Los Angeles Metro-area Regarding a First Stage System of Rapid Transit* Los
    Angeles
South California Rapid Transit District, 1968 *A Final Report to the People of the
    Los Angeles Metro-area Regarding a First Stage System of Transit* Los Angeles
State of California, 1964 *California Migration 1955 – 60* Financial and Population
    Research Section, Department of Finance, Sacramento, CA
Statistical Yearbook US Bureau of the Census, editions: 1940, 1950, 1960, and
    1970, Department of Commerce, Washington, DC
Steinbeck J, 1939 *The Grapes of Wrath* (Doubleday, New York)
Stenger F, 1968, "Kronecker product extensions of linear operators" *SIAM Journal
    of Numerical Analysis* **5** 422 – 435
Stimson H G, 1955 *The Rise of the Labor Movement in Los Angeles* (University of
    California Press, Berkeley, CA)
Swett I (Ed.), 1951, "Los Angeles Railway History" *Interurban* special issue,
    number 11
Taaffe E, 1956, "Air transportation and the US urban distribution" *Geographical
    Review* **46** 219 – 239
Taeuber K E, Taeuber A F, 1965 *Negroes in Cities* (Aldine, Chicago, IL)
Thom R, 1974 *Stabilité Structurelle et Morphogenèse* Coll 10-18 (Union Générale
    d'Edition, Paris)
Thompson W S, 1955 *Growth and Changes in California's Population* (Haynes
    Foundation, Los Angeles)
Topalov C, 1974 *Les Promoteurs Immobiliers* (Mouton, Paris)
Torgerson W S, 1958 *Theory and Methods of Scaling* (John Wiley, New York)
Tucker L R, 1963, "Implications of factor analysis of three-way matrices for
    measurement of change" in *Problems in Measuring Change* Ed. C Harris
    (University of Wisconsin Press, Madison, WI)

Tucker L R, 1964, "The extension of factor analysis to three dimensional matrices" in *Contributions to Mathematical Psychology* Eds N Frederiksen, H Gulliksen (Holt, Rinehart and Winston, New York)

Tucker L R, 1965, "Experiments in multi-mode factor analysis" in *Proceedings, 1964 Invitational Conference on Testing Problems* (Educational Testing Service, Princeton, NJ)

Tucker L R, 1966, "Some mathematical notes on three-mode factor analysis" *Psychometrika* **31**(3) 279–311

Tucker L R, 1972, "Relations between multi-dimensional scaling and three-mode factor analysis" *Psychometrika* **37**(1) 3–27

Ulam S M, 1962 *Adventures of a Mathematician* (Charles Scribener's Sons, New York)

US Bureau of the Census, *Census Tracts, Los Angeles–Long Beach Standard Metropolitan Statistical Area* 1940, 1950, 1960, 1970 [Final Report PHC(1)-117], Department of Commerce (US Government Printing Office, Washington, DC)

Van Arsdol M Jr, Maurice D, Schnerman L A, 1971, "Redistribution and assimilation of ethnic populations: the Los Angeles case" *Demography* **8** 459–480

Von Foerster H, 1960, "On self-organizing systems and their environments" in *Self-organizing Systems* Eds M C Yovitz, S Cameron (Pergamon Press, New York)

Von Neumann J, 1966 *Theory of Self-reproducing Automata* Ed. A W Burks (University of Illinois Press, Urbana, IL)

Warner S B, 1962 *Streetcar Suburbs: The Process of Growth in Boston: 1870–1900* (Atheneum, New York)

Weber M, 1958 *The City* (Free Press, New York)

West N, 1939 *The Day of the Locust* (Penguin Books, Harmondsworth, Middx)

White M, White L, 1962 *The Intellectual versus the City* (MIT Press, Cambridge, MA)

Williams R L Jr, 1956, "Negro's migration to Los Angeles: 1900–1946" *Negro Historical Bulletin* **19** 102–108

Wilson A G, 1982 *Catastrophe Theory and Bifurcation* (Croom Helm, Beckenham, Kent)

Winograd S, Cowan J D, 1963 *Reliable Computation in the Presence of Noise* (MIT Press, Cambridge, MA)

Winther O O, 1946, "The use of climate as a means of promoting migration to Southern California" *Mississippi Valley Historical Review* **33** 411–424

Wirth L, 1938, "Urbanism as a way of life" *American Journal of Sociology* **44**(2) 1–24